The British Monarchy: A Complete Guide to Britain's Kings and Queens

An Anglophile's Complete Guide to Royal British History

Other Books by Anglotopia

101 Budget Britain Travel Tips
101 London Travel Tips
101 UK Culture Tips
Anglotopia's Guide to British Slang
Londontopia's Guide to Cockney Slang
Great Britons: Top 50 Greatest Brits
Great Events in British History
Great British Houses
Anglotopia Guide to Bridgerton
101 Oxford Travel Tips
Anglotopia's Dictionary of Cockney Slang

Other Books by Jonathan Thomas

Adventures in Anglotopia
Anglophile Vignettes
Visions of Anglotopia
End to End: Britain From Land's End to John O'Groats

THE BRITISH MONARCHY: A COMPLETE GUIDE TO BRITAIN'S KINGS AND QUEENS

An Anglophile's Complete Guide to Royal British History

By
Anglotopia

Copyright © 2025 by Anglotopia LLC
Cover Design by Anglotopia LLC
Cover Copyright © 2025 Anglotopia LLC

Anglotopia LLC supports the right to free expression and the value of copyright. The purpose of copyright is to encourage writers and artists to produce the creative works that enrich our culture.

The scanning, uploading, and distribution of this book without permission is a theft of the author's intellectual property. If you would like permission to use material from the book (other than for review purposes), please contact info@anglotopia.net. Thank you for your support of the author's rights.

Anglotopia Press - An Imprint of Anglotopia LLC
www.anglotopia.press

Printed in the United States of America

1st US Edition: February 1st, 2025

Published by Anglotopia Press, an imprint of Anglotopia LLC.
The Anglotopia Press Name and Logo is a trademark of Anglotopia LLC.

Print Book interior design by Jonathan Thomas, all fonts used with license.

All images of Monarchs used in this book are in the public domain.

All other photos and art used in this book are in the public domain in the USA or in the Creative Commons.

Print ISBN: 978-1-955273-43-5

TABLE OF CONTENTS

Introduction 1
Methodology 3
What is the UK? 5
William the Conqueror 9
William II 17
Henry I 23
Stephen 29
Empress Matilda 35
Henry II 39
Richard I, the Lionheart 45
John 53
Henry III 59
Edward I 65
Edward II 73
Edward III 79
Richard II 85
Henry IV 91

Henry V 97
Henry VI 103
Edward IV 109
Edward V 115
Richard III 119
Henry VII 127
Henry VIII 133
Edward VI 141
Jane 147
Mary I 153
Elizabeth I 159
James I 165

Charles I   173
Oliver Cromwell   181
Charles II   189
James II   197
William & Mary   203
Anne   209
George I   215
George II   221
George III   227
George IV   235
William IV   241
Victoria   249
Edward VII   257
George V   263
Edward VIII   271
George VI   275
Elizabeth II   283
Charles III   289
Appendix 1: Current Line of Succession   295
Appendix 2: Burial Places of the Monarchs   300
Appendix 3: Ten Events That Shaped the Crown   302
Appendix 4: A Guide to Britain's Royal Palaces   306
Appendix 5: Royal Films: A Guide to the Best Movies About the British Monarchy   311

Appendix 6: Royal Television: The Best Shows About the British Monarchy   314
Appendix 7: Royal Protocol: A Guide to Titles, Styles, and Etiquette
Appendix 8: The Uncrowned   319
Appendix 9: The Interregnum   322
Appendix 10: The Acts of Union   329

Appendix 11: Royal Eras: A Journey Through British History 331
Appendix 12: The House of Windsor: A Very British Rebranding 336
Appendix 13: Where Every Monarch Was Born 338
Appendix 14: Abdication Crisis 340
Appendix 15: The Regency Era 347
Appendix 16: What is the Crown? 354
Appendix 17: The Crown Jewels 356

INTRODUCTION
The Story of British Monarchy

When we think of British history, we often think of it through its monarchs. From William the Conqueror to Charles III, the story of Britain has been shaped by the men and women who wore its crown. This book traces that story through nearly a thousand years of British monarchy, from 1066 to the present day.

Why start at 1066? The Norman Conquest marks a clear beginning point - it's the last successful foreign invasion of England, and every monarch since William has traced their legitimacy back to his victory at Hastings. More practically, the historical record becomes much clearer and more reliable from this point forward.

But this isn't just a chronological list of rulers. Each monarch's story reveals something about how Britain evolved from a medieval kingdom into a modern democracy. We see the transformation from absolute monarchy to constitutional rule, from religious upheaval to established church, from isolated island to global empire, and back again.

Along the way, we'll encounter extraordinary characters: warrior kings like Richard the Lionheart, reformers like Henry II, tyrants like John, powerful queens like Elizabeth I and Victoria, and modernizers like Elizabeth II. We'll also meet those who briefly held or claimed the throne - figures like Lady Jane Grey, Empress Matilda, and even Oliver Cromwell, whose stories help us understand how British monarchy evolved.

This book aims to make these stories accessible while maintaining historical accuracy. Each chapter provides key facts, important events, and cultural legacy, along with details about relevant historical sites you can visit today. We've also included information about how these monarchs have been portrayed in film and television, showing how their stories continue to captivate us.

This book is a survey, we are not able to go in-depth on each monarch, so consider the selections here a jumping-off point for further research. We give you enough to get you interested, then provide a list of further research you can explore to learn more about every one of these Kings and Queens. There is no end to historical scholarship!

Understanding the British monarchy helps us understand Britain itself - its laws, its traditions, its institutions, and its peculiarities. These stories of power, personality, and nation-building have shaped not just Britain but much of the modern world.

Whether you're a student of history, a royal enthusiast, or simply curious about how Britain came to be what it is today, these stories of Britain's monarchs offer fascinating insights into one of the world's oldest and most enduring institutions.

METHODOLOGY

Why Start with William?

When telling the story of British monarchs, one must choose a starting point. While Britain's royal history stretches back into the mists of time, with legendary kings like Arthur and historical figures like Alfred the Great, we chose to begin this chronicle with William the Conqueror in 1066. This decision wasn't arbitrary – it marks the last successful foreign conquest of England and establishes a continuous line of succession that leads directly to the current monarch, King Charles III.

The Norman Conquest represents more than just a change in leadership; it transformed English society, law, language, and culture. William brought with him continental feudalism, built lasting monuments of stone, and established record-keeping practices that give us far more reliable historical information than we have for previous periods. The Domesday Book, commissioned by William in 1086, provides us with an unprecedented snapshot of medieval England and marks the beginning of more systematic historical documentation.

But history isn't just about smooth transitions and unbroken lines. Some of the most fascinating chapters in British royal history involve disruptions, challenges, and alternate claims to the throne. That's why I've included several figures who might be considered "interruptions" in the traditional succession.

Take the tumultuous period known as the Anarchy, when Empress Matilda and King Stephen fought for the crown. Matilda was the designated heir of Henry I, but Stephen, her cousin, seized the throne. Their civil war split England and ultimately led to a compromise that put Matilda's son on the throne as Henry II. Their story illustrates how succession rules were still evolving and how powerful personalities could shape the destiny of the nation.

Similarly, Lady Jane Grey's brief nine-day reign might seem

like a historical footnote, but it encapsulates the religious and political tensions that dominated Tudor England. Though she never had a coronation, her tragic story – from teenage queen to executed prisoner – illuminates the dangerous politics of royal succession in the sixteenth century.

Perhaps the most controversial inclusion is Oliver Cromwell, who wasn't a monarch at all but rather Lord Protector during the Interregnum. After the execution of Charles I, Britain experimented with non-monarchical rule for the first and only time in its modern history. Cromwell's inclusion is essential for understanding how the monarchy evolved – the Restoration that followed his death brought significant changes to how British monarchs ruled, leading eventually to the constitutional monarchy we know today.

Throughout this book, you'll find both de facto rulers (those who held actual power) and de jure monarchs (those with legal claims to the throne). Some reigned for decades, while others held power for mere days or weeks. Each of their stories adds to our understanding of how the British monarchy has evolved over nearly a thousand years.

From William the Conqueror to Charles III, the British monarchy has survived civil wars, religious upheavals, plague, revolution, and the transition from absolute to constitutional rule. By including both the main line of succession and its various interruptions, this book aims to tell the complete story of how the British monarchy has adapted and endured through centuries of change.

The tales of these monarchs – whether they ruled for decades or days, whether they were crowned in Westminster Abbey or never crowned at all – help us understand not just British history, but how power, personality, and circumstance shape the course of nations.

WHAT IS THE UK?

A Tale of Four Countries

When we think of British monarchs, we often imagine them ruling over the United Kingdom as we know it today. But for most of history, this wasn't the case. The story of how England, Scotland, Wales, and Ireland came together – and how Ireland later partly separated – is a complex tale spanning nearly a millennium.

When William the Conqueror arrived in 1066, he became King of England only. Wales was a patchwork of independent principalities, Scotland was its own kingdom, and Ireland was divided into various kingdoms. Each had its own rulers, laws, and customs.

Wales was the first to join England, though not peacefully. After centuries of border conflicts, Edward I conquered Wales in 1283. He made his son "Prince of Wales" – a tradition that continues today with the monarch's heir. Wales was formally united with England by Henry VIII's Laws in Wales Acts of 1535 and 1542.

Scotland remained independent much longer, despite several English attempts at conquest. The two kingdoms shared a monarch for the first time in 1603 when James VI of Scotland inherited the English throne from his cousin Elizabeth I, becoming James I of England. However, they remained separate countries with different parliaments, laws, and systems of government. It was a union of Crowns, not of countries.

This situation changed dramatically in 1707 with the Act of Union. England (including Wales) and Scotland joined to create the Kingdom of Great Britain. This wasn't just a personal union under one monarch – it created a single parliament and unified political system. The Scottish Parliament was dissolved, though Scotland kept its own legal and education systems, which remain distinct today (and they were given back a Parliament in 1999).

Ireland's story is more complicated. English monarchs had claimed lordship over Ireland since the 12th century, but real control varied. In 1542, Henry VIII declared himself King of Ireland. When England and Scotland united in 1707, Ireland remained a separate kingdom under the same monarch. In 1800, another Act of Union created the United Kingdom of Great Britain and Ireland.

However, this union wouldn't last. After centuries of conflict and a war of independence, most of Ireland separated from the UK in 1922 to become the Irish Free State (later the Republic of Ireland). The six counties in the northeast remained part of the UK as Northern Ireland, creating the United Kingdom of Great Britain and Northern Ireland – the country we know today.

So when we read about early medieval English kings, we need to remember they ruled only England (and sometimes France…). By the Tudor period, they controlled Wales too. From 1603 they ruled Scotland as well, but as a separate kingdom until 1707. And while they claimed authority over Ireland for centuries, Ireland's relationship with the British crown remained complex and contentious until the partition of 1922.

This explains why the titles of British monarchs have changed over time. Elizabeth I was Queen of England and Ireland. Her successor James was King of England, Scotland, and Ireland. Queen Anne ended her reign as Queen of Great Britain and Ireland. And Elizabeth II was Queen of the United Kingdom of Great Britain and Northern Ireland, a title now held by Charles III.

The United Kingdom as we know it today is relatively young – just over a hundred years old in its current form. It's the product of centuries of gradual union, conquest, and separation, reflecting the complex relationships between four nations that share one crown.

Through all of this change, one thing has endured - the Monarchy - and with that The Crown (as a concept).

WILLIAM THE CONQUEROR (1066–1087)

The Battle of Hastings in 1066 was the swiftest, most effective, and most brutal military occupation ever seen and is believed by many to have been the most important battle in English history. Leading the victorious Norman invaders was William, a Norman duke known after 1066 as William the Conqueror, King of England. William completely transformed England, transferring all land from English freemen and Saxon-Danish nobility to his Norman followers, suppressing revolts by massacring entire villages and recording the new lay of the land for the benefit of generations to come in his famous Domesday Book.

Key Facts about William the Conqueror

- William the Conqueror was born in 1027, son of Robert the Devil and Herleva, daughter of William the Tanner.
- William became King of England on December 25th, 1066, aged 39.
- William married Matilda of Flanders, had ten children, and died on September 9th, 1087, aged 60.

A Brief Sketch of William the Conqueror

William the Conqueror was bred for battle at a young age. His father, Robert, the Devil Duke of Normandy, and his mother, Herleva, daughter of a burgher of Falaise known as William the Tanner, were not married. Herleva was married off to a Norman baron against her will but maintained a romantic relationship with Robert the Devil throughout his short life. When Robert died in 1035, William was just 8 years old. Despite the fact that his mother was married to another man, William was Robert's only son and thus became the Duke of Normandy.

Over the succeeding twenty years, William protected his Dukedom against the King of France, who continually plotted to invade Normandy and assassinate William, and against English rebels whose aim was to create anarchy in his duchy. Throughout William's childhood and adolescence, Norman nobles fought each other for power, with the battle lines often drawn between those in support of William and those against him. It is thought that up to four of William's custodians were killed during the early years of his dukedom. In 1047, William was victorious in quashing a Norman rebellion with the support of King Henry of England, but the years between 1045 and 1060 were relentlessly bloody and chaotic.

In the early 1050s, William married Matilda of Flanders in a union that was forbidden by Pope Leo IX. The papal sanction was eventually secured a few years later with the founding of two monasteries in Caen. William's marriage to Matilda secured his position and gave him important allies, as Flanders was a powerful French territory with links to the French monarchy and German emperors. William arranged for his allies to hold powerful positions in the Norman church and, in later years, took control of the neighboring territory of Maine.

William the Conqueror was a second cousin of King Edward the Confessor of England (William's father was the nephew of Edward's mother), and during the late 1050s, with no natural heir from King Edward, William became a real contender for the English throne. William claimed that Edward had already promised the throne to him, but on his deathbed in 1066, Edward named English Earl Harold Godwinson his successor.

The Battle of Hastings

By the time William invaded England in 1066, he had the support of the wealthiest barons and knights in Flanders and Brittany and had amassed a huge army and fleet of invasion barges. On the 14th of October, 1066, the Battle of Hastings began and lasted for one day. Harold's army of foot soldiers and archers offered a worthy opponent to William's army of cavalry. The decisive moment in the battle came with the death of Harold, who fell with arrow wounds to his head. King Harold's mother, Gytha, is said to have offered William the weight of her son's body in gold if she could have it in order to perform a proper burial. William refused and promised instead to throw Harold's body into the sea. Later, it was claimed Harold's body was buried at Waltham Abbey.

William was crowned King of England at Westminster Abbey on Christmas Day 1066 and immediately set about the tremendous transformation of the English nation. As England's first total conqueror, William united the country in complete subjugation. The predominantly Saxon-Danish English nobility who earned the majority of land in England were either killed at Hastings or completely expropriated by the new king. Three-quarters of the whole territory of England was shared out amongst around 5000 of William's followers and speculators from Brittany and Flanders, with the last quarter staying in the possession of the King. William's newly created magnates were required to contribute knights to his army as well as to defend local garrisons. This new feudal system structure meant that William was able to crush every rebellion against his rule successfully, including the Welsh and Danish attacks.

William used the lawlessness of constant but uncoordinated rebellions to justify the terrifying massacre and brutal suppression of any area that challenged his rule and many that didn't. William ordered the building of many new castles, keeps, and mottes and used these new fortifications as bases of aggression from which his armies could occupy the English countryside and retreat to safety when threatened. The central keep of the Tower of London was built high, outside the city walls, in order to ensure the domination of any would-be invaders.

During William's reign, royal power was at its peak. Observing the old, established Saxon laws, William set up ecclesiastical courts to settle marital and spiritual matters, banishing bishops from the shire court and administering 'King's Justice.' William also introduced a clerical bureaucracy separate from the church that was answerable only to him.

In 1085, William ordered the compilation of the Domesday Book. His scribes undertook a tremendous survey, recording the landholdings held by himself and his vassals throughout the entire country. Each listing records the holding, its owner, who owned it before the Conquest, and its value. The manuscript is still in existence, held at the National Archives in Kew, London, and offers a unique insight into land ownership, taxation, and way of life in Medieval England.

William the Conqueror was a brutal king who reduced many English villages to desolate graveyards during his rule. However, the 'revolt of the earls' of 1075 led to an invasion by The Danish King's brother Cnut, who saw William suffer his first defeat at the Castle Dol in Brittany. A rebellion led by William's oldest son, Robert, in 1077 and 1078 saw Normandy raided and William nearly killed in battle. In 1079, King Malcolm of Scots raided the River Tweed, and William's slow response led the Northumbrians to rebel against the Bishop of Durham and Earl of Northumbria.

William also fought in rebellions on the continent in the early 1080s. William's son Robert again rebelled, this time with support from the French king. In 1083, William's wife Matilda died, and just four years later, William joined her. In July 1087, William was fighting in an expedition against the French Vexin, a clash instigated by his son Robert, and was taken ill. It's unclear what illness he succumbed to or what injuries he sustained, but after being taken to the priory of Saint Gervase at Rouen, William died on 9th September 1087.

William was buried at the abbey-aux-hommes, but his tomb was disturbed many times. As promised, Normandy was bequeathed to William's eldest son, Robert, while custody of England was given to his second son, William. A decision that would inevitably lead to more war.

Legacy of William the Conqueror

William the Conqueror is one of the best-known monarchs in British history. Victor of the famous Battle of Hastings in 1066, William the Conqueror was the first man to successfully invade and conquer the whole of England.

The consequences of William the Conqueror's reign as king of England are complex and long-lasting. Immediately following William's death, his sons Robert and William went to war over control of England and Normandy, and the battles continued for many years, leading to the revolt of Maine and a resurgence of aristocratic power in Normandy. In England, William the Conqueror changed the church and aristocracy, influenced the English language, and altered the way land was owned and taxed forever. William created a fusion of English and Norman systems of power to create a new kingdom that lasted well into the Middle Ages. England's ties with Scandinavia were severed, and her ties with France were tightened, an alliance that has lasted to the present day.

William the Conqueror instigated the writing of the Domesday Book, the oldest statistical survey of life in England ever created.

Films and TV Shows Featuring William the Conqueror

- Lady Godiva of Coventry (1955)
- A Choice of Kings (1966) TV Play
- William the Conqueror (1982)
- Royal Blood: William the Conqueror (1990) TV series
- William the Conqueror (2015)

Further Research

- Douglas, David (1964) William the Conqueror
- Bates, David (2001) William the Conqueror
- Carpenter, David (2004) The Struggle for Mastery: The Penguin History of Britain 1066 to 1284
- Hugh, Thomas (2007) The Norman Conquest: England After William the Conqueror
- Huscroft, Richard (2009) The Norman Conquest

Locations Related to William the Conqueror

- Hastings Battlefield, in which William defeated King Harold II and became known as William the Conqueror. A Battle Abbey was built by William to commemorate the dead.

- William the Conqueror is buried at the Abbaye aux Hommes located in Caen, Normandy.
- Hastings Castle was built from timber in the months following the Battle of Hastings and then rebuilt in stone four years later.
- Westminster Abbey, where William the Conqueror was crowned king.
- Windsor Castle was commissioned by William the Conqueror, as were many other castles, including Corfe Castle, Durham Castle, Dover Castle, and Warwick Castle.

WILLIAM II
(1087–1100)

William II, also known as William Rufus, was the second son of William the Conqueror and was King of England from 1087 until his death in 1100. Despite his relatively short reign, William II played a significant role in the history of England. In this article, we will explore the life, reign, and legacy of this controversial monarch.

Key Facts about William II

- William II, also known as William Rufus, was the second son of William the Conqueror and Matilda of Flanders.
- He was probably born between 1056-1060 in Normandy, France, and was sent to England to be educated when his father became king in 1066.
- William II was known for his love of hunting and his military skills, which he showcased in campaigns against Scotland and Wales.
- His reign was marked by conflict with the Church and with Scotland, as well as by his own love of luxury and disregard for the welfare of his people.
- William II died in 1100, possibly assassinated by an arrow while hunting in the New Forest.

Early Life and Education

William II was born in sometime between 1056 and 1060 in Normandy, France. He was the second son of William the Conqueror and Matilda of Flanders. When his father became King of England in 1066, William II was sent to England to be educated. He was known for his love of hunting and his military skills, which he showcased in campaigns against Scotland and Wales.

Reign

William II ascended to the throne in 1087 following the death of his father. His reign was marked by conflict with the Church, which he often clashed with over issues of power and money. William II was known for his love of luxury, and he spent lavishly on his court and on his own personal pleasures, such as hunting and feasting.

One of the most controversial events of William II's reign was the death of his younger brother, Richard, who was killed in a hunting accident in the New Forest in 1075. There has been much speculation that William II was responsible for his brother's death, but there is no firm evidence to support this theory.

William II's reign was also marked by conflict with Scotland, which he invaded and defeated in 1091. He also campaigned against Wales, although he was unable to achieve a decisive victory.

Death

William II of England, commonly known as William Rufus, met his end in a mysterious and controversial manner in the New Forest on August 2, 1100. While out hunting with a small party, an arrow fatally struck him in the chest. The circumstances surrounding his death have been the subject of speculation and intrigue for centuries. Some historians believe it was a simple accident, a case of mistaken identity in the thick woods, while others suspect foul play, suggesting that his brother, Henry, who stood to gain from his demise, may have orchestrated the killing.

William Rufus' reign was marked by turbulence and conflict, and his death only added to the instability. His relationship with the Church was fraught with tension, as he clashed with Archbishop Anselm over issues of ecclesiastical authority and the king's right to appoint bishops. Additionally, his aggressive policies in Wales and Scotland fueled resentment among the native populations, further complicating matters. His sudden death without a clear successor plunged England into a period of uncertainty and set the stage for a power struggle among the nobility.

The death of William II had profound implications for the future of England. With his passing, his younger brother Henry seized the opportunity to assert his claim to the throne, quickly securing support from key nobles and clergy. Henry was crowned king within days of William's death, ushering in a new era for England. However, suspicions lingered regarding the circumstances of William Rufus' demise, fueling rumors and conspiracy theories that endure to this day.

Legacy

William II's reign was marked by controversy and conflict, and he was often portrayed as a cruel and selfish monarch. He was known for his love of luxury and his disregard for the Church, which made him unpopular with many of his subjects.

Despite these controversies, William II played a significant role in the history of England. He strengthened the power of the monarchy and established a centralized system of government that would endure for centuries. He also laid the foundation for the development of a strong military, which would prove crucial in the wars that would shape England's future.

William II's reign also saw the emergence of a new class of wealthy landowners who would come to play a significant role in the politics and economy of England. This class, which was made up of the descendants of the Norman conquerors, would dominate English society for centuries.

Further Research

Here are some books and documentaries about William II of England:

- William Rufus: The Red King – Frank Barlow
- William II: The Red King – John Gillingham
- The Reign of William Rufus and the Accession of Henry I – E.A. Freeman

Locations Related to William II

- Winchester Castle – William II was crowned at Winchester Cathedral and often held court at Winchester Castle.
- Winchester Cathedral – William was buried in Winchester Cathedral.
- The Rufus Stone – The Rufus Stone is a historical monument located in the New Forest, Hampshire, England. It marks the traditional site where King William II was fatally shot with an arrow while hunting in the forest on August 2, 1100. The stone itself is a large block of granite, inscribed with a plaque recounting the events of William Rufus' death.
- The New Forest – The New Forest is the site of the hunting accident that led to the death of William II.
- Tower of London – William II made significant additions to the Tower of London during his reign.
- Durham Cathedral – William II invaded and defeated the Scottish army near Durham Cathedral in 1091.
- Carlisle Castle – William II besieged Carlisle Castle during his campaign against Scotland.
- York – William II held court at York and made significant additions to York Castle.
- Wales – William II campaigned against Wales during his reign but was unable to achieve a decisive victory.

HENRY I
(1100–1135)

King Henry I of England, born on September 1068, was the fourth son of William the Conqueror and Matilda of Flanders. He was the king of England from 1100 until his death in 1135. He is often called the Lion of Justice for his legal reforms and for being a just ruler. Henry's reign was marked by significant achievements and struggles, mostly notably the legacy of his succession, which led to a dark period in English history called the Anarchy.

Key Facts about Henry I

- Henry I was the fourth son of William the Conqueror and Matilda of Flanders, born in September 1068.
- Henry I was King of England from 1100 until his death in 1135.
- He was known as the Lion of Justice for his legal reforms and for being a just ruler.
- Henry I defeated his brother Robert Curthose in the Battle of Tinchebrai in 1106 and captured him.
- His Charter of Liberties established the principle that the king was subject to the law and limited the king's power.

Life and Early Reign

Henry I's early years were marked by political turmoil and strife between his father and brothers. His father, William the Conqueror, had divided his kingdom among his sons, which led to conflicts. After William's death in 1087, Henry supported his brother William Rufus in the fight for the throne against their elder brother Robert Curthose. After William Rufus's 'accidental' hunting death in August 1100, Henry quickly claimed the throne and was crowned king.

During his early reign, Henry I focused on consolidating power and establishing peace in the country. He married Matilda of Scotland (also known as Edith), daughter of Malcolm III of Scotland, to secure peace with Scotland. He also secured alliances with the nobles and the Church by granting them favors and privileges.

Legal Reforms and Governance

Henry I's reign was significant for his legal reforms and governance. He appointed able and learned men to key positions in the government, such as the chief justice and chancellor. He also introduced legal reforms that strengthened the royal authority and improved the administration of justice. He established a system of royal justices who traveled throughout the country to administer justice and hear cases. He also introduced the concept of the writ, which allowed people to appeal to the king's court for justice. Henry I also issued the Charter of Liberties, which was a precursor to the Magna Carta. The Charter of Liberties was a document that listed the rights of the barons and the Church and limited the king's power. It also established the principle that the king was subject to the law.

Henry was viewed as a tough yet efficient ruler by his peers. He adeptly managed the barons in England and Normandy. In England, he utilized the existing Anglo-Saxon system of justice, local government, and taxation while also bolstering it with additional institutions such as the royal exchequer and itinerant justices. Normandy also saw the implementation of a growing system of justices and an exchequer. Many of Henry's officials were "new men" from humble origins rather than from high-status families, and they advanced through the ranks as administrators. Henry promoted ecclesiastical reform, although he became entangled in a serious dispute in 1101 with Archbishop Anselm of Canterbury, which was eventually resolved through a compromise solution in 1105. He backed the Cluniac order and played a significant role in appointing senior clergy in England and Normandy.

Military Campaigns and Succession

King Henry I of England led several significant military campaigns during his reign, showcasing his prowess as a formidable military commander. One of his most notable military achievements was the Battle of Tinchebrai in 1106, where he decisively defeated his elder brother Robert Curthose, Duke of Normandy. This victory solidified Henry I's control over Normandy and effectively ended the threat posed by his brother's claim to the English throne, securing Henry's position as the undisputed ruler.

In addition to his triumph at Tinchebrai, Henry I also conducted successful military campaigns against the Welsh and the Scots, asserting his authority and expanding his influence into these regions. These campaigns demonstrated Henry's strategic acumen and his ability to effectively command his forces in diverse geographical and political contexts. His military successes not only strengthened his hold on the English crown but also enhanced his reputation as a skilled and respected leader in both domestic and foreign affairs.

Henry I's military campaigns were pivotal in shaping the geopolitical landscape of his era and consolidating his authority as a monarch. His adeptness in military strategy and his ability to secure significant victories against internal and external threats contributed to his legacy as a powerful and influential ruler in English history.

Henry I's reign was marked by his struggle to secure the succession. He had only one legitimate son, William Adelin, who died in a shipwreck in 1120. After his son's death, Henry I named his daughter Matilda his succesor and heir, which led to a succession crisis after his death in 1135; this is commonly known as The Anarchy and was one of the most turbulent and violent periods in English history. More on this in the next chapters.

Further Research

Books:

- Henry I: King of England and Duke of Normandy by

- Judith A. Green
  - Henry I: The Father of His People (Penguin Monarchs)
  - Henry I by C. Warren Hollister
  - The English and Their History by Robert Tombs (includes a chapter on Henry I)

Documentaries:

  - Kings and Queens of England: The Normans – Henry I (Season 1, Episode 3)
  - The Plantagenets: Henry I – The Father of His People (Season 1, Episode 2)
  - Monarchy with David Starkey: Henry I (Season 2, Episode 1)

Locations Related to Henry I

  - Reading Abbey – Henry I was buried there.
  - Falaise, Normandy – Henry I was born there.
  - Caen, Normandy – Henry I was educated there.
  - Bayeux Cathedral, Normandy – Henry I swore an oath to support his brother William Rufus there.
  - Tinchebrai, Normandy – Henry I defeated his brother Robert Curthose there in 1106.
  - Westminster Abbey – Henry I was hastily crowned there in 1100.
  - Tower of London – Henry I used it as a royal residence and a place to store his treasures.

STEPHEN (1135-1154)

King Stephen of England's reign was a tumultuous time in England's history, marked by political instability and conflict often called 'The Anarchy.' Stephen was the grandson of William the Conqueror, and he came to the throne after the death of his uncle, Henry I. However, his claim to the throne was disputed by Henry's daughter, Matilda, who had been designated as Henry's heir. This led to great instability in the kingdom.

Key Facts about King Stephen

- King Stephen of England reigned from 1135 to 1154 during a period of political instability and conflict known as 'The Anarchy.'
- He was the grandson of William the Conqueror and became King of England after the death of his uncle, Henry I.
- His claim to the throne was disputed by Henry's daughter, Matilda, which led to great instability and conflict in the kingdom.
- The conflict during his reign was characterized by its brutality, with widespread violence and destruction across England.
- Despite some progress in terms of governance and administration, his reign was largely defined by the impact of the Anarchy on English society and the lasting scars it left on the country.

The Life and Reign of King Stephen

Stephen was the grandson of William the Conqueror, and he came to the throne after the death of his uncle, King Henry I. His claim to the throne was contested by his cousin, the Empress

Matilda, who was Henry's daughter and had been designated as his heir. Matilda's supporters argued that she had a stronger claim to the throne as the daughter of the previous king, while Stephen's supporters argued that he had been chosen by Henry as his successor.

The resulting conflict, known as The Anarchy, lasted for nearly two decades and had a profound impact on English society. Throughout Stephen's reign, there were numerous rebellions and uprisings as both sides fought for control of the country. The conflict was characterized by its brutality, with widespread violence and destruction across England.

One of the most significant rebellions during Stephen's reign was led by Empress Matilda herself. In 1139, Matilda landed in England with an army and began to seize territory in the south of the country. She was initially successful, but her campaign was eventually stalled by Stephen's forces, and she was forced to retreat. The conflict continued for several years, with both sides gaining and losing ground.

During this time, Stephen faced numerous challenges from other factions within England. One significant turning point was his treatment of Roger of Salisbury, who had been a powerful administrator and ally, having served as Henry I's chief justiciar. In 1139, Stephen arrested Roger and his family members, seizing their castles in a move that shocked the kingdom and damaged his reputation with the Church. Roger died that same year in custody. In 1141, the tide turned against Stephen when he was captured at the Battle of Lincoln. During his imprisonment, Matilda gained control of London and styled herself "Lady of the English," though she was never crowned queen. However, her arrogant behavior alienated the Londoners, and Stephen's wife Matilda of Boulogne rallied support for his cause. Stephen was eventually released in exchange for Robert of Gloucester (Matilda's half-brother), and the conflict continued.

Despite the ongoing violence and instability, Stephen was able to make some progress in terms of governance and administration. He established a number of new castles and fortifications throughout the country, which helped to strengthen his control over the territories he held. He also worked to develop a system of royal justice, which included the establishment of new courts and the appointment of new judges.

However, Stephen's reign was ultimately defined by the constant conflict and violence that characterized the Anarchy. The conflict took a heavy toll on the people of England, who suffered from widespread destruction and displacement. The country was left deeply divided, with many regions controlled by local warlords and factions rather than the central government.

In 1153, the conflict finally came to an end with the signing of the Treaty of Wallingford. Under the terms of the treaty, Stephen agreed to recognize Matilda's son, Henry Plantagenet, as his heir, effectively ending the dispute over the succession. Stephen also agreed to rule jointly with Henry until his death, ensuring a smooth transition of power.

Stephen died the following year, in 1154, having ruled for nearly 20 years. His reign was a period of great upheaval and conflict in English history, characterized by widespread violence and instability. While he made some progress in terms of governance and administration, his legacy is largely defined by the impact of the Anarchy on English society and the lasting scars that it left on the country.

Legacy of King Stephen

The legacy of the reign of King Stephen is one word: Anarchy. The period of conflict and instability known as the Anarchy had a profound impact on the country, with widespread violence and destruction causing significant social and economic upheaval. The legacy of this period can still be seen in the decentralization of power in England, with many regions retaining significant autonomy and local control. Additionally, the conflict contributed to the development of a system of royal justice and the establishment of new castles and fortifications throughout the country. Despite these advancements, however, the reign of King Stephen remains a cautionary tale of the dangers of political instability and the devastating impact it can have on society.

Portrayals of King Stephen

Stephen, the King of England, has been a popular historical figure who has been featured in several works of historical fiction. One such example is the detective series The Cadfael Chronicles, written by Ellis Peters, set in the years between 1137 and 1145. Peters' portrayal of Stephen's reign is a localized narrative primarily focused on the town of Shrewsbury and its surroundings. Despite his execution of the Shrewsbury defenders after the taking of the city in 1138, Peters depicts Stephen as a tolerant and sensible ruler. However, in contrast to this depiction, Stephen is portrayed in an unsympathetic light in both the historical novel The Pillars of the Earth, written by Ken Follett, and the TV mini-series adaptation of the same.

Further Research

- "Stephen and Matilda: The Civil War of 1139-53" by Jim Bradbury
- "The Anarchy: The Darkest Days of Medieval England" by Richard Kohn
- "Stephen: The Reign of Anarchy" by Carl Watkins
- "The Empress Matilda: Queen Consort, Queen Mother and Lady of the English" by Marjorie Chibnall (includes a chapter on King Stephen)

Site of Interest

- Oxford Castle, where Stephen was imprisoned during the conflict with Matilda.
- The Tower of London is where Stephen was kept prisoner after his capture at the Battle of Lincoln.
- Bristol Castle, which was besieged by Stephen's forces during the Anarchy.
- Fotheringhay Castle, where Matilda was born and where Stephen's son Eustace died.
- Wallingford Castle, where the Treaty of Wallingford was

signed, ended the conflict between Stephen and Matilda.

EMPRESS MATILDA (1141)

Empress Matilda, also known as Matilda of England, was one of the most intriguing and controversial figures of medieval England. She was born in 1102 and was the daughter of King Henry I of England. Her father, who had no male heir, declared Matilda as his successor and made the barons swear an oath to accept her as queen. However, after Henry's death, his nephew Stephen of Blois seized the throne, and Matilda was forced to fight for her right to rule.

Key Facts

- Matilda was the daughter of King Henry I of England, born in 1102 in London.
- Her father declared her his successor, but after his death, his nephew Stephen of Blois seized the throne.
- Matilda was backed by her half-brother Robert of Gloucester, who was a powerful baron and military leader during the civil war known as The Anarchy.
- Matilda's claim to the throne was based on her royal bloodline, but she faced opposition from those who believed that a woman could not be a good ruler.
- She was not crowned.
- Matilda's son, Henry, became King Henry II of England and founded the Plantagenet dynasty, which ruled England for over 300 years.
- She was not the 'Empress' of England but got the title from her marriage to the Holy Roman Emperor.

Early Life and Marriage

Matilda was probably born in Berkshire on February 7, 1102, and was the only surviving legitimate child of King Henry I and his wife Matilda of Scotland. She was well-educated and fluent in English, French, and Latin. She was married to Henry V, the Holy Roman Emperor, in 1114, when she was only 12 years old. The marriage was a political alliance between her father and the emperor, but it was not a happy one. Henry V died in 1125, and Matilda returned to England.

The Struggle for the Throne

In 1135, King Henry I died without a male heir. He had named Matilda as his successor, but his nephew Stephen of Blois seized the throne. Matilda, who was in Normandy at the time, immediately began to gather support for her cause. She was backed by her half-brother Robert of Gloucester, who was a powerful baron and military leader.

The civil war that followed, known as The Anarchy, lasted for nearly 20 years. Matilda's claim to the throne was supported by many of the barons, but Stephen was also popular with the people. The conflict was marked by battles, sieges, and political maneuvering. Matilda was captured by Stephen's forces in 1142, but she managed to escape from Oxford Castle and fled to France.

Matilda's son Henry, who was born in 1133, grew up in Normandy and became a skilled military leader. He invaded England in 1153, and after a series of negotiations, a peace treaty known as the Treaty of Wallingford was signed. Under the terms of the treaty, Stephen was allowed to remain on the throne for the rest of his life, but Henry was named as his successor.

Legacy

Matilda's legacy is mixed. She was a strong and determined woman who fought for her right to rule, but she was also seen as arrogant and aloof. Her claim to the throne was based on her royal bloodline, but she faced opposition from those who believed that a woman could not be a good ruler. The civil war that followed her father's death was a period of chaos and violence, and it led to the deaths of thousands of people.

Matilda's son, Henry, became King Henry II of England and was one of the most powerful monarchs in English history. He founded the Plantagenet dynasty, which ruled England for over 300 years. Matilda's daughter, also named Matilda, was married to Henry the Lion, Duke of Saxony, and became the mother of the Holy Roman Emperor Otto IV.

Further Research

- "Matilda: Empress, Queen, Warrior" by Catherine Hanley
- "Empress Matilda: A Legendary Medieval Warrior Queen" by Laurel A. Rockefeller

Locations Related to Empress Matilda

- London, where she was born in 1102.
- Winchester Castle, where she spent much of her childhood.
- Rouen Cathedral in Normandy, where she was buried after her death in 1167.
- The ruins of Wallingford Castle in Oxfordshire, where Matilda and Stephen signed the peace treaty.

HENRY II
(1154–1189)

Henry II was the first Plantagenet king of England, reigning from 1154 until his death in 1189. He was born in Le Mans, France, in 1133 and was the eldest son of the Count of Anjou. Henry was an ambitious and energetic ruler who expanded his territories through a combination of military conquest and strategic marriages. During his reign, he controlled England, substantial parts of Wales and Ireland, and much of France (including Normandy, Aquitaine, and Anjou), an area that altogether was later called the Angevin Empire, and also held power over Scotland and the Duchy of Brittany. He is perhaps best known for his turbulent relationship with Thomas Becket, the Archbishop of Canterbury, and the resulting murder of Becket in 1170. Despite this controversy, Henry was a successful king who made important legal and administrative reforms and laid the foundation for the strong centralized monarchy that would characterize England in the centuries to come.

Key Facts about Henry II

- Henry II was born in Le Mans, France, in 1133 and was the eldest son of the Count of Anjou.
- He became the first Plantagenet king of England in 1154 and reigned until his death in 1189.
- He expanded his territories through a combination of military conquest and strategic marriages.
- Henry had a turbulent relationship with Thomas Becket, the Archbishop of Canterbury, which resulted in Becket's murder in 1170.
- Despite the controversy, Henry was a successful king who made important legal and administrative reforms and laid the foundation for the strong centralized monarchy that would characterize England in the centuries to come.

Early Life and Rise to Power

Henry was born into a powerful family, the House of Anjou, one of the most prominent noble houses in France. His father, Count Geoffrey V of Anjou, died when Henry was only nine years old, and his mother, Empress Matilda, was the daughter of King Henry I of England. This connection to the English royal family would later play a crucial role in Henry's rise to power.

After his father's death, Henry was raised by his mother in Normandy. He received a high-quality education and developed a keen interest in learning and politics. He was also trained in warfare and became a skilled military commander.

In 1152, Henry married Eleanor of Aquitaine, a powerful and wealthy French duchess who had previously been married to King Louis VII of France. This marriage brought Henry vast territories in France, including Normandy, Anjou, Maine, and Aquitaine, making him one of the most powerful rulers in Europe.

In 1154, upon the death of King Stephen of England, Henry was crowned King Henry II of England. He was only 21 years old at the time, but he was already a seasoned politician and military leader.

Military Conquests and Strategic Marriages

During his reign, Henry II expanded his territories through a combination of military conquest and strategic marriages. He launched several military campaigns in Wales, Scotland, and Ireland, consolidating English control over these regions.

Henry also made strategic alliances through marriage. He arranged for his daughter, Matilda, to marry Henry the Lion, Duke of Saxony, and his son, Richard the Lionheart, to marry Berengaria of Navarre. These marriages strengthened Henry's position in Europe and helped him to build a powerful network of allies.

Turbulent Relationship with Thomas Becket

One of the most significant controversies of Henry's reign was his relationship with Thomas Becket, the Archbishop of Canterbury. Becket was a close friend and advisor of Henry's, but their relationship deteriorated when Becket was appointed Archbishop in 1162.

Becket began to resist Henry's attempts to exert control over the Church, and their disagreements soon turned into open conflict.

At one point, Henry reportedly uttered the infamous phrase, "Will no one rid me of this turbulent priest? (some quotes attribute it as 'troublesome priest')." It wasn't expressed as an order, but in 1170, four knights loyal to Henry murdered Becket in Canterbury Cathedral, causing outrage throughout Europe.

Henry was not directly involved in Becket's murder, but he was widely blamed for inciting it. He was forced to do penance for his role in Becket's death, and the incident damaged his reputation and authority.

Legal and Administrative Reforms

Despite the controversy surrounding Becket's murder, Henry was a successful king who made important legal and administrative reforms. He introduced the concept of the common law, which established a set of legal precedents that could be applied to similar cases in the future. He also established a system of royal justices, which helped to centralize the legal system and make it more efficient.

Henry also made significant administrative reforms. He established the office of the Exchequer, which was responsible for managing the royal finances, and he created a system of royal officials who could be dispatched to different parts of the country to enforce the king's laws.

Death and Legacy

Henry II died in 1189 while on a military campaign in France. He was succeeded by his son, Richard the Lionheart, who would go on to become one of England's most famous monarchs.

Henry's legacy is complex. He was a successful monarch who expanded England's territories, introduced important legal and administrative reforms, and strengthened the monarchy. However, his turbulent relationship with Thomas Becket and his involvement in Becket's murder has overshadowed many of his accomplishments.

King Henry II of England was a powerful and influential monarch whose reign had a lasting impact on English history. He was a skilled military commander, a shrewd politician, and a reformer who laid the foundations for the centralized monarchy that would characterize England in the centuries to come.

Movies and TV Shows Featuring Henry II

Henry II has been featured in several modern plays and films. James Goldman's 1966 play "The Lion in Winter" portrays an imaginary encounter between Henry's family and Philip Augustus over Christmas at Chinon. It has been turned into an Academy Award-winning film and a TV remake in 2003. The character of the King in this play is fictionalized, and his passions and character are not entirely accurate.

The relationship between Henry and Thomas Becket has been a rich source of drama, as seen in the 1923 film "Becket," Jean Anouilh's play "Becket" (filmed in 1964), and T. S. Eliot's play "Murder in the Cathedral." The character of the King in these plays is also fictitious, created to enhance the drama between them.

Henry II is also a character in Alfred, Lord Tennyson's 1884 play "Becket," and A.V. Bramble played Henry II in the 1924 adaptation of Tennyson's play.

Beth Flintoff has written a trilogy of plays that feature Henry II, his mother Matilda, and grandfather Henry I. These plays are fictionalized accounts of historical events, with the first play, "Henry I of England," covering the foundation of Reading Abbey in 1121. The second play, "Matilda the Empress," shows Henry II as a child during The Anarchy period after Henry I's death when Matilda and her cousin Stephen were rivals for succession. In the concluding part, "Henry II," which premiered in October 2018 at Reading's Minster Church of St Mary the Virgin, the king is the main focus. The play takes place over the Easter weekend of 1164, during the dedication of the Abbey, of which Henry II was an important patron.

Further Research on Henry II

- Henry II and Eleanor of Aquitaine: Founding an Empire by Matthew Lewis
- The Restless Kings by Nick Barratt
- Henry II (Penguin Monarchs): A Prince Among Princes by Richard Barber
- King of the North Wind: The Life of Henry II in Five Acts by Claudia Gold
- Thomas Becket: Warrior, Priest, Rebel by John Guy

Locations Related to Henry II

- Chinon Castle: This medieval castle in France was a significant residence for Henry II and his court.
- Westminster Abbey: Henry II was crowned at Westminster Abbey in 1154.
- Anjou, France: Henry II's ancestral homeland, where he held extensive lands and power.
- Dover Castle: One of the key defensive strongholds, often used by Henry II to secure the English coast.
- Canterbury Cathedral: Associated with the infamous murder of Thomas Becket, the Archbishop of Canterbury, during Henry II's reign.
- Clarendon Palace: A royal residence and hunting lodge where important decisions and agreements were made.
- Fontevraud Abbey: Henry II's final resting place, where he is buried alongside his wife Eleanor of Aquitaine.
- Fontevraud Abbey: The final resting place of Henry II's wife, Eleanor of Aquitaine, and their son, King Richard the Lionheart.
- Woodstock Palace: A royal residence where Henry II imprisoned his wife Eleanor during a rebellion led by their sons.

RICHARD I, THE LIONHEART (1189–1199)

The reign of Richard the Lionheart was dominated by the Third Crusade, his ill-fated and costly siege of Jerusalem. Richard supported his father, King Henry II, in battle from a young age and became Duke of various French territories in his twenties. Despite spending as little as six months of his reign as a resident in England, Richard I is said to have been adored by his English subjects, who thought him to be a great warrior and pious hero.

Key Facts about Richard the Lionheart

- Richard I was born on the 8th of September, 1157, in Oxfordforshire, UK.
- Richard succeeded as King of England on July 6th, 1189, at the age of 31.
- He was married on May 12th, 1191, to Berengria of Navarre.
- Richard died on 6th April 1199. His body is buried at Fontrevault, but his heart is buried at Rouen.

The Life of Richard I

Richard was born in England and but spent most of his youth in France. Richard, the third son of King Henry II, great-grandson of William the Conqueror, and Eleanor of Aquitaine was never expected to ascend to the English throne.

Before his death, Henry II had planned to divide his and Queen Eleanor's lands between his three eldest sons. Henry was to control England, Anjou, Maine, and Normandy; Richard would control Aquitaine and Poitiers, and Geoffrey would control Brittany. Although Henry II was already ill and Henry the Young was the natural heir to the English throne, his impatience got the better of him, and on the advice of his mother, Queen Eleanor, he organized a revolt against the King. Henry's brothers, Richard and Geoffrey, supported his revolt, and all three sought the protection and support of King Louis VII of France.

Following years of war across England and France, the family was reconciled with Richard receiving a 'kiss of peace' from Henry II during a peace treaty on the 23rd of September, 1174. Peace did not last long, however, and over the next ten to fifteen years, fighting between the King and his sons continued until finally, in 1183, King Henry the Younger was killed in battle.

In 1189, Richard again tried to take Henry's throne by force and defeated Henry II's army at Ballans. The crown slipped from Henry II's weary head two days later and was placed directly onto the head of Richard, who was now next in line to the throne. Richard was considered worthy of the English crown by many of the most influential people of the time, having proven his political agility and military skill by suppressing revolts by the rebellious nobles who repeatedly challenged his father's authority.

Richard officially became Duke of Normandy on the 20th of July, 1189, and was crowned King of England on the 3rd of September, 1189, at Westminster Abbey. During his coronation, Richard banned all women and Jews from the Abbey and had any Jews who did attempt to attend stripped and flogged. These actions instigated a pogrom massacre in London where many Jews were killed and Jewish homes and businesses destroyed. Richard distributed a Royal Writ ordering that the violence against Jews must stop, but it seems this was loosely enforced, and the violence spread to other cities such as York and Norwich.

Despite this civil unrest, Richard continued with his plans to launch a Third Crusade to Jerusalem, hoping to seize the holy land from its current ruler, Saladin, with the help of King Philip II of France. In order to raise a crusader army, Richard recklessly liquidated positions and lands belonging to the crown. He plundered the treasury and made all those occupying official posts in the Kingdom pay huge sums to retain them. During his rapacious pursuit of quick cash, he was said to announce, 'I would have sold London if I could have found a buyer.' Leaving his brother John in charge of England, Richard set off on his crusade in the summer of 1190.

Over a year later, Richard was no closer to Jerusalem than Sicily. It was around this time that Richard's mother, Eleanor of Aquitaine, who was by now 69 years old, traveled to Sicily to introduce Richard to the young Berengaria of Navarre. It was sound tactical judgment to lay claim to Navarre, considering its position bordering the Gascony area of Aquitaine, so Richard agreed to the marriage. Soon after, Richard captured the island of Cyprus, occupying a key strategic position in the maritime channels to Jerusalem and benefiting from much-needed financial gain. Richard and Berengaria were married on May 12th, 1191, at the Chapel of St George and enjoyed a double coronation as Richard was crowned King of Cyprus and Berengaria was crowned Queen of England and Cyprus.

Richard and his forces aided in the capture of Acre on the coast of what was then Saladin's Empire in June of 1191. Following the seizure, Richard and Philip seriously offended Leopold V, Duke of Austria, by removing Leopold's banner from where it was raised, a slight the Duke took as a signal to leave the crusades. Philip left soon after, and his relationship with Richard was tarnished by Richard's insistence on claiming all of Cyprus for himself.

Richard's crusading army made two major advancements towards the capture of Jerusalem in the following months, but each time they came within sight of Jerusalem, they only turned back without launching an attack. Dissension among the crusading army's leaders, poor weather, and news from England that Philip and Richard's brother John were plotting to overthrow him all led Richard to call off his great crusade and come to a settlement with Saladin. The pair came to an agreement on the 2nd of September, 1192, and embarked on a three-year truce.

Richard's journey home was not an easy one. Bad weather forced him to dock his ship at Corfu, which was then ruled by a Byzantine emperor who considered Richard an enemy due to his capture of Cyprus. Richard escaped only to become shipwrecked on the coast of central Europe. Richard was captured near Vienna by Duke Leopold V of Austria, the same Duke he had humiliated in Acre. The Duke held Richard in Durnstein Castle before handing him over to Henry VI, Holy Roman Emperor, who held him in

Trifels Castle. Both Duke Leopold and Henry VI found themselves excommunicated by Pope Celestine for their part in Richard's detention, as it was illegal to imprison a crusader.

The emperor demanded 150,000 marks (65,000 pounds of silver) be paid for Richard's release. At the time, this represented between 2 to 3 times the annual income of the English crown. Eleanor of Aquitaine worked hard to raise the funds for her son's release by taxing the English people heavily for over a year. John, Richard's brother, and his ally King Philip did not wish to see Richard return and tried to pay the Emperor to keep Richard imprisoned, but to no avail. Richard returned to England in February of 1194.

During his imprisonment, Philip had taken control of Normandy. Bizarrely, Richard forgave his brother John for his revolt, securing his claim to the throne on Richard's death. Richard left for France with his army, waging war with King Philip to regain Normandy for the English. He was successful in building the vast Château Gaillard high up on the River Seine in order to protect his land.

Legend has it that Richard I was killed by a young boy employed as an archer, defending his castle walls. It is thought that Richard had killed the boy's parents. The wound caused by the arrow became gangrenous, and, knowing his days were numbered, he ordered that the boy be brought to him so that he could ask for his forgiveness. Richard died on the 6th day of April, 1199.

Legacy of Richard I

Richard is an iconic figure remembered for his wars and crusades. An accomplished military engineer, Richard's skill at organizing an army and the logistics of defending a castle have gone down in history. Richard's peace treaty with Saladin, Sultan of Egypt, also had a lasting effect on the global politics of the Middle Ages as a friendship emerged between the Muslim and Christian adversaries and opened up the possibility of negotiation between people of differing faiths.

Some believe Richard to have been a good King, a kind and generous man, and a talented and brave soldier. But there are also those who consider Richard to have been a terrible King, one who cost England dearly, both in fortune and in lives, for his unsuccessful crusade and his foolish capture and ransom. Richard was a man of war, and his love for England extended only as far as her resources, which he plundered mercilessly to fund his blood lust. He spent no more than six months in England during his ten years' reign.

Films and TV Shows Featuring Richard I

- The Crusades(1935)
- The Adventures of Robin Hood(1938)
- Ivanhoe(1952)
- The Men of Sherwood Forest(1954)
- The Lion in Winter(1968)
- Robin and Marian(1976)
- Lionheart(1987)
- Robin Hood(2010)
- Richard The Lionheart(2013)
- Richard the Lionheart: Rebellion(2014)

Further Research

- Miller (2013) Richard the Lionheart: The Mighty Crusader
- Madden, Thomas F.(2005), Crusades: The Illustrated History
- Gillingham, John (2002)Richard I,
- Turner, Ralph V, Heiser, Richard R (2000), The Reign of Richard Lionheart
- Flori, Jean (1999), Richard the Lionheart: Knight and King
- Harvey, John (1948), The Plantagenets

Locations Related to Richard I

- There is a statue of Richard I on horseback outside of the Palace of Westminster, London.
- Richard built Chateau Gaillard in Normandy, the ruins of which can be visited by the public.

- Richard I died at the Chateau du Chalus-Chabrol. The castle is still standing and can be visited by the public.
- Richard I's remains are buried in three locations; his entrails are in Chalus, his heart is in Rouen, and the rest of his body is in Fontevraud Abbey in Anjou. All three tombs can be visited by the public.

JOHN (1199–1216)

King John is thought to be the antithesis of King Richard, the Lionheart who preceded him. If Richard was tall, strong, brave, and an accomplished military leader, John was short, weak, cowardly, and completely unskilled in the art of war. After attempting to steal the English crown from his brother Richard, who had entrusted John to look after his Kingdom while he led the Third Crusade, John legally inherited the throne in 1199 when Richard the Lionheart died. King John is remembered today for his sealing of the Magna Carta, a document sealed under pressure to avoid a full-scale civil war. John lost all English territories in France, his treasure, his crown, and his life at the age of 49.

Key Facts about King John

- John was born on December 24th, 1167, in Oxford, England.
- He became King of England on April 7th, 1199, aged 32.
- John was married twice, first to Isabella of Gloucester, whom he divorced in 1200, and second to Isabella of Angouleme, with whom he had five children.
- He died at 49 of dysentery and is buried at Worcester Cathedral.

The Life of King John

The youngest of the nine children of King Henry II and Queen Eleanor, John was born into a dynasty already at war over titles and inheritance. Shortly after his birth, he was sent, along with his sister Joan, to Fontevault Abbey. Neither of his parents had any involvement in his upbringing, and it is thought that a future in the church was encouraged.

Yet, as soon as he was old enough, John joined in the scheming and treachery within the royal family wholeheartedly. John joined his brothers in a revolt against King Henry II when Henry was already dying. He later plotted against his brother Richard when he was overseas leading the Third Crusade. His childhood nickname, Lackland, a cruel joke referring to his lack of inheritance due to his late and unexpected birth (Eleanor was 45 when she gave birth to John, a very old pregnancy by the standards of the Middle Ages), followed him throughout his life.

John is thought to have been the favorite son of King Henry II, and there is much evidence of this. John was originally betrothed to Alais and heiress to Humbert III of Savoy when he was just five years old. At the same time, King Henry II transferred ownership of three prominent castles and estates into John's name. In 1176, King Henry had the sisters of Isabelle of Gloucester disinherited so that he could betroth her to John, securing her vast fortune for him. Then, in 1177, Henry dismissed the Lord of Ireland and replaced him with John, who was just ten years old. It is these acts that are thought to have instigated the animosity between King Henry and his other sons that led to years of uncertainty and revolt.

John's rule of Ireland was unsuccessful, to say the least. He failed to make allies among the Anglo-Norman settlers, offended the native Irish, and failed to stabilize the country. Within six months, John was withdrawn from his position and sent home. Soon after, Henry II's eldest son, Geoffrey, died, and tensions within the family grew. Richard was afraid Henry would choose John as his successor, so he, along with Philip II of France, launched a war against him. John's support was supposed to be with his father, Henry, but he treacherously changed sides late in the war when it became clear that his father's health was waning and he was likely to lose the fight.

During Richard's reign, John was married to Isabella of Gloucester and given valuable lands in various English counties in an attempt to buy his loyalty while Richard was away fighting the Third Crusade. It was agreed that John would leave England and remain a resident elsewhere for the next three years to deter him from launching any real threat to Richard's crown. However, the political system Richard had set up to rule in his absence quickly fell apart, leaving John free to set up his own royal court. John fought with

Richard's chancellor, William Longchamp, a conflict that resulted in Longchamp being held in the Tower of London while John took control of the city and had its citizens recognize him as heir to the throne.

Desperate to find a powerful ally before his big brother returned from his crusade and found out what he had been up to, John sought the friendship of King Philip II of France. Philip had recently returned from Richard's crusade, feeling ill towards the King. Despite John's scheming and the civil war that broke out between followers of Richard and John in England, Richard forgave his younger brother on his return, remarking that John was but "a child who has had evil counselors."

Although Arthur of Brittany, four-year-old son of oldest son Geoffrey, was named heir to Richard's throne, John was crowned King of England on April 7th, 1199, at Westminster Abbey. John's ten-year marriage to Isabel of Gloucester was childless, so once he became King, the marriage was annulled quickly. Less than a year later, John kidnapped Isabella of Angouleme from her fiancée Hugh X de Lusignan, Count of Lusignan, and married her in a ceremony on 24th August 1200. Isabella was between twelve and thirteen years old at the time she became Queen of England, young even for medieval standards, but the King was thought to be besotted by her. Between the years 1207 and 1215, Isabella bore John five healthy children who all lived into adulthood and took up powerful positions in the English nobility. John also acknowledged up to 12 illegitimate children, many of whom were the result of his seducing the wives and children of his barons. Incredibly, following John's death, Isabella returned to Angouleme to marry her original fiancée, Hugh IX le Brun, with whom she gave birth to a further nine children.

As a direct result of John's aggressive approach to securing Isabella's hand in marriage, King Philip II confiscated all of the couple's French lands, and war ensued. Early in his reign, John lost the regions of Normandy, Anjou, and Maine. Anjou and Maine had defected on the death of Richard, choosing Arthur as their lord. John had Arthur killed, and in retaliation, King Philip occupied Normandy, Anjou, and Maine. John attempted to regain the territories he had lost, but due to a lack of resources, bad treatment of allies, and general incompetence, he lost all English territories on the continent to Philip of France except the Duchy of Aquitaine.

In 1207, King John fell out with Pope Innocent III over who should become the next Archbishop of Canterbury. This disagreement led to the Pope excommunicating John and placing England under Church law, an act that made any christenings or marriages performed in the country invalid without the Pope's personal consent. The English people were horrified, and King John became more unpopular than ever. It took until 1213 for John to reconcile with the pope in a formal agreement that involved the exchange of cash and was thought to be humiliating to the King.

The loss of all of England's French territories led to the Baron's Revolt, and John was forced to agree to the Magna Carta, granting certain rights to English men and women, in order to avoid a full-scale civil war. Although important politically and symbolically, Magna Carta did not bring about an end to war, and after two years of fighting, King John became gravely ill. John's personal treasure was lost when his carriage was washed away in the Wash, Lincolnshire, and just a few days later, he met with his death. King John was succeeded by King Henry III.

Legacy of King John

As is the nature of historiography, historian's opinions on King John have changed over time. John's reign is remembered for his huge military defeats, most notably his loss of Normandy to Philip II of France in the first few years of his reign. Although it is difficult to gauge public opinion during the Middle Ages, when very little was recorded by the mostly illiterate masses, it is thought that John was an unpopular King. His taxes were high, his foreign campaigns were unsuccessful, and his private life was said to be immoral.

However, King John does have his supporters. As a regular judge at the Royal Courts, John was thought to have been diligent and fair, and he implemented a fastidious approach to record-taking that the archivists of today will thank him for.

John managed to aggrieve the Pope of the time, almost all

of his powerful Barons, and King Philip II of France during his reign, leading many to conclude that he was inept in the political subtlety needed to be a successful monarch. John was forced to seal the Magna Carta, a document so important it has been preserved to the present day, and eventually lost his throne under the threat of a devastating civil war.

Film and TV Shows Featuring King John

- Ironclad (2011)
- Robin Hood (2010)
- The Lion in Winter (2003)
- Ivanhoe (1997) TV Show
- The Life and Death of King John (1984)
- Ivanhoe (1952)
- King John (1899) Short Silent Film

Further Research

- Morris, Marc (2015) King John: Treachery, Tyranny and the Road to the Magna Carta
- Turner, Ralph V. (2009) King John: England's Evil King?
- Church, Stephen D. (2007) King John: New Interpretations
- Lloyd, Alan. (1972) The Maligned Monarch: a Life of King John of England.
- Holt, James Clarke. (1963) King John

Locations Related to King John

- King John spent most of his childhood at Fontevrault Abbey in Anjou. Nothing remains of the original building, but the area has been designated a UNESCO World Heritage Site.
- The Magna Carta is on display at the British Library in London, UK.
- An effigy of King John can be found in Worchester Cathedral.

HENRY III
(1216–1272)

Henry III was one of the longest-reigning monarchs in English history, reigning from 1216 to 1272. His rule was marked by political turmoil, religious conflict, and economic hardship, but it also saw significant cultural and artistic achievements. Henry III was known for his patronage of the arts, particularly architecture, and he oversaw the construction of several notable buildings, including Westminster Abbey and the rebuilt Westminster Palace. Despite his many accomplishments, Henry III's reign was also marked by challenges to his authority, including a series of baronial rebellions that threatened to undermine his rule and reshape English governance.

Key Facts about Henry III

- Henry III was only nine years old when he became king of England in 1216, following the death of his father, King John.
- Henry III was a devout Christian who made several pilgrimages to holy sites throughout his reign, including Santiago de Compostela in Spain.
- He was a prolific builder, and his patronage of architecture led to the construction of many significant buildings, including the famous Westminster Abbey.
- Henry III's reign saw the first use of the term "parliament" to refer to the English council of nobles and clergy who advised the king.

A Brief Look at the Life of Henry III

Henry III was born on October 1, 1207, in Winchester, England, to King John and Isabella of Angouleme. His father's reign had been marked by political turmoil, including a conflict with the

English barons that led to the signing of the Magna Carta in 1215. Following King John's death in October 1216, nine-year-old Henry III was crowned king of England.

During the early years of his reign, Henry III faced a series of challenges to his authority. One of the most significant of these was the threat of invasion by Prince Louis of France, who had been invited to England by the rebellious barons. In 1217, however, the English forces, led by William Marshal, defeated the French at the Battle of Lincoln, securing Henry III's position as king.

For much of his reign, Henry III struggled to maintain control over his realm, particularly in the face of the powerful barons who held significant political and military power. In 1258, a group of barons led by Simon de Montfort formed a council that effectively governed England for the next two years. This period, known as the "Provisions of Oxford," saw significant reforms to English governance, including the establishment of a council of nobles and clergy that would advise the king.

However, Henry III's reign was not entirely marked by political turmoil. He was a devout Christian and made several pilgrimages to holy sites throughout his reign, including to Santiago de Compostela in Spain. He was also a prolific builder, and his patronage of architecture led to the construction of many significant buildings, including the famous Westminster Abbey.

One of Henry III's most significant achievements was his patronage of the arts, particularly architecture. He oversaw the construction of several notable buildings, including Westminster Abbey and the rebuilt Westminster Palace. He was also a significant patron of the arts, commissioning works from some of the most prominent medieval artists of his time.

Henry III's reign saw the first use of the term "parliament" to refer to the English council of nobles and clergy who advised the king. While the precise origins of the English parliament are unclear, it is generally agreed that it evolved from the council of advisors that surrounded the king.

One of the key figures of Henry III's reign was Simon de Montfort, who led the baronial rebellion that challenged the king's authority in the mid-13th century. De Montfort was a formidable military leader and a skilled politician, and his rebellion led to significant changes in English governance. However, he was eventually defeated by the king's forces at the Battle of Evesham in 1265.

Another key figure of Henry III's reign was William Marshal, who played a significant role in securing the young king's position following his father's death. Marshal was a skilled military leader and a trusted advisor to the king, and he played a key role in several of the major conflicts of the early years of Henry III's reign.

Overall, Henry III's reign was marked by both significant achievements and significant challenges. His patronage of the arts and architecture left a lasting legacy, while his struggles to maintain control over his realm highlighted the complex political landscape of medieval England. Despite the challenges he faced, Henry III's reign played a significant role in shaping the history of England and its monarchy.

Legacy of Henry III

Henry III's reign was marked by both significant achievements and challenges. His patronage of the arts and architecture left a lasting legacy that you can still see in England's built landscape, while his struggles to maintain control over his realm highlighted the complex political landscape of medieval England. His rule also saw the first use of the term "parliament" to refer to the English council of nobles and clergy who advised the king. Although Henry III faced many challenges to his authority, his reign laid the foundation for the development of the English monarchy and the growth of parliamentary governance in the centuries to come. His reign also saw significant cultural and artistic achievements, which helped to shape the identity of England as a nation and a center of European culture.

Cultural Depictions of Henry III

Henry is a character in Purgatorio, the second part of Dante's Divine Comedy, which was completed in 1320. In the book, the King is portrayed sitting alone in purgatory, separated from other failed rulers such as Rudolf I of Germany, Ottokar II of Bohemia, Philip III of France, Henry I of Navarre, as well as Charles I of Naples and Peter III of Aragon. It is unclear why Dante depicted Henry sitting separately, but it could be a reference to England not being part of the Holy Roman Empire. Another possibility is that Dante had a favorable opinion of Henry due to his unusual piety. In the same work, Canto VII. 132, Dante also salutes Henry's son, Edward.

In William Shakespeare's play King John, Henry appears as a minor character referred to as Prince Henry. However, in modern popular culture, Henry has a minimal presence and has not been a prominent subject of films, theatre, or television. Several historical novels feature him as a character, including Longsword, Earl of Salisbury: A Historical Romance (1762) by Thomas Leland, The Red Saint (1909) by Warwick Deeping, The Outlaw of Torn (1927) by Edgar Rice Burroughs, The De Montfort Legacy (1973) by Pamela Bennetts, The Queen from Provence (1979) by Jean Plaidy, The Marriage of Meggotta (1979) by Edith Pargeter, and Falls the Shadow (1988) by Sharon Kay Penman.

Further Research

- Henry III: The Rise to Power and Personal Rule, 1207-1258 (Volume 1) (The English Monarchs Series)
- Henry III: Reform, Rebellion, Civil War, Settlement, 1259-1272 (Volume 2) (The English Monarchs Series)
- Henry III Paperback by Darren Baker
- Henry III (Penguin Monarchs): A Simple and God-Fearing King by Stephen Church

Locations Related to Henry III

- Born at Winchester Castle
- The Great Hall at Winchester Castle (built by Henry)
- Crowned in Gloucester Cathedral (with a second coronation at Westminster Abbey later)
- Buried in Westminster Abbey

EDWARD I
(1272–1307)

Edward I, also known as "Edward Longshanks," was born on June 17, 1239, in Westminster, London. He was the eldest son of King Henry III and Queen Eleanor of Provence. Edward was a tall and imposing figure, standing at 6'2", and was known for his military prowess, administrative skills, and legal reforms. His reign as King of England from 1272 to 1307 was marked by significant achievements that transformed England both domestically and internationally. In this article, we will explore the life, reign, and legacy of Edward I.

Key Facts about Edward Longshanks

- Edward I was born on June 17, 1239, in Westminster, London.
- He reigned as King of England from 1272 to 1307, a total of 35 years.
- Edward was known for his military prowess, administrative skills, and legal reforms.
- He was responsible for the conquest of Wales and the subjugation of Scotland (which was depicted in Braveheart).
- Edward was a towering figure, standing at 6'2", which was considered very tall for his time.

Early Life and Education

Edward was raised in a turbulent political climate, where his father, King Henry III, struggled to maintain his grip on power. In 1254, when Edward was 15 years old, he was married to Eleanor of Castile, the daughter of King Ferdinand III of Castile. The marriage was a strategic alliance that helped secure peace between England and Castile.

Edward received an excellent education, which prepared

him for his future role as king. He was fluent in several languages, including Latin, French, and Italian, and was well-versed in the classics, history, and law. He also had a keen interest in military strategy and was an accomplished horseman and swordsman.

During the Second Barons' War, Edward's father faced a rebellion led by Simon de Montfort, who had become increasingly dissatisfied with his father, Henry III's rule. The conflict culminated in the Battle of Lewes in 1264, where de Montfort's forces defeated the royal army and captured Edward I. He was held captive for several months. The war ultimately resulted in significant changes to the political landscape of England and led to the establishment of the first parliament.

The Crusader

Edward I was a significant figure during the Crusades. He was an ardent supporter of the Crusades and saw it as an opportunity to defend Christendom against the Muslim threat. Edward was particularly interested in the Ninth Crusade, which took place between 1271 and 1272. He was one of the few European rulers who actively supported this campaign, and he personally led a contingent of English knights to the Holy Land. Edward's involvement in the Crusades not only demonstrated his religious zeal but also helped him establish himself as a powerful ruler on the international stage.

Edward's involvement in the Crusades was not limited to his participation in the Ninth Crusade. He also played a significant role in the defense of Acre, one of the last remaining Christian strongholds in the Holy Land. In 1271, Acre was under siege by the Muslim forces, and Edward responded by sending a large contingent of knights to assist in its defense. Edward's forces played a vital role in lifting the siege and securing Acre's safety. His leadership and military prowess during this campaign earned him the nickname "Hammer of the Saracens."

Edward's involvement in the Crusades helped establish him as a significant figure in medieval Europe. His religious zeal and military prowess earned him the respect and admiration of his contemporaries, and his participation in the Ninth Crusade and defense of Acre helped strengthen England's position on the international stage. Edward's legacy as a king who was committed to defending Christendom against the Muslim threat is still remembered today, and he remains a popular figure in the history of the Crusades. While on his way home to England after his adventures, he was informed his father had died and he was King.

Reign as King of England

Edward's reign as king was marked by significant achievements, which transformed England both domestically and internationally. He worked tirelessly to strengthen the power of the monarchy and the rule of law, which helped establish England as a leading European power.

One of Edward's most significant achievements was his military campaigns in Wales and Scotland. Edward was determined to bring Wales under English control, and he launched a series of military campaigns that lasted over two decades. In 1284, he established the Statute of Rhuddlan, which reorganized the governance of Wales and created the position of Prince of Wales, which has since been held by the heir to the English throne. Wales, which was a principality, was incorporated into England as if it didn't exist. Wales would not exist as a separate political entity for centuries after that.

Edward's campaigns in Scotland were equally successful. He invaded Scotland in 1296 and captured the Scottish king, John Balliol, who was forced to abdicate. Edward then installed a series of English governors in Scotland, which led to a rebellion by Scottish nationalists (which included William Wallace, depicted in the film Braveheart, which is not very historically accurate). Edward responded by launching a brutal campaign that culminated in the Battle of Falkirk in 1298, where he defeated the Scottish army and secured English control over Scotland.

Domestically, Edward was also a visionary ruler who introduced significant legal reforms that helped strengthen the rule of law. He established the Model Parliament, which provided a forum for the king to consult with his subjects and seek their advice on important matters of state.

Legacy of Edward Longshanks

Edward's legacy as a king who transformed England both domestically and internationally cannot be overstated. His military campaigns in Wales and Scotland helped establish England as a leading European power, while his legal reforms strengthened the rule of law and established the principle of parliamentary sovereignty. It also cemented full English control of the island of Great Britain.

Edward's impact on English society can still be felt today. The position of Prince of Wales, which he created in 1284, is still held by the heir to the English throne. The Model Parliament, which he established in 1295, evolved into the modern-day Parliament, which plays a vital role in British politics. Most people would be familiar with him from his portrayal in the film Braveheart. While the characterization might be accurate, many of the facts are not (it's still a fantastic film!).

Movies and TV Shows Featuring Edward I

The Famous Chronicle of King Edward the First, a theatrical play by George Peele, dramatized Edward's life. Edward I was a popular figure in historical fiction during the Victorian and Edwardian eras. Novels from this period featuring Edward include Truths and Fictions of the Middle Ages (1837) by Francis Palgrave, Forest Days; or Robin Hood (1843) by G. P. R. James, The Lord of Dynevor: A Tale of the Times of Edward the First (1892) by Evelyn Everett-Green, Simon de Montfort; or, The third siege of Rochester Castle by Edwin Harris (1902), and De Montfort's squire. A story of the battle of Lewes by the Reverend Frederick Harrison (1909). The Prince and the Page: A Story of the Last Crusade (1866) by Charlotte Mary Yonge depicts Edward's involvement in the Ninth Crusade and portrays him as a chivalrous and brave figure.

Halcott Glover's play, The King's Jewelry (1927), focuses on Edward's relationship with England's Jewish community, while Geoffrey Trease's The Baron's Hostage (1952) portrays Edward as a young man participating in the Battle of Evesham.

Some novels with a contemporary setting also feature Edward, portraying him in a negative light. The Brothers of Gwynedd quartet by Edith Pargeter, for example, depicts Edward as the antagonist of the Welsh heroes. Edward also appears in The Reckoning and Falls the Shadow by Sharon Penman, The Wallace and The Bruce Trilogy by Nigel Tranter, and the Brethren trilogy by Robyn Young, a fictional account of Edward and his involvement with a secret organization within the Knights Templar.

Hungarian poet Janos Arany's ballad The Bards of Wales tells the story of the 500 Welsh bards who were burned at the stake by King Edward I of England for refusing to sing his praises during a banquet at Montgomery Castle after the Plantagenet conquest of Wales (but this did not actually happen). The poem was meant as a veiled attack against Emperor Franz Joseph and Tsar Nicholas I of Russia for their roles in the defeat of the Hungarian Revolution of 1848 and for the repressive policies in the Kingdom of Hungary that followed the end of the uprising.

In the film Braveheart, Edward Longshanks is portrayed as a ruthless and cunning king who is determined to bring Scotland under English control. He is depicted as a manipulative leader who uses his power and influence to achieve his goals, regardless of the cost. His treatment of the Scottish people is brutal, and he is shown ordering the execution of William Wallace and other Scottish rebels. The portrayal of Edward Longshanks in Braveheart is one of a cold and calculating monarch who is willing to do whatever it takes to maintain English dominance.

Further Research

- A Great and Terrible King: Edward I and the Forging of Britain by Marc Morris
- Edward I (The English Monarchs Series) by Professor Michael Prestwich
- Edward I (Penguin Monarchs) Part of: Penguin Monarchs by Andy King
- Daughters of Edward I by Kathryn Warner

Locations Related to

- Westminster, London – where Edward I was born in 1239
- Castile, Spain – where Edward's wife, Eleanor of Castile, was from
- Wales – where Edward launched a series of military campaigns to bring it under English control
- Rhuddlan, Wales – where Edward established the Statute of Rhuddlan in 1284, which reorganized the governance of Wales
- Scotland – where Edward invaded in 1296 and secured English control over the country
- Falkirk, Scotland – where Edward defeated the Scottish army in the Battle of Falkirk in 1298
- The Tower of London – where Edward I imprisoned his Scottish rival, John Balliol
- The English Channel – which Edward used to transport troops and supplies during his military campaigns
- The Palace of Westminster – where Edward established the Model Parliament in 1295
- The city of York – where Edward held a series of important councils and meetings during his reign.

EDWARD II
(1307–1327) (deposed)

Ultimately, a failure as a king, Edward II spent the majority of his reign battling with the baronial lords of the time who constantly rebelled and sought to gain power over the king and control of the country. Edward II incurred large debts during his years as King and oversaw the Scots' famous victory at Bannockburn by Robert the Bruce. Criticized for his habit of taking close personal friends and lavishly bestowing them with titles and wealth, Edward was constantly at odds with his nobles. Betrayed by his wife, in politics and matrimony, Edward was forced to renounce his throne to his son before dying a sad death while held captive at Berkeley Castle.

Key Facts about Edward II

- Edward II was born on the 25th of April 1284 at Caernarvon.
- He succeeded to the English throne on 7th July 1307, aged 23, and became the King of England, Overlord of Ireland and Scotland, and Duke of Aquitaine.
- Edward II was married in 1308 to Isabella of France, daughter of King Philip IV. Isabella was nicknamed the She-Wolf and, after 19 years of marriage, was instrumental in having Edward deposed and killed.
- Following his abdication from the throne and ten months of imprisonment, Edward II was killed on 22nd September 1327.

The King Betrayed By His Wife

The fourth surviving son of King Edward I and his first wife, Eleanor of Castile Edward II, endured a childhood marked by loss. Eleanor of Castile was separated from Edward through the majority of his childhood and died when he was just seven years old following an extended illness. Edward I was fighting in three countries over the next few years of young Edward's life. When Edward I remarried, he focussed his time on his new family and rarely saw his other sons.

Raised by a dedicated Royal Household, Edward was given a religious education by Dominican friars. Edward enjoyed horse riding and music but was criticized for his regular association with laborers and other members of the lower class. An image of Edward as a somewhat shallow and irresponsible person took seed during his childhood years and set him on a course of hostility with his court that he would struggle with for the rest of his life.

During 1297 and 1298, Edward II was left as the acting regent of England while his father fought a campaign in Flanders against the French King Philip IV. As part of a peace treaty, Edward was betrothed to Isabella, King Phillip's daughter, who was then only seven years old. Edward was taken to Scotland with his father in 1300 to command a division and was declared the Prince of Wales in 1301. The young prince was being groomed for a future as King.

According to some historians, the single most significant person in Edward's life was not his father, his wife, or his priest but his childhood playmate, Piers Gaveston. Piers was the son of a noble knight from Gascony and was brought to Edward's household as a companion to the young prince. Edward's life was filled with Gaveston, and contemporary chroniclers of royal lives have launched in-depth investigations into whether or not the pair were intimate. The details of the relationship remain unclear, but in 1306, Gaveston was knighted by King Edward I a few days after the Feast of Swans before being promptly exiled by him in 1307.

Just one month after his father's death, the newly crowned Edward II brought Galveston back from exile and made him the Earl of Cornwall, a title generally reserved for the royal family, and married him to the wealthiest lady in the land, Margaret de Clare. As if that wasn't enough, Edward appointed Gaveston regent of England while he went to France for his wedding to 16-year-old Isabella of France. None of this was well-received by the English aristocracy. In fact, the special treatment given to young Galveston was so badly received by the aristocracy that Edward's own Council launched a revolt.

Thomas of Lancaster, a Marcher Lord who was in the enviable position of being a cousin to both the King and his new queen and holding five powerful earldoms, led the revolt against Edward. Within a year of his accession, Edward was forced by his Council to take the Earldom of Cornwall back from Gaveston and again sent him into exile. In response, Edward appointed Gaveston as his Lord Lieutenant of Ireland, a move that further enraged the Barons.

Within one year, Gaveston returned to Edward's court thanks to Edward's efforts, which involved a complicated game of favors between the Pope and the monarchy of France. When Gaveston's influence over government and excessive spending of the country's revenue got too much for the Barons, they forced the appointment of 21 Lord Ordainers who took over the management of the economy.

Tensions between the unpopular king and the barons remained high, and the earls opposed to the king, led by the powerful and wealthy Earl of Lancaster, kept their personal armies mobilized. In 1312, the barons had Galveston excommunicated by the Archbishop of Canterbury and seized him following a short siege. Accused of being a traitor, Gaveston was executed.

The storm clouds parted for just a moment to welcome Edward and Isabella's first child into the world, a son who would go on to become Edward III, but soon things got even worse for the unhappy king. In 1314, seven years into his reign, Edward came up against Robert the Bruce in the Battle of Bannockburn and suffered a defeat that gained Scotland its independence. It would take three centuries for the English to recover this loss, and the huge debts left by Edward's Scottish campaign made him even more unpopular with the people.

In the tense time that followed the loss of Scotland, Lancaster was able to insert himself as the leader of the Lord Ordainers, effectively the leader of the formal government of England. Excluded and despised, Edward turned to his friends, most notably the Lord le Depenser and his son, who he pampered with favors and titles, just as he had pampered Gaveston.

The Earl of Lancaster and Roger de Mortimer, Earl of March, formed a powerful enough alliance to wage war with the king, and a civil war ensued. The le Depensers were banished, but Edward managed to capture both Lancaster and Mortimer. Lancaster was executed, and Mortimer was held in the Tower of London. By now, it was known to all that Edward's wife, Isabella, was having an affair with Mortimer. In 1323, Isabella took matters into her own hands, contriving Mortimer's escape from the Tower into France and following with her son Edward III, heir to the English throne.

In September 1326, the ambitious trio landed in Suffolk with an army and declared the young prince-governor of the country. With no army and no support from his people, Edward II was easily captured, his companions, the le Depensers, were hanged, and he was imprisoned in Kenilworth to await his fate. After being forced to abdicate by a representative delegation of barons, clergy, and knights who agreed that Edward II was unfit to lead the country, his son Edward III was proclaimed King of England at Westminster Abbey on 20 January 1327.

Conveniently, Edward II died in custody on 21st September. Little is known about the circumstances of his death, but it is thought that Mortimer likely arranged for his murder. Mortimer's dominance did not last long, however. He and Isabella soon fell out of favor with the populace as they amassed and spent a huge fortune. In 1330, King Edward III initiated a coup d'etat, arresting and executing Mortimer on charges of treason. But that's the story of a different king.

Legacy

King Edward II's legacy is not a particularly glorious one. Unpopular with his baronial lords, his court, and his people, Edward's reign was primarily spent avoiding his duties as king and buying the affection of his so-called 'favorites.' A dismal reign, Edward's time on the throne saw English defeat at the Battle of Bannockburn. Much writing on Edward II following his death has focussed on his relationship with Piers Gaveston and alluding to his possible homosexuality. An unpopular and inadequate king, Edward II was nonetheless a source of fascination, particularly to the Victorians who learned about his life from the likes of Charles Dickens and Charles Knight.

Film and TV

- Braveheart (1995)
- Marlowe (1991)
- Edward II (1991)
- Edward II (1970) (TV Movie)
- Edward II (1982) (TV Movie)

Further Research

- Mortimer, Ian, and Warner, Kathryn (2015) Edward II: The Unconventional King
- Jones, Dan (2013) The Plantagenets
- Phillips, Seymour (2011) Edward II (The English Monarchs Series)
- Doherty, Paul (2004). Isabella and the Strange Death of Edward II
- Haines, Roy Martin (2003). King Edward II: His Life, his Reign, and its Aftermath

Locations to Visit

- Caerphilly Castle is the place where Edward II spent his last weeks in hiding.
- Warwick Castle is the location where Piers Gaveston was tried and killed.
- Bannockburn was the place where England was defeated by the Scots under Robert the Bruce during Edward II's reign.
- Edward II's place of death, Berkeley Castle in Gloucestershire, UK
- Edward II's burial site is Gloucester Cathedral in Gloucestershire, UK.

EDWARD III
(1327–1377)

Edward III was the king of England for 50 years, during which time he turned the country into one of the most powerful military forces in Europe, initiated the beginning of the Hundred Years' War with France, made huge developments to the English Parliament and led the country through the devastating Black Death. Initially a much-admired king whose main interests were warfare and the extension of the Kingdom of England, Edward III became unpopular in his later years as his military campaigns failed, the economy suffered, and his health deteriorated.

Key Facts about Edward III

- Edward III was born at Windsor Castle on 13 November 1312.
- He succeeded as King of England, Duke of Aquitaine, and Overlord of Ireland on 20 January 1327, aged 14.
- Edward III married Philippa, daughter of the Count of Flanders, in January 1328. The couple had 14 children together.
- The king died of a stroke on 21 June 1377, aged 64, having reigned for 50 years.
- The Fifty-Year King

Battle of Crecy Froissart

Edward III did not have a particularly stable upbringing. Edward, the first son of King Edward II, was a notorious royal failure. Edward was used by his mother, Isabella, and her new lover, Lord Mortimer, to remove his father from the throne forcibly.

In 1325, King Charles IV of France demanded that King Edward II perform homage to the English Duchy of Aquitaine. Unwilling to leave England and ignorant of the plot that his wife

Isabella and her exiled lover Mortimer were forming against him, Edward II sent his son Edward in his place. Isabella promptly had the young Edward engaged to Philippa of Hainault and, with the support of the French King, launched an invasion against England. King Edward II was forced to relinquish his throne, and the new king, Edward III, was crowned in January 1327.

At first, Edward was a puppet in the administration of Mortimer, the de facto ruler of England. Mortimer and Isabella were instantly unpopular as they had signed a costly treaty with King Charles IV of France. This treaty proved to be even more damaging than first thought, as Charles died almost immediately, giving Edward a legitimate claim to the French throne that was now forfeited.

Edward was married to Philippa in January 1328; despite the fact that Edward was only 15 at the time of the marriage and Philippa was just 13, the couple managed to have a son within two years. Having suffered the indignity of being ruled by his mother's lover for long enough and as the proud new father of a legitimate heir, Edward took violent action against the unpopular and unsuccessful Mortimer. When a parliament was called at Nottingham Castle, Edward and a group of close friends dragged Mortimer from Isabella's bed in the middle of the night and executed him as an 'enemy of the state.'

Edward took to the throne with gusto and immediately set out to prove himself as a worthy king by renewing the war against the Scots. But Scotland was already at war with itself. On one side was King David II, and on the other, the pretender Edward Balliol, a representative of 'The Disinherited,' a group of English magnates who had lost land in Scotland due to the peace accord. Edward supported Balliol, while King Philip VI of France supported King David II and gave him refuge. Philip confiscated Edward's title to Aquitaine, so Edward threw the match into the powder keg and made his claim to the French throne, starting what became the Hundred Years' War.

In 1339, King Edward III invaded France and laid claim to the throne. Victory over France would lead to the expansion of an already lucrative wool trade with Flanders and wine trade with Gascony, as well as opportunities for feudal taxes and all-out plundering of French towns. The invasion was popular with the English public.

The first few years of the Hundred Years' War went brilliantly for Edward. In a significant naval battle in 1340, the English Navy destroyed almost the entire French fleet at Sluys. In 1342, Edward overran Brittany, and in 1346, he landed in Normandy and defeated the French King Philip VI at Crecy. At the same time, Queen Philippa was fighting independently in the north, defeating the Scots at Neville's Cross and capturing King David II of Scotland.

Edward's costly war went on with no end in sight until it was forced to pause in 1348 while England fought an invisible enemy, the bubonic plague. The Black Death killed 1.5 million people in England alone over the next few years. One-third of the population of England died of the plague, and what remained of the decimated population was neither able nor willing to fund a war overseas. Serious fighting did not begin again until the mid-1350s when Edward's oldest son, Edward, later known as the Black Prince, won the Battle of Poitiers and captured King John II, the youngest son of Philip VI.

This was to be the most glorious moment of Edward III's aggressive reign. At one time, the King of Scots was held in the Tower of London, and the King of France was held in Windsor Castle. England owned a great deal of land in France, and the French central government had totally collapsed. However, the final push that would have seen Edward III crowned King of France never came, and in 1360, Edward renounced his claim to the throne and, in return, was awarded extended territory around Aquitaine and the bastion of Calais, now owning almost one-quarter of France.

Edward's attempt nine years later to claim his title as King of France proved to be too little too late, and the rest of his reign was a disaster, militarily and politically. All five of Edward's sons were granted ducal titles with a deed to English territory, and Edward created the Duchy of Cornwall to provide the heir to the throne with an income independent of the sovereign or the state.

By the mid-1360s, Edward was increasingly relying on his sons to manage his military efforts and state affairs. Lionel of Antwerp, the king's second surviving son, led a campaign in Ireland where he hoped to exert control over the autonomous Anglo-Irish lords in charge there. The venture was a disaster, and in April 1364, John II of France died in captivity in England, having failed to raise his ransom, restarting the war with France. Edward's younger son, John of Gaunt, led a disastrous campaign in France that culminated in the 1375 Treaty of Bruges and left only Calais, Bordeaux Bayonne, and Brest in English hands.

Public opinion about King Edward III and his reign shifted dramatically. Previously seen as a chivalrous, victorious, and strong King, Edward was now seen as weak and was accused of leaving his duties in the hands of his advisors, who were running England's economy into the ground. Following Queen Philippa's death in 1369, Edward took a mistress by the name of Alice Perrers, who, in the mid-1370s, was thought to hold too much power over the weakened king and was banished from court by parliament.

Largely deserted by his family, Edward was alone with Alice Perrers when he died of a stroke in June 1377. So the story goes, Alice Perrers looked at Edward's prone body, stripped the rings from his royal fingers, and left.

Legacy Today

During his lifetime, King Edward III was an extremely popular king. Edward created the Order of the Garter, creating a sense of camaraderie amongst his peerage, a peerage that he purposefully expanded during his reign by creating many new earls and dukes. Edward's popularity extended out from the nobility to the lower classes, thanks in part to his reputation as a fearless warrior. The people of England were united in their fear of a French invasion and turned to Edward, a war-hungry king, for reassurance. Edward III's reign saw key developments in the establishment of the English Parliament and a strong revival of the English language in literature and law. Only one thing has scarred the reputation of the chivalrous warrior king, and that is the length of his reign: Edward III won some of the most important battles of the Middle Ages but died with only three castles to show for them.

Film & TV

- "World Without End" (2012) TV series
- "Eduard III" (1961) TV movie
- "The Death of King Edward III" (1911)

Further Research

- Ormrod, Mark (2013) "Edward III" (English Monarchs Series) (The English Monarchs Series)
- Mortimer, Ian (2008) "The Perfect King: The Life of Edward III, Father of the English Nation"
- Bothwell, J. (2001). "The Age of Edward III".
- Waugh, S.L. (1991). "England in the Reign of Edward III".

Locations to Visit

- Edward III was born at Windsor Castle.
- His famous roundtable is located in Winchester.
- In York, visitors can see York Minster, where Edward's marriage to Queen Philippa of Hainault, York Abbey, where Edward kept his chancery, and York Castle, where Edward kept his Exchequer.
- Edward III is buried at Westminster Abbey

RICHARD II (1377–1399) (deposed, died 1400)

Richard II succeeded to the English throne at the age of ten and, by the age of fourteen, was playing a major role in English politics, particularly the Peasants' Revolt of 1381. But his reign was blighted by the ambitions of his powerful uncles, most notably John of Gaunt, who constantly threatened Richard with rebellion. More interested in art and culture than war and aggression, Richard sought to bring an end to the Hundred Year's War and created an atmosphere of refinement and decadence in the royal court. Thought to have been a tyrannical king during his later reign, Richard was unpopular with the masses, and when Henry of Bolingbroke [John of Gaunt's son] captured Richard, had him deposed, and later probably murdered him, he was met with little resistance from Richard's former subjects.

Key Facts about Richard II

- Richard II was born on January 6th, 1367, in Bordeaux.
- On June 16th, 1377, Richard became the King of England, Wales, and Ireland, aged ten.
- Richard II was married twice, once in January 1382 to Anne of Bohemia and for a second time in September 1396 to Isabella of Valois, who was just nine years old at the time of their union.
- Richard II abdicated his throne on September 29th, 1399, and was deposed by Parliament on the same day. He died at Pontefract either by self-starvation or murder.
- Richard was the son of Edward the Prince of Wales, known as the Black Prince, and his wife Joan, the 4th Countess of Kent, and was born at the Archbishop's Palace in Bordeaux, Aquitaine, on January 6th, 1367.

The Tragic Boy King

At nine years old, Richard's father, The Black Prince, died, leaving Richard the titles Prince of Wales and Duke of Cornwall. Richard had an older brother, Edward of Angoulême, who died at five years old, making Richard first in line to the English throne. A year later, Richard's grandfather, King Edward III, died, leaving him the title King of England.

At first, Richard II submitted to the government of a regency council, but in 1381, aged fourteen, he intervened in the increasingly violent Peasant's Revolt. Richard personally came to an amicable agreement with the leaders of the revolt that successfully ended the uprising, but when his council took over, rescinded the pardons, and had the leaders hanged, Richards's reputation suffered a drop it never fully recovered from.

While the rule of his grandfather, Edward III, was marked by almost constant military aggression and wars overseas, Richard II had little interest in expanding his kingdom abroad through violence. Instead, the reign of Richard II was notable for Richard's constant struggle to defend his throne against his three powerful uncles, the dukes of Lancaster, York, and Gloucester. John of Gaunt, the Duke of Lancaster, constantly schemed to take the throne from Richard and passed on his ambitions to his son, Henry of Bolingbroke.

Richard was married to Anne of Bohemia, daughter of Holy Roman Emperor Charles IV and sister of King Wenceslaus IV of Bohemia, for clear political reasons in order to foster a relationship with a strong central European ally against France. Their marriage turned out to be a success both politically and personally as they appeared to be completely devoted to each other throughout their twelve years of marriage, although their union did not provide Richard with an heir.

Known to be an autocratic leader, Richard amassed a household of over 10,000 people and used allies within Parliament to support his absolute rule over the kingdom. Known as an aesthete with a refined interest in culture and the arts, Richard cultivated a refined atmosphere at his court and believed strongly in the royal prerogative, which basically meant, in simple terms, that he could do no wrong.

But Parliament, supported by Richard's unhappy and powerful uncles and led by the influential Earls of Warwick, Derby, Arundel, Nottingham, and the Duke of Gloucester, continued to pressure the King to cooperate with them. Eventually, this pressure turned to violence, and the unruly lords took up arms and drove some of Richard's allies, officials in the royal household, into exile. In 1387, control of government was taken over by this group of aristocrats who called themselves the Lords Appellant. In response, Richard launched a coup d' état in 1388 and resumed a personal government, gradually diplomatically partnering with the opposition.

In 1394, Queen Anne died suddenly from the plague, and due either to grief or the lack of the Queen's modifying influence, Richard became ever more despotic and extravagant, leading to renewed revolt from his enemies in Parliament. Richard was re-married in September 1396 to Isabella of Valois, daughter of King Charles VI of France, who was just shy of seven years old at their wedding. This union further stabilized the truce in place with France, which, up to this point, had been a 28-year pause in the Hundred Years War. Richard insisted on referring to himself as the King of France and refused to give back ownership of Calais.

In order to placate his uncle, John of Gaunt, Richard legitimized John's four illegitimate children. John had been engaged in an affair with Katherine Swynford for many years throughout both of his marriages, and their children were almost as old as John's heir, Henry of Bolingbroke. This simple act, presumably poorly thought out by the King, came to govern the succession of the English throne in the coming years. All of John's children, now legitimized by the King, enjoyed huge gains in prestige and wealth, and John was temporarily pacified.

Three lords now stood in the way of Richard's almost complete domination: the Duke of Gloucester, the Earl of Arundel, and the Earl of Warwick. Arundel was the first to be arrested and promptly executed, Warwick was taken next, heavily fined, and exiled, and finally, Gloucester was sent to Calais, where he died in suspicious circumstances in prison [supposedly instigated by Thomas de Mowbray]. The killing was not over yet. The influential

Earl of Derby, John of Gaunt's son and heir, accused Thomas de Mowbray, the Duke of Norfolk, of treason, an accusation Richard decided to settle by means of a joust to the death. The battleground was set in Coventry in front of a crowd of thousands of people, but just as the deed was about to be done, Richard canceled the joust and banished both Dukes out of England and out of his sight.

Soon after John of Gaunt died, but with Henry, formerly the Earl of Derby, in exile, Richard refused to give him his due inheritance. Henry responded by landing in Yorkshire to 'claim his father's duchy' and, while he was at it, the throne of England as well. Henry captured King Richard and brought him to the Tower of London, where he forced him to abdicate his throne on September 29th, 1399, before a mixed committee of officials and peers.

The next day, at a meeting of Parliament in Westminster Hall, Henry is said to have risen from his place on the duke's bench and cried out, 'I challenge this kingdom and crown.' In London, Henry's claim was met with great acclaim, and his place on the throne secured, but as always, there were those who did not agree with his claim and, due to a complicated genealogy, opposed him as a usurper. Henry dealt with this opposition in the same way Richard would have, provoking his enemies to reveal themselves and having them killed. The constant threat of a swell in support of Richard led to his [alleged] murder in Pontefract Castle on February 14th, 1400. Henry V later had his body buried in Westminster Abbey.

Legacy Today

Richard II's legacy has been shaped so significantly by Shakespeare's play based on his life that it's difficult to know what we would think of the King if this play had never been written. Ultimately, it was Richard's inability or unwillingness to work in conjunction with Parliament and his unwavering belief in the royal prerogative that led to his downfall. Although an unsuccessful king overall, Richard showed promise as a young king, and his role in suppressing the Peasant's Revolt of 1381 has not been forgotten.

Film & TV

- Richard II (1997)
- The Wars of the Roses (1989) TV series
- The Tragedy of King Richard II (1970) TV
- An Age of Kings (1960) TV series
- Richard of Bordeaux (1955) TV
- Richard II (1954) TV
- The Tragedy of King Richard II (1950) TV

Further Research

- Dodd, Gwilym (ed.) (2000). The Reign of Richard II
- Bennett, Michael J. (1999). Richard II and the Revolution of 1399
- Gillespie, James; Goodman, Anthony (eds.) (1998). Richard II: The Art of Kingship
- Saul, Nigel (1997). Richard II
- Goodman, Anthony (1992). John of Gaunt: The Exercise of Princely Power in Fourteenth-Century Europe
- Steel, Anthony (1941). Richard II. Cambridge: Cambridge University Press.

Locations to Visit

- Richard was born at the Archbishop's Palace in Bordeaux, died in Pontefract Castle in Yorkshire, and is buried in Westminster Abbey.
- Richard surrendered to Henry of Bolingbroke at Flint Castle in Wales. The remains of the castle are open to the public.

HENRY IV
(1399–1413)

Henry IV is one of the most intriguing figures in English history. Born in 1367, he was the son of John of Gaunt, the Duke of Lancaster, and his wife, Blanche of Lancaster. He grew up in a time of great turbulence in England, with the Hundred Years War raging on the continent and the Black Death devastating the country.

Key Facts about Henry IV

- Henry IV was born in 1367 as the son of John of Gaunt, the Duke of Lancaster, and his wife, Blanche of Lancaster.
- He became the King of England in 1399 after deposing his cousin Richard II in a coup.
- He faced many challenges during his reign, including the rebellion led by the Welshman Owain Glyndwr and the ongoing Hundred Years War with France.
- Despite these challenges, Henry IV was generally successful in maintaining his grip on power and promoting justice and fairness.

A Brief History of His Life

Henry's father, John of Gaunt, was one of the most powerful men in England, but his legitimacy was always in question. John of Gaunt's parents were Edward III of England and his wife, Philippa of Hainault. There were some doubts about John of Gaunt's legitimacy due to rumors about Edward III's affairs. In any case, John of Gaunt was never able to claim the throne for himself, and his son Henry was only able to do so after a series of dramatic events.

Henry IV came to the throne in 1399 after deposing his cousin Richard II in a coup. Richard had been a weak and unpopular king, and Henry was able to win the support of the nobility and the common people by promising to rule with justice and fairness. He was crowned on October 13, 1399, and set about consolidating his power.

One of the most important things Henry did during his reign was to pass the Statute of Prerogative, which limited the king's power and gave more authority to Parliament. This was a significant step towards modern democracy, and it laid the foundation for the constitutional monarchy that exists in England today.

Henry also faced many challenges during his reign. The most significant of these was the rebellion led by the Welshman Owain Glyndwr, which began in 1400 and lasted for over a decade. Glyndwr was able to gain the support of many Welsh nobles and commoners, and his forces were able to inflict several defeats on the English army. However, Henry was ultimately able to suppress the rebellion, and Glyndwr disappeared into obscurity.

Despite these challenges, Henry IV was generally successful in maintaining his grip on power. He was able to win the support of the nobility by granting them lands and titles, and he was popular with the common people for his efforts to promote justice and fairness. He was also successful in promoting trade and commerce, which helped to stimulate the economy.

Henry IV died in 1413 at the age of 46. He was succeeded by his son, Henry V, who would go on to become one of England's most celebrated monarchs. Although Henry IV's reign was relatively short and marked by many challenges, he was an important figure in English history. His efforts to limit the power of the monarchy and promote justice and fairness laid the foundation for the modern democratic state, and his successes in promoting trade and commerce helped to lay the foundation for England's economic prosperity.

Henry IV was a complex figure who faced many challenges during his reign. He was able to consolidate his power and win the support of both the nobility and the common people, and he made significant contributions to the development of modern democracy and the economy. Although many challenges and struggles marked his reign, he remains an important figure in English history, and his legacy continues to be felt to this day.

Movies and TV Shows Featuring

- Almost two hundred years after his death, Henry became the subject of two plays by William Shakespeare, Henry IV, Part 1 and Henry IV, Part 2, and was featured prominently in Richard II.
- Ian Keith in The Black Shield of Falworth (1954), with Tony Curtis
- John Gielgud in Chimes at Midnight (1965), a merger of several Shakespeare plays
- Carl Wharton in Henry IV – Part 2 (2012), a film by The Co-operative British Youth Film Academy.
- Ben Mendelsohn in The King (2019), a film by Netflix
- The Hollow Crown (BBC)
- Numerous BBC dramas and plays

Further Research

- Henry IV: The Righteous King by Ian Mortimer
- Henry IV (The English Monarchs Series)

Locations Related to Henry IV

- Bolingbroke Castle: This was the birthplace of Henry IV, and he lived here for some time before becoming the King of England.
- Coventry: The city was a significant location during the Peasants' Revolt of 1381 and also played a significant role in the rebellion led by Owain Glyndwr in the early 15th century.
- Wales: Henry IV faced a rebellion led by Welshman Owain Glyndwr, which lasted for over a decade and was a significant challenge to his reign.
- France: The Hundred Years War with France was ongoing during Henry IV's reign, and he was able to win several significant victories against the French.
- London: As the capital city of England, London was the

center of political and economic power during Henry IV's reign, and he spent much of his time there.
- York: The city played a significant role in the rebellion led by the Archbishop of York, which challenged Henry's authority in the early years of his reign.
- East Anglia: This region was one of the most prosperous areas of England during Henry IV's reign, and he made efforts to promote trade and commerce there.
- Scotland: Henry IV faced several challenges from Scotland during his reign, including a rebellion led by the Earl of Northumberland in 1402.
- Kenilworth Castle: The castle was a significant location during the rebellion led by Owain Glyndwr, and it was besieged by Welsh forces in 1403.
- Canterbury: The city was a significant location during the Peasants' Revolt of 1381 and was also the site of several important events during Henry IV's reign.

HENRY V
(1413–1422)

Henry V, born in 1386, was the son of King Henry IV and Mary de Bohun. He was the second English king from the House of Lancaster and ruled from 1413 until his death in 1422. Henry V is known for his military victories in the Hundred Years' War against France, particularly his triumph at the Battle of Agincourt in 1415. However, his reign was also marked by political and religious turmoil, as well as his early death at the age of 35.

Key Facts about Henry V

- Henry V was born in Monmouth, Wales, on August 9, 1386, and was the eldest son of King Henry IV and his first wife, Mary de Bohun.
- Henry V is known for his military victories in the Hundred Years' War against France, particularly his triumph at the Battle of Agincourt in 1415.
- Henry V became king upon the death of his father in 1413 and was crowned at Westminster Abbey on April 9, 1413, at the age of 26.
- Henry V signed the Treaty of Troyes in 1420, which recognized him as the heir to the French throne and made him regent of France during the lifetime of King Charles VI.
- Henry V's reign was marked by political and religious turmoil, and his early death at the age of 35 left England in a state of uncertainty.

Early Life and Ascension to the Throne

Henry V was born in Monmouth, Wales, on August 9, 1386. He was the eldest surviving son of King Henry IV and his first wife, Mary de Bohun. As a young prince, Henry was known for his piety and his interest in military affairs. He received a rigorous education, studying Latin, French, and English literature, as well as military strategy and tactics.

In 1399, Henry's father overthrew King Richard II and took the throne as Henry IV. Henry V was appointed Prince of Wales and became his father's heir. However, there were several attempts to overthrow Henry IV throughout his reign, including a rebellion led by his own son, Henry Percy, in 1403.

Henry V became king upon the death of his father in 1413. He was crowned at Westminster Abbey on April 9, 1413, at the age of 26. At the time, England was in a state of political and religious turmoil, with many factions vying for power. However, Henry V was determined to restore order and stability to the kingdom.

Military Victories in France

One of the defining moments of Henry V's reign was his victory at the Battle of Agincourt in 1415. This battle was part of the Hundred Years' War between England and France, and it was a major victory for the English. Despite being outnumbered, the English army defeated the French with a combination of archery and hand-to-hand combat.

Henry V continued to wage war against France, winning several more victories, including the capture of the city of Harfleur. In 1420, he signed the Treaty of Troyes, which recognized him as the heir to the French throne and made him regent of France during the lifetime of King Charles VI. This treaty was a major diplomatic triumph for Henry V and gave him control over much of northern France.

However, Henry V's military campaigns took a toll on his health. He suffered from dysentery and other illnesses, and his constant travels and battles left him exhausted.

Religious and Political Turmoil

Henry V's reign was also marked by religious and political turmoil. He faced several rebellions, including one led by his former friend and ally, Richard, Earl of Cambridge, in 1415. Henry V put down these rebellions with force, executing many of the rebels and confiscating their lands.

Henry V was also deeply involved in the religious conflicts of his time. He did not support the Lollards, a group of reformers who challenged the authority of the Catholic Church. He also supported the Church's efforts to suppress heresy and enforce orthodoxy.

Legacy of Henry V

Despite his short reign, Henry V left a lasting legacy. He is remembered as a skilled military commander who won several major victories against France. He is also known for his piety and his support of the Church. However, his reign was also marked by political and religious turmoil, and his early death at the age of 35 left England in a state of uncertainty.

Henry V's son, Henry VI, inherited the throne at the age of nine months. His reign was marked by even greater instability and conflict, including the Wars of the Roses, which would ultimately lead to the end of the House of Lancaster and the rise of the House of York. However, Henry V remained a symbol of English military prowess and national pride, and his legacy continues to be celebrated to this day.

Movies and TV Shows Featuring Henry V

- There have been several cultural depictions of Henry V in movies and TV shows. Some notable examples include:
- Shakespeare's plays – Henry V is the protagonist of William Shakespeare's plays Henry IV, Part 1, Henry IV, Part 2, and Henry V.
- Henry V (1989) – a film directed by and starring Kenneth Branagh as Henry V.
- The Hollow Crown (2012) is a TV series that features Tom Hiddleston as Henry V.
- Henry V (1944) – a film directed by and starring Laurence Olivier as Henry V.

- The King (2019) is a film that portrays the rise of Henry V, starring Timothée Chalamet as the lead.
- Battlefield Britain (2004) – a TV documentary series that features a detailed account of the Battle of Agincourt, one of Henry V's most famous military victories.

Further Research

- Henry V by William Shakespeare
- Henry V: The Warrior King of 1415 by Ian Mortimer
- Henry V: The Life of the Warrior King & the Battle of Agincourt by Teresa Cole
- Henry V by Christopher Allmand
- Henry V: The Scourge of God by Desmond Seward
- The Life and Times of Henry V by Peter Earle
- Henry V: A Guide to the Play by Harold Bloom
- Henry V: The English King Who Invaded France by Anne Curry
- Henry V: The Practice of Kingship by Gwilym Dodd
- Henry V: The Rebirth of Chivalry by Malcolm Vale

Locations Related to Henry V

- Monmouth, Wales (birthplace of Henry V)
- Westminster Abbey, London (site of Henry V's coronation as king and where he is buried)
- Agincourt, France (site of Henry V's famous victory in the Hundred Years' War)
- Harfleur, France (city captured by Henry V during his military campaigns in France)
- Rouen, France (city captured by Henry V during his military campaigns in France)
- Troyes, France (site of the signing of the Treaty of Troyes, which made Henry V regent of France)
- Meaux, France (city besieged by Henry V during his military campaigns in France)
- Bois de Vincennes, France (site of the assassination of

John the Fearless, an event that had political implications for Henry V)
- Southampton, England (departure point for Henry V's military campaigns in France)
- Eltham Palace, London (one of Henry V's favorite residences)

HENRY VI
(1422–1461 and 1470–1471)

Henry VI (6 December 1421 – 21 May 1471) was King of England from 1422 to 1461 and again from 1470 to 1471. He also held the contested title of King of France from 1422 to 1453. As the sole offspring of Henry V, Henry VI ascended to the English throne at just eight months old following his father's death and inherited the French throne shortly thereafter upon the death of his maternal grandfather, Charles VI. His reign was marked by political instability, military defeats, and mental illness. Despite his many shortcomings, Henry VI is remembered as a pious and kind-hearted monarch who was committed to peace and justice.

Key Facts about Henry VI

- Henry VI became king at the age of nine months, making him one of England's youngest monarchs.
- He suffered from mental illness, which caused him to have frequent bouts of insanity.
- Henry VI was known for his piety and devotion to religion.
- He was overthrown twice during his lifetime, once by the House of York and later by the House of Lancaster.
- Henry VI was the last Lancastrian king of England, and his reign marked the end of the Hundred Years' War.

Early Life and Reign of Henry VI

Born during the third phase of the Hundred Years' War (1337–1453), Henry's uncle, Charles VII, challenged the English claim to the French throne, which had been secured by the Treaty of Troyes in 1420. Henry remains the only English monarch to have been crowned King of France, a ceremony that took place in Notre Dame de Paris in 1431. During his early years, England was governed by a regency, marking a high point in English power in France. However, by the time Henry was deemed mature enough to rule in 1437, England's position had weakened due to various military, diplomatic, and economic challenges. Henry's reign witnessed significant military losses in France and escalating political and financial turmoil in England, exacerbated by growing divisions among the nobility.

When Henry VI reached his majority at the age of 15, he took control of the government and tried to pursue a policy of peace and reconciliation with France. However, his efforts were hampered by the growing power struggle between the nobles, the financial burden of the Hundred Years' War, and the outbreak of the Wars of the Roses, a series of dynastic conflicts between the rival houses of Lancaster and York.

In contrast to his father, Henry VI was known for being timid, shy, and averse to conflict, qualities that contributed to his eventual mental instability after 1453. His reign saw the near-total loss of English territories in France. In 1445, Henry married Margaret of Anjou, Charles VII's niece, in an attempt to secure peace. This policy failed, leading to the resumption of war and rapid French reconquest of lands held by England, including Normandy and Aquitaine. By 1453, Calais was the only English-controlled territory left in France. Henry's popularity at home declined in the 1440s, particularly after it became known that the county of Maine had been secretly ceded back to France. This led to significant political unrest, culminating in the 1450 lynching of his key adviser, William de la Pole, 1st Duke of Suffolk, and a major rebellion. Political factions exacerbated the unrest, as regional magnates with private armies, including soldiers returning from France, caused widespread disorder and dominated the government.

From 1453 onwards, Henry suffered multiple mental breakdowns, rendering him incapable of governing. His authority was usurped by rival nobles, notably Richard, 3rd Duke of York, and Edmund Beaufort, 2nd Duke of Somerset, who vied for control. Queen Margaret, far from remaining neutral, became a significant political figure, wielding substantial influence. Amidst ongoing military failures in France and domestic instability, the Queen and her supporters were accused of mismanagement by Henry's cousin, the increasingly popular Duke of York. The conflict between Margaret and York over control of the incapacitated king's government escalated into a fierce dispute over succession, leading to the Wars of the Roses, a series of civil wars that began in 1455.

On 4 March 1461, Henry was deposed by the Duke of York's son, who ascended as King Edward IV. Despite continued resistance led by Margaret, Henry was captured in 1465 and imprisoned in the Tower of London. He briefly regained the throne in 1470 with the support of the Earl of Warwick, but Edward reclaimed power in 1471 and killed Henry's only son, Edward of Westminster, at the Battle of Tewkesbury. Henry was re-imprisoned in the Tower and died there on the night of 21 May 1471, possibly murdered on King Edward's orders. Initially buried at Chertsey Abbey, his remains were later moved to Windsor Castle in 1484. After his death, Henry was informally venerated as a saint and martyr, with miracles attributed to him, and he is remembered for founding Eton College, King's College, Cambridge, and, alongside Henry Chichele, All Souls College, Oxford. William Shakespeare dramatized Henry's life in a trilogy of plays, portraying him as a weak and easily influenced ruler, particularly by his wife, Margaret.

Legacy of Henry VI

Despite his many shortcomings, Henry VI is remembered as a pious and kind-hearted monarch who was committed to peace and justice. He was known for his piety and devotion to religion and founded Eton College and King's College, Cambridge, two of England's most prestigious educational institutions.

Henry VI is also remembered as a patron of the arts and a great lover of music and literature. He commissioned the building of St. George's Chapel at Windsor Castle, which is considered one of the finest examples of Gothic architecture in England.

Movies and TV Shows Featuring Henry VI

- The Hollow Crown: The Wars of the Roses (2016)

- The White Queen (2013)
- Henry VI, Part 1 (1983)
- Henry VI, Part 2 (1983)
- Henry VI, Part 3 (1983)

Books and Documentaries About Henry VI

- Henry VI: A Good, Simple and Innocent Man by James Ross
- The Reign of Henry VI by R.A. Griffiths
- The Wars of the Roses: The Fall of the Plantagenets and the Rise of the Tudors by Dan Jones
- The Last Lancastrian: A Story of Margaret Beaufort by Samantha Wilcoxson

Locations Related to Henry VI

- Eton College, Windsor
- King's College, Cambridge
- Windsor Castle
- Westminster Abbey
- St. George's Chapel, Windsor

EDWARD IV
(1461–1470 and 1471–1483)

Edward IV of England was a pivotal figure in English history, having ruled the country twice during the 15th century. As the first Yorkist king, he played a significant role in the Wars of the Roses, which saw the House of York and the House of Lancaster vying for the throne. Throughout his reigns (he was deposed, then restored), Edward IV proved himself to be a skilled military strategist, a charismatic leader, and a shrewd politician.

Key Facts about Edward IV

- Edward IV was the first Yorkist king of England, having seized the throne from Henry VI in 1461.
- He is known for his victory at the Battle of Towton, which was the largest and bloodiest battle fought on English soil.
- He was deposed and then restored to the throne.
- He was married to Elizabeth Woodville, a commoner who was renowned for her beauty and charm.
- Edward IV died at the age of 40, leaving behind two young sons, the elder of whom would later become King Edward V (but was never crowned and deposed, possibly murdered).

Early Life

Edward IV was born on April 28, 1442, in Rouen, France, where his parents had fled to escape the violence of the Hundred Years' War. He was the eldest son of Richard, Duke of York, and Cecily Neville. From an early age, Edward showed a keen interest in military matters and was trained in the art of warfare by his father.

In 1460, Edward's father and younger brother were killed in battle, leaving him as the head of the House of York. Edward then claimed the throne from the Lancastrian King Henry VI, who was deemed unfit to rule due to his bouts of mental illness. Edward was crowned king in 1461 at the age of 19.

Reign

Edward IV ascended to the throne in 1461 after a series of decisive battles against the Lancastrians, culminating in the Battle of Towton on March 29, 1461. This battle is often described as the largest and bloodiest conflict of the Wars of the Roses, with estimates of the dead ranging from 20,000 to 28,000 men. Edward's victory at Towton solidified his claim to the throne and marked the beginning of his reign.

Towton was not just a battle; it was a turning point. Edward's forces, though outnumbered, used a combination of clever tactics and advantageous weather conditions to overcome the Lancastrian army. The victory allowed Edward to enter London unopposed and be crowned King of England despite the Lancastrian King Henry VI still being at large.

Early Reign and Domestic Policies

Edward IV's early reign was characterized by his efforts to stabilize the kingdom and assert his authority. He focused on winning the loyalty of his subjects through various means, including generous grants of land and titles. This strategy helped to secure the support of many powerful nobles, although it also led to some resentment and jealousy among those who felt overlooked or marginalized.

Edward's reign was also marked by his patronage of the arts. He supported the work of numerous artists and craftsmen, commissioning portraits, tapestries, and other works that celebrated his reign and the Yorkist cause. His patronage extended to the construction of several significant buildings, including the Chapel of St. George at Windsor Castle, which remains one of the finest examples of Gothic architecture in England.

Foreign Policy and the French Campaigns

In addition to his domestic policies, Edward IV pursued an active foreign policy aimed at reasserting English control over lost territories in France. One of his notable successes was the recapture of the strategic port of Calais in 1467, which had been a focal point of English military and economic interests since the reign of Edward III. Edward's efforts in France, however, were complicated by shifting alliances and the complex political landscape of the time.

Edward's reign saw fluctuating relations with France. Initially, he sought to forge alliances to strengthen his position, including an attempt to marry his sister Margaret to Charles the Bold, Duke of Burgundy, which would have bolstered his position against the French King Louis XI. However, the death of Charles in 1477 and the subsequent decline of Burgundy as a powerful entity weakened Edward's position in continental politics.

Internal Challenges and Rebellion

Edward IV's reign was not without its challenges. He faced several uprisings and conspiracies, the most significant being the rebellion led by his own brother, George, Duke of Clarence. Clarence, who was initially a staunch supporter of Edward, grew increasingly dissatisfied with his position and sought to claim the throne for himself. In 1478, Edward ordered Clarence's arrest and subsequent execution for treason, a move that underscored the seriousness of the threat he posed to the stability of the kingdom.

Another notable challenge to Edward's authority came from Richard Neville, Earl of Warwick, also known as the "Kingmaker." Initially a key supporter of Edward, Warwick eventually turned against him due to political disagreements and personal grievances. In 1470, Warwick managed to temporarily restore the deposed Henry VI to the throne, forcing Edward into exile. However, Edward returned to England in 1471, defeated Warwick at the Battle of Barnet, and reclaimed his throne.

Restoration and Consolidation

After his return to power, Edward IV worked to consolidate his position and strengthen the Yorkist hold on the throne. He implemented a series of administrative reforms aimed at improving the efficiency of government and increasing royal revenues. One of his notable achievements was the introduction of a more systematic approach to the collection of taxes, which helped to stabilize the kingdom's finances.

Edward's later reign was also marked by his efforts to build a stable and prosperous kingdom. He sought to promote trade and commerce, encouraging the growth of industries such as wool and cloth production, which were vital to the English economy. His policies helped to lay the foundations for the economic prosperity that would characterize the early Tudor period.

Legacy and Death

Edward IV died unexpectedly on April 9, 1483, at the age of 40, leaving behind a complex legacy. His sudden death plunged the kingdom into another period of uncertainty, as his young son Edward V was declared king but was soon deposed by his uncle Richard, Duke of Gloucester, who became Richard III. The instability that followed Edward IV's death eventually led to the rise of the Tudor dynasty, with Henry VII emerging as the new ruler after defeating Richard III at the Battle of Bosworth in 1485.

Edward IV's reign is remembered for its military successes, particularly in securing the throne and maintaining relative peace and stability during a turbulent period in English history. His ability to command loyalty and manage conflicts, coupled with his patronage of the arts and efforts to promote economic growth, left a lasting impact on the kingdom. However, the internal challenges he faced, including the betrayal of close allies and family members, highlight the complexities and dangers of ruling during the Wars of the Roses.

Edward's legacy has been somewhat overshadowed by the events that followed his death. His younger brother, Richard III, seized the throne from Edward's young son, Edward V, and is widely believed to have had him and his younger brother, Richard, Duke of York, murdered in the Tower of London. This event, known as the Princes in the Tower, has cast a shadow over Edward's reign and his legacy.

Films and TV Shows Featuring Edward IV

- The White Queen (2013)
- The Hollow Crown (2012)
- The Wars of the Roses (1965)
- Richard III (1955)

Books and Documentaries About Edward IV

- The Wars of the Roses by Alison Weir
- The Last White Rose: The Secret Wars of the Tudors by Desmond Seward
- Edward IV by Charles Ross
- The Plantagenets: The Warrior Kings and Queens Who Made England by Dan Jones

Locations Related to Edward IV

- The Tower of London, where Edward's two sons were imprisoned and subsequently murdered.
- The site of the Battle of Towton, which took place near the village of Towton in Yorkshire.
- The Palace of Westminster, where Edward was crowned king in 1461.

EDWARD V
(Uncrowned)
(1483 - Deposed)

Edward V of England may have been one of the shortest-reigning monarchs in the country's history, but his legacy has endured for centuries. Despite never being officially crowned, his brief reign is remembered for the political intrigue and tragedy that surrounded it. In this article, we will explore the life and reign of Edward V, as well as his legacy and the various depictions of him in popular culture.

Key Facts about Edward V

- Edward V was the eldest son of King Edward IV and his queen, Elizabeth Woodville.
- He was born in Westminster on November 2, 1470.
- After his father's death in 1483, Edward V was declared king at the age of 12, but he was never crowned.
- He and his younger brother, Richard, were placed in the Tower of London by their uncle, Richard III, and were never seen in public again.
- Edward V's fate remains a mystery, but he is widely believed to have been murdered by his uncle.

Early Life

Edward V was born in Westminster on November 2, 1470, to King Edward IV and his queen, Elizabeth Woodville. He was the eldest of their ten children and was considered a healthy and lively child. Edward's childhood was spent in the lap of luxury, surrounded by the comforts and privileges of royalty. He was well-educated and showed a keen interest in music and literature from an early age.

Reign

Edward V's reign began on April 9, 1483, following the death of his father. However, his uncle, Richard, Duke of Gloucester, declared that Edward IV's marriage to Elizabeth Woodville was invalid, and therefore, his sons were illegitimate. Richard then had himself declared king and placed Edward V and his younger brother, Richard, in the Tower of London for their own protection. They were never seen in public again, and it is widely believed that they were murdered on Richard's orders.

Legacy

Despite his brief reign and tragic end, Edward V's legacy has endured throughout history. He is remembered as a symbol of innocence and victimhood, as well as a tragic figure in the history of the English monarchy. His story has been the subject of countless books, films, and documentaries, and his fate remains a topic of debate and speculation to this day.

Edward V's story is a tragic one, filled with political intrigue and mystery. Despite his short life, his legacy has endured for centuries, and his fate remains a topic of debate and speculation. From books and documentaries to films and TV shows, his story has captured the imagination of people all over the world, ensuring that his memory will live on for generations to come. Speculation about the fate of the princes is still much discussed today, with new theories being presented every few years.

Books About Edward V

- The Princes in the Tower by Alison Weir
- The Daughter of Time by Josephine Tey
- The Murder of the Princes in the Tower by David Baldwin
- Richard III and the Princes in the Tower by A.J. Pollard
- Locations Related to Edward V
- The Tower of London
- Westminster Abbey

- St. George's Chapel, Windsor Castle
- Ludlow Castle, Shropshire

RICHARD III
(1483–1485)

Richard III is now as talked about in the 21st century as he was in the 15th. In 2012, a skeleton was found buried under a council car park in the town of Greyfriars in Leicester, England. Following a series of state-of-the-art tests involving advanced carbon dating and DNA matching, experts were able to confirm the skeleton was that of Richard III.

The last King of England to die on the battlefield, the last of the Plantagenet dynasty, and the last male of the House of York, Richard's death marked the end of the Middle Ages. Despite now being in possession of his skeleton, the real Richard III is difficult to uncover. A vicious child-killing monster, as immortalized by Shakespeare during the 16th century, or a worthy and unfairly-ousted King, Richard III's reign marks a bloody end to a bloody period in English history.

Key Facts about Richard III

- Richard III was born on October 2nd, 1452, at Fotheringay Castle, Northamptonshire.
- Richard ascended to the throne at the 'request of parliament' on June 25th, 1483.
- In 1472, Richard married Anne Neville, daughter of Richard Earl of Warwick, who was known as 'The Kingmaker'.
- Richard III died in combat at the famous Battle of Bosworth on August 22nd, 1485.

A Primer on Richard III

During the Middle Ages, forecasting who would be the next to sit on the English throne was not a simple case of following the royal bloodline. Murder, rebellion, exile, invasion, and civil war all played a part in the Game of Thrones that made it impossible to judge where the crown would next land. Richard III's life was an endless drama of plotting and planning, by purportedly very devious means, to become the King of England. Even once he was crowned King, Richard could not sleep soundly in his bed, well aware of the role reversal that had taken place and that he was now the one who must watch his back.

Born in 1452, Richard was the twelfth child of Richard Plantagenet, the 3rd Duke of York, and his wife, Cecily Neville. The 3rd Duke contested the throne of King Henry VI, arguing that he himself was the rightful heir. The Duke's followers were known as 'Yorkists,' while those loyal to King Henry VI were known as Lancastrians. As the son of the leader of the Yorkists, Richard was born into the heart of a period of English history marked by extreme political instability and regular civil warfare known as the War of the Roses.

Richard was born and raised for battle. In 1461, his older brother Edward was crowned King Edward IV following the Lancastrian defeat at the Battle of Towton. Aged just nine years old, Richard was named the Duke of Gloucester and made a Knight of the Garter and a Knight of the Bath. The majority of Richard's childhood was spent training to become a warrior of the battlefield under the tutelage of his cousin Richard Neville, 16th Earl of Warwick, at Middleham Castle in Yorkshire. It's here that Richard met his future wife, Warwick's daughter, Anne Neville.

Despite his close relationship with Richard, Warwick organized a revolt against King Edward IV in 1470, which Edward's brother George supported. Richard stayed loyal to the King and was forced to flee to Burgundy. The exile did not last long, though, as Richard was a skilled warrior and played a crucial role in the battles of Barnet and Tewkesbury, which saw Edward return to the throne in early 1471.

Richard III's nickname was Richard Crookback, although it is unknown whether this slur was used during his lifetime or added as an epithet following his demise by the victorious Tudors. Various accounts of the king suggest that his posture was indeed crooked, his right side hunched and his left arm withered. Following the recovery of Richard III's skeleton in 2012, an osteoarchaeologist was able to use 3D imaging and printing technology to map the King's spine and confirmed that he had, in fact, developed idiopathic scoliosis as an adolescent.

Richard was married in 1473 at the age of twenty-one. His bride was Anne Neville, daughter of the Earl of Warwick. Anne was only sixteen years old when her marriage to Richard was arranged, and incredibly, she was already a widow as she had been wed at the age of thirteen by Henry VI's heir, Edward Prince of Wales. Richard's older brother, George, was already married to Anne's older sister, Isabel, and the question of who would inherit what from the sisters' huge inheritance caused a rift between the brothers that lasted until George's death.

In 1483, Edward IV died, and his son, Edward V, succeeded him to the throne. As he was only twelve years old at the time, Edward V was appointed a Lord Protector to ensure his safety against the widowed Queen's family, who were plotting to seize the throne. This Lord Protector was Richard III, who was advised to move Edward and Edward's younger brother, nine-year-old Prince Richard, to the Tower of London for their own safety. During the young King and Prince's incarceration, it became known that Edward IV's marriage to their mother, Elizabeth Woodville, had been declared invalid, and thus, Edward V and his brother were illegitimate and without any kind of claim to the throne.

Apparently, at the behest of the citizens of London, Richard was petitioned to assume the throne and accepted. On the 6th of July in 1483, Richard III was crowned at Westminster Abbey. What happened next has been the subject of speculation ever since. Soon after Richard III's coronation, Edward and Richard, or 'the princes in the tower' as they later became known, disappeared. Popular opinion held that Richard had had the princes killed to avoid any future dispute as to the legitimacy of his accession and had either hidden or destroyed the bodies to avoid detection.

At this point, Richard could not have known that the real threat to his crown would come not in the form of child princes but in the form of Henry Tudor. The Earl of Richmond, Henry Tudor, was a Lancastrian who had been resident in France for twelve years on the advice of Henry VI, who knew all too well how risky it was for an heir to the English throne to be resident in England. Some of the most powerful lords in England were part of a plot to oust Richard III, crown Henry Tudor, and marry him to Elizabeth of York, creating a union of the two heirs of Red and White Rose factions, effectively ending the War of the Roses.

Henry attempted a premature invasion of England in 1485. Unable to defeat Richard's impressive navy, Henry's invasion only succeeds in alerting Richard to his aims and helping him to identify Henry's support in England so that he can behead them.

During their marriage, Richard and his wife Anne Neville had one son, Edward of Middleham. Unfortunately, Edward died in 1484, thought to have been just ten years old and already the Prince of Wales and direct heir to the English throne. Anne is said to have been so distraught that she herself became gravely ill. During this period, Richard began to court his niece, Elizabeth of York, whose hand was promised to his enemy, Henry Tudor. Richard was already accused of killing Elizabeth's two brothers, and with his recently bereaved wife still living, this behavior did not sit well with the English public, whose opinion of him is thought to have suffered dramatically.

The invasion was inevitable, and on the 7th of August, 1485, Henry Tudor set foot on English land via Wales and met with Richard at Bosworth Field near Leicester. A two-hour battle ensued, and Richard met his end at the sword of Henry's bodyguard. Richard's crown fell from his head as he was struck down, and Lord Stanley placed it promptly and symbolically on Henry Tudor's head.

Legacy of Richard III

Richard III has one of the most complex legacies of any British monarch. Both those for and against the King offer extreme views on his character and reign. For some, Richard was a child killer, a lecherous man, and a terrible ruler. For others, he was capable and kind, a fearsome warrior on the battlefield who was unfairly plotted against and lost his throne in a despicable way. Historian Polydor Vergil said of Richard in 1520, "His courage also high and fierce, which failed him not in the very death."

While Richard was on the throne, he established the Council of the North, bringing stability and economic prosperity to the previously neglected north of England. He created a court of requests where those without the funds to pay a lawyer could air their grievances and invented the concept of bail, whereby those accused of crimes could retain their liberty and property while awaiting trial. Richard also implemented a Royal Charter that removed restrictions on printing books and had laws that were previously only written in French translated into English.

However, most of what is thought and said about Richard III comes not from historians but from his representation by William Shakespeare, who wrote his play Richard III under the gaze of Elizabeth I, England's last Tudor Queen. Shakespeare's Richard is a grotesque figure, and some say his play is a propaganda piece to gain favor with the Queen.

Films and TV Featuring Richard III

- The Life and Death of King Richard III (1912)
- Tower of London (1939)
- Richard III (1955)
- Richard III (1995)
- Richard III (1996) TV Documentary
- Richard III: The King in the Car Park (2013) TV Film

Further Research

- Langley, Phillipa and Jone, Michael (2013) The King's Grave: The Search for Richard III
- Baldwin, David (2012) Richard III
- Carson, Annette (2009) Richard III: The Maligned King
- Tey, Josephine (1951) The Daughter of Time
- William Shakespeare (16th Century) King Richard III

Locations Related to Richard III

- It is possible to visit the site of the battle of Bosworth,

during which Richard II lost his life.
- Crosby Hall was the home of Sir John Crosby, who rented the property to Richard as a London home for him and his family. A modern house stands on the site of this original house with a plaque to mark the hall's existence and its links to the king.
- Richard was born in Fotheringay Castle, but little remains of his family's home. It is possible to visit the remains of the castle, and it's still an impressive church.

HENRY VII
(1485–1509)

Henry VII secured his right to the throne of England at the famous Battle of Bosworth Field (1485), where his army defeated that of King Richard III and killed him. Henry ended the Wars of the Roses and began the great dynasty of the House of Tudor, stabilizing a country scarred by years of civil war and political upheaval and uniting Europe, at least for a time. When he wasn't fighting rebel forces intent on ousting him from the throne, Henry spent his time collecting revenue in ways that were revealed after his death to have been less than legal, but it was a full treasury he left behind on his death in 1509.

Key Facts about Henry VII

- Henry VII was born on 28 January 1457 at Pembroke Castle.
- He proclaimed himself 'King of England and of France, and Lord of Ireland' on 22 August 1485 after the Battle of Bosworth.
- Henry VII was married on 18 January 1486 to his third cousin, Elizabeth of York, the eldest child of Edward IV and sister of Edward V.
- Henry VII died (21 April 1509) of tuberculosis aged 52, having reigned 23 years.
- Henry VII's questionable claim to the English throne came about by chance when King Richard II decided to legitimize Henry's great-grandmother and her siblings.

The Life of Henry VII

Richard II's uncle, John of Gaunt, was in a long relationship with a lady called Katherine Swynford despite the fact that he was married to another woman. Together, John and Katherine had four children who were, by law, bastards born out of wedlock and not entitled to claim any inheritance or titles from John.

Richard was in a constant state of political warfare with his uncles, including John of Gaunt, and feared John's legitimate son, Henry, Earl of Derby, was plotting to take his throne (which he later did and became King Henry IV). So, to satisfy his uncle and block Derby from the throne, Richard II had John and Katherine's four children, the Beauforts, as they later became known, legitimized.

Henry VII's grandmother was the widow of Henry V, Catherine of Valois, and Sir Owen Tudor, a former gentleman usher at Queen Catherine's court. Catherine and Owen's first child, Edmund Tudor, was Henry VII's father and half-brother of King Henry VI. As a half-brother to the King, Edmund was made the Earl of Richmond. Edmund married Lady Margaret Beaufort, the King's cousin and a great-granddaughter of John of Gaunt and Katherine Swynford. Edmund was captured while fighting for Henry VI in South Wales against the Yorkists and died while 13-year-old Margaret was pregnant with Henry.

Born and raised a Welshman, Henry was primarily raised in Wales. Following the Battle of Tewkesbury, which saw his fellow Lancastrians all but wiped out, Henry was sent to live in France in exile. By 1483, Henry's mother was promoting him in powerful circles as the next king, an alternative to Richard III. On Christmas Day 1483, Henry pledged to marry Elizabeth of York, King Edward IV's eldest daughter and heir.

With the support of his mother, wife, and the King of France, Henry was confident of his entitlement to the throne and began to raise an army to invade England. Richard III attempted to have him extradited from Brittany, but Henry escaped to France, where he was greeted with a gift of French troops. Henry landed in Pembrokeshire in 1485 and marched towards England with an army of 5,000 soldiers. Richard III's army significantly outnumbered that of Henry, but during the famous Battle of Bosworth Field on 22 August 1485, many of Richard's key allies switched sides or simply left the battlefield. Richard III was killed, effectively ending the War of the Roses and making Henry VII the next king.

King Henry VII's coronation took place at Westminster

Abbey on 30 October 1485. To help solidify his position as the rightful king not only by conquest but also by inheritance, Henry honored his pledge to marry Elizabeth of York. The wedding took place at Westminster on 18 January 1486, successfully united the warring houses of York and Lancaster, and gave any children of Henry and Elizabeth a strong claim to the throne.

Henry took all of the precautions he could think of against potential revolts and usurpers to his throne. He had 10-year-old Edward, Earl of Warwick, arrested and taken to the Tower of London for fear that he may have a rival claim to his throne. But despite his best efforts, the early years of Henry's reign were troubled by rebellions. In 1486, the rebellion of the Stafford brothers and Viscount Lovell threatened Henry's throne.

In 1487, Yorkist troops led by a boy, Lambert Simnel, who claimed to be the Earl of Warwick, invaded England, and in 1490, a man, Perkin Warbeck, claiming to be Richard, one of the 'Princes in the Tower' invaded Ireland in 1491 and later England in 1495 with the support of James IV of Scotland. In an attempt to protect himself, Henry founded the 'Yeoman of the Guard,' a personal bodyguard that still exists and is the oldest British military corps in existence.

When he wasn't fighting rebellions and executing anyone with even the most tenuous connection to his throne, Henry VII was examining the royal accounts. Henry tightened the royal administration and perfected his own ruthless system for collecting revenue, resulting in a surplus in the national accounts by the time he died. Henry cared little for the interference of Parliament and summoned it seven times for a total of 25 weeks over his entire reign of 24 years.

Henry and his wife Elizabeth had seven children together, and rather than adopting the costly and aggressive strategy of invasion and war favored by some of his predecessors, Henry used dynastic royal marriages to make alliances in Europe and establish the Tudor dynasty in England. Henry and Elizabeth's daughter, Margaret, was married to James IV of Scotland, Mary was married to Louis XII, King of France, and Arthur Tudor married Catherine of Aragon. When Arthur died suddenly in 1502, Henry VII sought and arranged a papal dispensation from Pope Julius II that gave permission for his younger son Henry, who would go on to become Henry VIII, to marry Catherine, his brother's widow. This dispensation would later play a key role in Henry VIII's separation of the Church of England from the Roman Catholic Church.

Queen Elizabeth died on 11 February 1503 from infection, a result of childbirth on 2 February 1503, and Henry is thought to have been overcome by grief. Immediately following Elizabeth's death, Henry became gravely ill and almost died himself. Although he made vague plans to remarry and have more children, Henry was alone for the remainder of his life and died of tuberculosis at Richmond Palace on 21 April 1509, tended to by his mother, who followed him to the grave two months later.

Legacy Today

Henry VII is credited with ending the War of the Roses and founding the great and powerful Tudor dynasty. Despite spending the majority of his reign defending his shaky claim to the English throne through brutal and extreme measures, Henry was also able to strengthen the English government and rebuild the royal finances. Although he won his throne through battle, like the sovereign powers of Louis XI of France and Ferdinand II of Aragon, Henry's approach to statecraft was multi-faceted and forward-thinking. By marrying his children into powerful royal families in the likes of Scotland and Aragon, Henry increased England's influence in Europe and secured the closest thing to peace in the Middle Ages.

Film & TV

- "The White Queen" (2013) TV series
- "Henry VIII"(2003) TV Series
- "Looking for Richard" (1996)
- "Richard III" (1995)
- "Shadow of the Tower" (1972) TV series
- "An Age of Kings" (1960) TV series
- "Richard III" (1955)
- "Richard III" (1912) silent film

Further Research

- Weir, Alison (2008) Henry VIII: King and Court
- Bacon, Francis and Thompson, Brian (2007) The History of the Reign of King Henry VII
- Cunningham, Sean (2007) Henry VII
- Chrimes, S.B. (1999) Henry VII the English Monarch Series
- Penn, Thomas (2011) Winter King: Henry VII and the Dawn of Tudor England

Locations to Visit

- Henry VII was born in Pembroke Castle in Wales.
- Bosworth Battle Heritage Centre is located in Leicestershire, United Kingdom.
- Henry VII frequented the medieval Eltham Palace. Henry VIII and his siblings were raised there.
- He died at Richmond Palace, which no longer exists, but was buried at Westminster Abbey.

HENRY VIII
(1509–1547)

Divorced, beheaded, died; divorced, beheaded, survived. This grim little rhyme was once used by English History teachers to help their students memorize the sad fates of the six wives of Henry VIII (it's out of fashion because it's actually incorrect). One of the most infamous monarchs in British history, Henry VIII, believed deeply in the idea of the divine right of the sovereign to rule precisely as he pleased. During his reign, Henry brought about the dissolution of the monasteries, separated the Catholic Church, and became the head of his self-styled Church of England. Henry VIII's obsession with creating a male heir to his throne led to him being married six times, and he dealt with anyone who stood in his way by beheading them. An arrogant and ruthless man who brought about the phrase 'heads will roll,' Henry eventually produced a male heir called Edward. Edward VI ruled as a child for a mere six years before his sister, the powerful and long-reigning Queen Elizabeth, took over.

Key Facts about Henry VIII

- Henry VIII was born on June 28th, 1491 at Greenwich.
- Henry became King of England and Lord of Ireland on 5th April 1509, aged 17.
- He was first married on 11th June 1509 to Catherine of Aragon. This marriage was annulled in 1533, leaving Henry free to marry five more times in his lifetime.
- Henry VIII died on January 28th, 1547, of kidney disease, gout, and a circulatory disorder.

The Life of Henry VIII

Henry VIII was the second son of his father, Henry VII, and Elizabeth of York, and, as such, was not expected to ascend to the

English throne. Instead, Henry was raised to take on the role of Archbishop of Canterbury and was educated by the best tutors in the land, with a focus on Latin, French, and Theology. Just one year after Arthur, Henry's older brother, married Catherine of Aragon, Arthur died, and the widowed Catherine was betrothed to 12-year-old Henry. Henry was reluctant to marry Catherine, perhaps for religious reasons, and it was thought that the marriage was only encouraged by Henry VII to keep Catherine's substantial dowry in the family.

On Henry VIII's ascension to the throne, he suddenly agreed to marry Catherine, stating that the match had been his dying father's last wish. Henry VIII became King of England and Lord of Ireland on 22nd April 1509. Just two days after Henry and Queen Catherine's coronation, which was a grand and festive affair, Henry arrested his father's two most disliked ministers, charged them with high treason, and had them executed. This first act of violence marked the beginning of his merciless approach to ruling his kingdom, and execution became Henry's primary tactic for dealing with any kind of opposition to his will.

During Henry's early years as King, he was mainly concerned with the uniting of Europe, acting as a mediator between the most powerful political personalities of the time: Ferdinand of Aragon, Emperor Maximillian, Pope Julius II, and King Louis XII of France. A short war in France was the result of Henry's negotiations.

In the following years, Henry's interest in European politics waned, and he passed over most of his foreign policy affairs to his chancellor, Thomas Wolsey. Wolsey encouraged Henry to write a religious book against the church-reforming doctrines of Luther that were circulating illegally at the time. This work led to Henry being awarded the title Defender of the Faith.

Queen Catherine had given birth four times in the eight years between 1510 and 1518, and of the six pregnancies, only one child survived, a girl named Mary. Henry did not recognize Mary as his heir and is known to have had mistresses throughout this time. One of his mistresses, Elizabeth Blount, gave birth to his son in 1519 and named him Henry FitzRoy. Although illegitimate, the boy was made Duke of Richmond. In time, Henry FitzRoy may have been legitimized and, as a result of the Second Succession Act, may have eventually become King had he not died suddenly, aged just 17, married but childless.

Henry's displeasure at Catherine's inability to provide him with a male heir was in part superstitious; he believed God's displeasure at his union with his brother's widow had left them unable to create a male heir, but Henry also had a new mistress named Lady Anne Boleyn whom he intended to marry. Henry colluded with Cardinal Wolsey in pressuring Pope Clement VII to annul the previous Pope's dispensation that Henry and Catherine could marry, deeming the marriage null and void. But Pope Clement had only recently been reinstated as Pope following a period of imprisonment by Emperor Charles V, who was Catherine of Aragon's nephew. The annulment was never secured, Wolsey was ruined, and Henry took matters into his own hands.

Thomas Cromwell now entered the picture as Henry VIII's chief minister. Cromwell pushed through a series of acts that challenged papal power in England and led to the Protestant Reformation of England. Catherine's daughter was declared illegitimate in the Act of Succession in 1533; the Acts of Supremacy of 1534 recognized Henry VIII's status as the Supreme Head of the Church of England, and the Act in Restraint of Appeals abolished the right of citizens to appeal to Rome. This final act led to Henry VIII's excommunication from the Catholic Church.

Henry's marriage to Catherine was annulled, but not before he had already married his current love interest, Anne Boleyn, in secret. Anne gave birth to their first child in 1533, a girl named Elizabeth. Anne was pregnant two more times, each ending in a miscarriage. In retaliation for the lack of a male heir, Henry had Anne executed by beheading on charges of treason, incest, and adultery, along with five men she was accused of having sex with, one of them her own brother.

Henry's next wife was Jane Seymour, daughter of Sir John Seymour, who he married in May 1536, just days after Anne's execution. Jane was able to give Henry a son, Edward, but sadly, she died in childbirth. Next, Henry married Anne of Cleves on the advice of Thomas Cromwell. Anne was a Lutheran Catholic and a good match for the young King, but Henry was said to have been displeased by her appearance, and the marriage was not consummated. It's unclear exactly why, but Thomas Cromwell, once a close advisor to the King and responsible for the accumulation of the King's huge wealth and dissolution of the monasteries, now became an enemy in court. Cromwell was tried for treason and executed on July 28th, 1540.

The King's attentions now turned to the teenage Catherine Howard, daughter of the King's political enemy, the Duke of Norfolk. They were married in secret in 1540 when the King was 49 years old, and she was just 17. Henry was said to have been besotted with his new Queen, but soon after the marriage, it came to light that Catherine was having affairs with two men on her staff. All three were beheaded. In the same year, Henry sanctioned the destruction of shrines to saints, and over the next few years, all of England's remaining monasteries were dissolved, and property and assets transferred to the crown.

Henry's last wife, Catherine Parr, was a wealthy widow and a religious reformer who often argued with Henry over theological matters. She is thought to have narrowly escaped execution because of her propensity to provoke Henry into rages with her radical Protestantism. Catherine Parr reconciled Henry with his daughters Mary and Elizabeth and helped usher in an Act of Parliament in 1543 that put both Mary and Elizabeth back in line to the English throne.

In his later years, Henry VIII was in very bad health; he was obese and suffered from gout thought to be linked to inactivity due to a leg injury sustained many years before. Recently, it has been suggested that Henry VIII may have suffered from Type II Diabetes. Henry died on 28th January 1547 in the Palace of Whitehall; his body was laid to rest in St George's Chapel in Windsor Castle alongside his third wife, Jane Seymour.

Legacy of Henry VIII

Henry's radical changes to the English Constitution asserted the supremacy of the sovereign over all others, created the Church of England, and initiated the English Protestant Reformation.

To some, Henry's changes to the church-state relationship were positive, strengthening the position of the English monarchy against the papacy in Rome and acquiring the monastery's wealth, which could be put to better use. To many, Henry was a ruthless and foolish man who made massive changes to the very fabric of English society for his own selfish ends and created a dangerous Protestant-Roman Catholic divide that plagued his kingdoms for years to come. The wealth of the monasteries never helped to ease the lot of the poor; instead, they improved the wealth of the aristocracy and funded wars overseas.

Henry's lifelong obsession with creating a Tudor dynasty and a long line of successors to the throne ended with the short rule of one son, Edward, and the long rule of one daughter, Elizabeth, who died childless.

Films and TV Shows Featuring Henry VIII

- Henry VIII(1911)
- Anna Boleyn(1920)
- Tower of London(1939)
- Anne of the Thousand Days(1969)
- Henry VIII and His Six Wives(1972)
- Crossed Swords(1977)
- The Other Boleyn Girl(2008)
- The Tudors (TV Show)
- Wolf Hall (TV Show)

Further Research

- John Guy (2014) Henry VIII: The Quest for Fame
- Helen Simpson (2013) Henry VIII
- Alison Weir (2011) Henry VIII: King and Court
- Alison Weir (2011) The Six Wives of Henry VIII
- David Starkey (2002) The Reign of Henry VIII: The Personalities and the Politics
- Shakespeare's Henry VIII (17th Century)

Locations Related to Henry VIII

- Eltham Palace is where Henry VIII spent the majority of his childhood. The Medieval Hall still survives, although much of the building dates back to the 1930s.
- Hampton Court Palace was Henry's home for the majority of his reign. You can visit his private apartments by taking a tour.
- Leeds Castle was visited several times by Henry during his life, and during his marriage to Catherine of Aragon, the castle was renovated for her use.
- The Tower of London has a special part to play in Henry VIII's reign. The King had many enemies incarcerated here and also ordered a number of executions. Most notably, his second wife, Anne Boleyn, was murdered here.
- Windsor Castle is the oldest castle in the world that still has residents. Both Henry VIII and his third wife, Jane Seymour, are buried here.
- Henry is responsible for the dissolution of the monasteries. Lindisfarne Priory, Penshurst Place, Castle Acre Abbey, and Fountains Abbey were all disbanded and fell into ruin during Henry VIII's reign.

EDWARD VI (1547–1553)

Edward VI was the son of Henry VIII and his third wife, Jane Seymour. Despite his short reign, he is known for being a significant figure in English history, as his reign saw the establishment of the Church of England as a Protestant church. Since he was a child when he succeeded to the throne, his reign was mostly governed by Edward Seymour, his uncle, who made lasting changes to England during the Protestant Reformation.

Key Facts about Edward VI

- Edward VI was born in 1537 and ascended to the throne at the age of 9.
- He was the first monarch to be raised as a Protestant.
- His reign saw the introduction of the Book of Common Prayer and the establishment of the Church of England as a Protestant church.
- Edward VI was known for his intelligence and love for learning, especially in theology and languages.
- He died at the age of 15, most likely due to tuberculosis.

His Short Life and Reign

Edward VI, born on October 12, 1537, at Hampton Court Palace, was the only son of King Henry VIII and his third wife, Jane Seymour. His mother died due to childbirth complications when Edward was merely a few weeks old. Later on, he was entrusted to the care of his stepmother, Katherine Parr, who was a fervent Protestant. Under her tutelage, Edward was immersed in the burgeoning ideas of the Reformation, embracing Protestantism.

Ascending to the throne at the tender age of nine, Edward VI's reign bore the indelible marks of his formative years. However, the true reins of power during his minority were often held by a regency council, with various figures vying for influence in the Royal Court. Although officially established to govern in his stead, the de facto ruler during much of his reign was Edward Seymour, Duke of Somerset, who served as Lord Protector and effectively wielded authority over England (confusingly also named Edward...).

Under Seymour's guidance, Edward's reign saw significant strides towards establishing Protestantism as the state religion. The Church of England underwent profound transformations, with the introduction of the Book of Common Prayer in 1549 solidifying its Protestant character. Edward's fervent support of the Reformation manifested in his efforts to reform education, law, and finance, leaving an enduring imprint on the trajectory of England's religious and political landscape.

Edward VI's early years were characterized by the delicate balance of power as factions within the court maneuvered for control. Despite his nominal position as king, Edward's youth and inexperience left him largely dependent on the guidance of regents and advisors. Chief among these was his uncle, Edward Seymour, who wielded immense influence as Lord Protector.

Seymour's regency was not without its challenges as he navigated the treacherous waters of court politics and faced opposition from rival factions, including the conservative Catholic contingent. Yet, his vision for England as a Protestant nation drove his policies, leading to sweeping reforms that reshaped the fabric of English society.

Under Seymour's stewardship, the Protestant Reformation gained momentum, with the Church of England undergoing radical changes to align with Protestant doctrine. Monastic lands were dissolved, and the wealth of the church was redirected to the crown, consolidating royal power and funding Edward's ambitious agenda for reform.

Education emerged as a focal point of Seymour's reforms, with efforts to expand access to learning and promote Protestant teachings. Schools were established, and the curriculum was revamped to instill the principles of the Reformation in the next generation of English citizens.

In the realm of law, Seymour sought to modernize and

streamline the legal system, laying the groundwork for future legal reforms. His efforts aimed to create a more equitable and efficient system of justice, reflecting the ideals of the emerging Protestant ethos.

Economically, Seymour's policies aimed to bolster England's financial stability and promote economic growth. Initiatives were launched to encourage trade and industry, laying the foundation for England's emergence as a global economic power in the centuries to come.

Despite his ambitious agenda, Seymour's regency was not without controversy. His authoritarian tendencies and heavy-handed approach to governance alienated many within the nobility and fueled discontent among the populace. Ultimately, his reign as Lord Protector was marked by both triumphs and tribulations, leaving a complex legacy that continues to shape perceptions of Edward VI's reign and the tumultuous era of the English Reformation.

Legacy

Edward VI's reign was short, but it had a significant impact on English history through the regency of Edward Seymour. His establishment of the Church of England as a Protestant church paved the way for the religious reforms of Elizabeth I and the development of the Anglican Church. Edward's reign also saw the introduction of several important reforms in education, law, and finance, which helped to modernize England. When he died, there was a succession mess.

Edward VI's reign was tragically cut short by his untimely death at the age of fifteen on July 6, 1553. Afflicted by a terminal illness, likely tuberculosis, Edward's passing left England in a state of uncertainty regarding the succession. His deathbed designation of Lady Jane Grey, a Protestant, and his cousin once removed, as his heir apparent, sparked a succession crisis. However, Edward's half-sister Mary, the daughter of Henry VIII and Catherine of Aragon, swiftly moved to assert her claim to the throne. Supported by powerful allies and buoyed by popular sentiment, Mary successfully deposed Lady Jane Grey and was proclaimed Queen of England on July 19, 1553, marking the beginning of her tumultuous reign as Mary I (more on that here).

Movies and TV Shows Featuring Edward VI

- "The Tudors" (2007-2010)
- "The Six Wives of Henry VIII" (1970)
- "Elizabeth R" (1971)
- "The Virgin Queen" (2005)
- "Wolf Hall" (2015)

Books and Documentaries:

- "Edward VI: The Last Boy King" by Stephen Alford
- "The Reign of Edward VI" by James Anthony Froude
- "Edward VI: The Lost King of England" by Chris Skidmore
- "The Children of Henry VIII" by Alison Weir

Locations Related to Edward VI:

- Hampton Court Palace – the place of Edward's birth and childhood
- Westminster Abbey – where Edward was crowned king.
- Westminster Chapel in Windsor - Where Edward is buried.
- Greenwich Palace – where Edward spent much of his reign and where he died

JANE
(uncrowned)
(1553 - Deposed)

The 'nine-day Queen,' Lady Jane Grey, is one of the most tragic figures in the history of the monarchy. At just 16 years old, the pious and learned young woman had little desire to be proclaimed the Queen of England, but through the political machinations of her father, the Duke of Suffolk, and the powerful Duke of Northumberland, Edward VI's will made it so. Lady Mary Tudor, daughter of Henry VIII and rightful heir, did not take this coup lying down and raised enough followers to overthrow Jane in just nine days. Following a stint in the Tower of London, Lady Jane Grey was beheaded aged just sixteen or seventeen years old.

Key Facts

- Lady Jane Grey was born in Leicestershire in 1537.
- She was married at the age of 16 to Lord Guildford Dudley, the youngest son of the Duke of Northumberland.
- Lady Jane Grey was secretly proclaimed the Queen of England and Ireland on July 10th, 1553, and reigned just nine days before she was seized and imprisoned in the Tower of London.
- Jane was executed by beheading on 12 February 1554, aged 16.

The Tragic Life of Jane Grey

Born in the autumn of 1537, Jane was the daughter of Lady Frances Brandon, the eldest daughter of Mary Tudor, Queen of France, younger sister of Henry VIII, and Henry Grey, the 1st Duke of Suffolk. Through her mother, Jane was the great-granddaughter of Henry VII.

In February 1547, aged around 10, Jane joined the household

of Thomas Seymour, Edward VI's uncle, and Katherine Parr, widow of Henry VIII and queen dowager. Under Katherine's influence, Jane received a strict protestant education and grew up to become one of the best-educated young women of her day. Queen Katherine died due to complications related to childbirth soon after Jane joined them, and Jane acted as chief mourner at her funeral. In October 1551, King Edward VI made Jane's father, Henry Grey, the Duke of Suffolk, and Jane began to appear at the King's Court.

Both Thomas Seymour and Jane's father, Henry Grey, used Jane as a pawn to further their own political ambitions and proposed her as a bride for Lord Hertford and the King himself. Neither of these plans came to fruition, though, and Lady Jane Grey ended up marrying Lord Guildford Dudley, son of John Dudley, 1st Duke of Northumberland and the most powerful man in the country, on 25 May 1553 at Durham House.

The Duke of Northumberland acted as regent to King Edward VI and was fiercely protestant. In February 1553, at the age of 15, King Edward became terminally ill. At this point, Jane was an heiress to the English throne according to her great-uncle King Henry VIII's will, but only on the condition that his son Edward and daughters Mary and Elizabeth died without issue.

When it became clear to him that Edward was dying, the Duke of Northumberland, who already had control of the government, persuaded Edward to sign a will that passed over six feasible claimants to the throne, declared both Mary and Elizabeth Tudor illegitimate, and assigned the succession to the Duke of Northumberland's daughter-in-law, Lady Jane Grey.

The Duke and his followers were desperate to stop Mary Tudor, Henry VIII's eldest daughter and Catholic, from taking the throne, and when Edward died on 6 July 1553, Jane was informed that she was now queen. Jane took the throne with reluctance and was officially proclaimed Queen of England when she took up residence in the Tower of London. Interestingly, Jane refuses to name her husband Dudley as king and makes him the Duke of Clarence instead.

On hearing of Edward VI's death, Lady Mary Tudor immediately left her residence at Hunsdon, foiling the Duke of

Northumberland's plot to kidnap her. From a safe place in East Anglia, Mary began to rally her Catholic supporters, of which she had many, and plan her next move.

As soon as the Duke left London to confront Mary, the privy council saw which way the wind was blowing and switched their allegiance from Jane to Mary, a trend that was adopted even by the Duke of Suffolk, Jane's own father. On 19 July 1553, Mary was proclaimed Queen of England, and Jane and her husband were imprisoned in the Tower.

The Duke of Northumberland was executed on 22 August 1553. Jane and her husband were both tried for high treason on 13 November 1553. Both pleaded guilty and were sentenced to death, a sentence that was suspended and might never have been carried out if it wasn't for a rebellion that had nothing at all to do with Jane. On Queen Mary's announcement that she would marry the future Philip II of Spain, a fellow Catholic, those who did not support her joined Sir Thomas Wyatt, The Younger's rebellion, including the Duke of Suffolk, Jane's father. After defeating the rebellion, Queen Mary ordered that Jane and her husband be beheaded along with the Duke of Suffolk.

On 12 February 1554, Guildford was taken to the public execution place at Tower Hill, beheaded, and his corpse taken back to the Tower, where Lady Jane was shown his corpse. Lady Jane was then taken to Tower Green, where she recited Psalm 51, blindfolded herself, and was beheaded. The Duke of Suffolk, Jane's father, was executed 11 days later, but her mother, the Duchess of Suffolk, was given a full pardon, remarried, and lived out her days at court with her two surviving daughters.

Legacy

Once seen either as a calculating usurper of the throne or an unwitting political pawn, Lady Jane Grey now has a legacy as the tragic heroine of the Reformation. No proven authentic portrait exists of Lady Jane Grey, which has allowed popular culture to take every liberty with her appearance and fully realize the image of a beautiful, romantic heroine destined to be a political and religious martyr. The tale of Lady Jane Grey, who will be 16 or 17 years old forever, became legendary thanks in part to The Book of Martyrs by John Foxe, which emphasized the young queen's piety and unrelenting faith.

TV and Film

- The Prince and the Pauper (2000) TV
- Lady Jane (1986)
- Elizabeth R (1971) TV series
- Crossed Swords (1977)
- Tudor Rose (1936)
- The Court of Intrigue (1923)

Further Reading

- Plowden, Alison (2011) Lady Jane Grey: Nine Days Queen
- Ives, Eric (2009). Lady Jane Grey: A Tudor Mystery
- De Lisle, Leanda (2009). The Sisters Who Would Be Queen: Mary, Katherine, and Lady Jane Grey. A Tudor Tragedy
- Cook, Faith (2005) Nine Day Queen of England: Lady Jane Grey
- Loades, David (1996). John Dudley, Duke of Northumberland

Locations to Visit

- The location of Lady Jane Grey's birth is not known, but she died at the Tower of London and is buried at St. Peter ad Vincula in London.

MARY I
(1553–1558)

Mary I began her life as a much-cherished and respected Tudor princess but during her adolescence was rejected by her father, King Henry VIII, who declared her illegitimate and isolated from the royal court. A devout Catholic, Mary took the throne from the pretender Lady Jane Grey after just nine days and began a campaign to restore Catholicism to England and undo the transformation to the Church of England her father King Henry VIII had begun. The method Mary chose was extreme persecution, and during her reign, she had approximately 300 Protestants burned at the stake. At the end of her life, Mary was the first Queen regnant of England, and was much-reviled and much-deserving of the sobriquet Bloody Mary.

Key Facts About Mary I

- Mary I was born on the 18th of February 1516 at Greenwich Palace.
- The first child of Henry VIII, Mary I succeeded as Queen of England Ireland on 19 July 1553, following the disastrous nine-day reign of Lady Jane Grey
- Mary I was married on 25 July 1554 to Philip of Spain, son of Holy Roman Emperor Charles V, and later King Philip II of Spain.
- Mary died at St. James Palace on the 17 November 1558 of cancer having reigned just five years.

The Life of Mary I

The only child of Henry VIII and his first wife, Catherine of Aragon, to survive childhood, Mary was doted on by her parents and enjoyed a lavish and loving childhood. Mary was extremely well-educated, and by the age of nine could read and write Latin and also studied French, Spanish, music, and dance. All was not well with Mary's parents, however, and realizing that Catherine of Aragon was unable to provide him with a male heir, Henry VIII had Mary, and Catherine was sent to Ludlow Castle in Wales where she held her own court.

Eager to secure the continuation of the Tudor dynasty with a male heir and, perhaps, already in love with Anne Boleyn, Henry VIII appealed to Pope Clement VII to have his marriage to Catherine annulled. The Pope refused, and yet Henry VIII married Anne Boleyn in 1533, who was already pregnant with his child. In May 1533 the Archbishop of Canterbury, Thomas Cranmer, declared Henry and Catherine's marriage void, Henry broke with the Roman Catholic Church altogether and declared himself the Supreme Head of the Church of England. Mary became Lady Mary, and her newborn sister, Elizabeth took her position in the line of succession.

It is thought that Mary was treated badly by her father during the next few years during which time she was persecuted by Anne Boleyn and was frequently ill. Little did Anne Boleyn know that her own daughter Elizabeth would suffer the same fate as Mary in the years to come. Despite the fact that her mother was gravely ill, Mary was not permitted to visit Catherine, and in 1536, Catherine died leaving Mary inconsolable.

Following her mother's death, Mary was encouraged by her Catholic advisers to acknowledge her mother's divorce and made an oath of loyalty to her father as the Supreme Head of the English Church. In the years that followed, Henry VIII worked his way through his next five wives with Mary enjoying a fairly stable place at her father's court. In 1543, Henry married his sixth wife, Catherine Parr, who convinced him to bring his family back together and return Mary and Elizabeth to the line of succession after Edward.

When Mary's half-brother Edward VI, a partisan Protestant came to the throne, Mary was harassed for her religious beliefs, but her response to these hardships and ill-treatment was to cling ever more fiercely to her Catholic faith. Edward died aged just 15, and following a disastrous attempt by the Duke of Northumberland to maintain a Protestant England by planting Lady Jane Grey on the throne, Mary finally claimed her throne after Jane was deposed by the Privy Council. Having proven her popularity, Mary rode into London on the 3rd of August 1553 with her sister Elizabeth in tow. Her accession took place on the 1st of October 1553 at Westminster Abbey.

At first, Mary's reforms were relatively mild although she did slowly begin to restore Catholicism in England by re-introducing Mass, reinstating deprived Bishops, and expelling married members of the clergy. Next, Mary reinstated old heresy laws that declared that anyone who practiced or believed in a religion different from that of the sovereign was committing treason. Finally, at the age of 37, Mary made it known that she intended to marry Philip of Spain, the eldest son, and heir of Holy Roman Emperor Charles V. She hoped that the union would produce a child who would become her Catholic heir, effectively removing Elizabeth from direct succession. This decision was very unpopular both with parliament and the public and a revolt began.

Thanks to the reinstated heresy laws Mary was able to legally have any member of the aristocracy who challenged her beheaded and around 300 Protestant 'heretics' burned at the stake. The first executions took place in early February and included prominent Protestants John Rogers, Laurence Saunders, and the Archbishop of Canterbury who was forced to watch fellow clergymen Bishop Ridley, and Bishop Latimer burned at the stake before he himself succumbed to the same fate. Even Mary's new husband Philip of Spain warned against these atrocities despite the fact that he was doing a very similar thing in the Netherlands at the same time.

The marriage of Mary and Philip was childless, and Mary suffered two 'false pregnancies' in 1555 and 1557 during which time she showed symptoms of pregnancy without actually being pregnant. Philip left England after just 13 months of marriage and returned only once in order to convince Mary to send England to war with France, an expedition that led to the loss of Calais after a tenure of 211 years. England received no share in the Spanish monopolies in New World trade and Mary's popularity continued to plummet as the burning of Protestants at the stake became even more frequent.

In ill health and finally accepting that she would never have a child, Mary withdrew to St James' Palace where she died during an influenza epidemic on 17 November 1558. It is thought that Mary may have suffered from ovarian or uterine cancer, and it is this cancer that may have killed her. Mary was interred in Westminster Abbey on 14 December 1558 in a tomb she would eventually share with her sister, Elizabeth.

Legacy Today

Her posthumous sobriquet, Bloody Mary, says much about Queen Mary I's legacy. The first woman to claim the throne of England, Mary was a popular queen during the early years of her reign and was loyally supported by the Roman Catholics of England. Mary has been seen as a bloodthirsty tyrant throughout most of history thanks in part to writings published in the years following her death that became popular with English Protestants. Mary's unpopularity wasn't only due to the horrendous executions carried out in her name, but a mixture of failed crops, military failure in France, and her failure to produce an heir combined to turn the public against her. Now, viewed through a more scholarly historical lens, Mary is seen as a bloody queen, but a queen who began the economic reforms, military growth, and expansion of the British Empire that made the Elizabethan era glorious.

Film & TV

- The Other Boleyn Girl (2008)
- The Tudors (2007) TV series
- The Virgin Queen (2005) TV series
- Elizabeth (1998)
- Lady Jane (1986)
- Elizabeth R (1971) TV series
- Marie Tudor (1966)
- Pearls of the Crown (1937).
- Tudor Rose (1936)
- Marie Tudor (1917)

Further Research

- Edwards, John (2011) Mary I: England's Catholic Queen
- Whitelock, Anna (2010) Mary Tudor: England's First Queen
- Duffy, Eamon (2009). Fires of Faith: Catholic England Under Mary Tudor
- Ridley, Jasper (2001). Bloody Mary's Martyrs: The Story of England's Terror
- Tittler, Robert (1991). The Reign of Mary I
- Loades, David M. (1989) Mary Tudor: A Life
- Erickson, Carolly (1978). Bloody Mary: The Life of Mary Tudor
- Prescott, H. F. M. (1952). Mary Tudor: The Spanish Tudor

Locations to Visit

- Mary and King Philip II took their honeymoon at Hampton Court Palace in London.
- For a time Mary held her own court at Ludlow Castle in Shropshire.
- Mary also lived in both Hatfield House in Hertfordshire with her half-sister Elizabeth and Hunsdon House in Hertfordshire following her mother's death.
- The Palace of Beaulieu in Boreham, Essex was granted to Mary I upon Henry VIII's death, as stated in his will. The property is now used as a private school.
- Mary assembled a military force and launched her attack on Lady Jane Grey's supporters from Framlingham Castle, Suffolk.
- Mary died at St James's Palace in London and is buried in Westminster Abbey.

ELIZABETH I
(1558–1603)

The fifth and final monarch of the highly influential, although relatively short-lived, rule of the Tudor dynasty, Elizabeth I, was the second daughter of Henry VIII. Elizabeth's relationship with her family was tense, to say the least. Her mother was executed by her father before she was three years old, she was proclaimed a bastard, rejected by her half-brother, imprisoned by her half-sister, and had Mary Queen of Scots executed for treason. Despite these Tudor complications, Elizabeth's reign lasted a long and overall successful 44 years. Cautious in foreign affairs and relatively tolerant in matters of religion, Elizabeth I helped to stabilize the English economy and strengthened the role of parliament. Remaining unmarried, Elizabeth inspired a popular following who admired her as a virginal goddess-like figure and was known to be a charismatic, if difficult, leader. Ruling England at a time when the arts flourished and discovery was high on the agenda, the Elizabethan era is remembered as a golden age of creativity and exploration.

Key Facts about Elizabeth I

- Elizabeth I was born on September 7th, 1533 at the Palace of Placentia in Greenwich.
- Elizabeth ascended as Queen of England on November 17th, 1558
- Known as the Virgin Queen, Elizabeth did not marry or have children and died on March 24th, 1603, aged 69, having reigned for 44 years.

A Brief Look at the Life of Elizabeth I

Elizabeth was the first daughter of King Henry VIII and his second wife Anne Boleyn. Born within wedlock and thus legitimately, Elizabeth should have automatically been third in line for the throne after her younger brother, Edward, and older sister Mary. However, the breakdown of Henry and Anne's marriage and Anne's subsequent execution under charges of adultery left Elizabeth both motherless and illegitimate.

Elizabeth's childhood was difficult and her future uncertain. Although her mother was beheaded before she was three years old, Elizabeth was not expelled from the royal circle and was raised and educated at Hatfield Palace by a series of highly sought-after tutors. By the time she reached adulthood, Elizabeth was one of the best-educated women in England and spoke six languages fluently.

Following Henry VIII's death, Elizabeth's brother Edward became King of England at the age of just nine. When he died six years later his will made clear that the Succession to the Crown Act of 1543 was not to be followed and both Mary and Elizabeth were excluded from the succession. He named Lady Jane Grey his heir, granddaughter of Henry VIII's sister. Jane was proclaimed Queen but was deposed after only nine days and Mary became Queen.

On the surface, Mary and Elizabeth were sisters, allies, and friends, although Elizabeth swore to being a true Roman Catholic, her education had been a protestant one and the sisters found themselves on opposite sides of a huge religious divide. When Elizabeth was implicated in Sir Thomas Wyatt's revolt against Queen Mary, Mary had her sent to the Tower of London and then placed under house arrest to protect her throne. Mary's popularity waned when she married Prince Phillip of Spain, a devout Catholic, and when Mary died and Elizabeth succeeded her the protestant masses were overjoyed.

Mary Queen of Scots, Elizabeth's cousin, questioned Elizabeth's legitimacy while on the Scottish throne, a move that would make life difficult for her later when she was forced to abdicate to her one-year-old son and seek refuge in England. In order to keep Mary Queen of Scots away from her Catholic enemies in Scotland and France, Elizabeth detained her in England, a detainment that ended up lasting a total of nineteen years. The freeing of Mary and her claim to the English throne became the focus of a huge Catholic rebellion. The other claimant to Elizabeth's throne, Queen Mary's husband, Phillip II of Spain, was also Catholic.

Queen Elizabeth is thought to have been more tolerant than Queen Mary in her approach to religious differences in her kingdom but support for Mary was wide-reaching and deeply felt, particularly among English Catholics who were being persecuted. Queen Elizabeth is thought to have imprisoned and executed a number of Catholic Bishops who refused to acknowledge a revised Book of Common Prayer recognizing her as the Head of the Church. International Catholic powers in Rome, Spain, and France financed and assisted Mary in her plots against Elizabeth, and in a 1570 bull, Pope Pius V announced that all of Elizabeth's subjects were to be released from their allegiance to her, condoning the withdrawal of the Queen from her throne.

Elizabeth reacted by making 'the intent' to convert English subjects to Catholicism a treasonable offense, carrying the death penalty. Many priests were executed and a cult of martyrdom ensued. Elizabeth's treatment of Catholic enemies in Ireland is said to have been particularly brutal and permanently affected Anglo-Irish relations. Eventually, after being shown proof of Mary Queen of Scot's involvement in plots to assassinate her, Elizabeth signed her death warrant and she was beheaded at Fotheringhay Castle on 8th February 1587.

Soon after Philip II, Queen Mary's husband and claimant to the English throne, assembled the Spanish Armada, a navy of over 130 ships that intended to invade England, overthrow the Queen, and re-establish Roman Catholicism as the state religion. After suffering dramatic losses on the coast of Ireland, the Spanish left, defeated.

Despite this success, England remained at war with Spain and was less successful in future costly campaigns. Elizabeth's wars put a financial strain on the crown and the country and left a huge deficit for her successor. The threat of invasion from Spain through Ireland and from France through Scotland was real and constant.

One of the Queen's main allies in her ongoing sea battles with the Spanish was Francis Drake, whom she had knighted for his circumnavigation of the globe between 1577 and 1580. The exploratory work of Drake and his contemporaries Walter Raleigh and Humphrey Gilbert led to the establishment of the East India

Company in 1600 and the beginning of a huge colonial empire that reached its peak in the Victorian Era.

However, in the later years of Elizabeth's reign, popular opinion of her fell. The standard of living of many of her subjects had dramatically declined thanks to the cost of ongoing wars, higher taxes, and poor harvests. This economic recession coincided with a period of greater repression of Catholics in England. In 1592, Elizabeth authorized commissions that allowed her to spy on Catholic households and interrogate Catholic subjects at will.

Elizabeth died at Richmond Palace on 24th March 1603 of complications related to old age. The date of her accession became a national holiday, one that lasted over 200 years.

Legacy of Elizabeth I

Elizabeth chose never to marry, instead using her potential to become a wife as a political tool. Known as 'The Virgin Queen', 'Gloriana' and 'Good Queen Bess', Elizabeth's reign is remembered as one of triumph. She married herself to England and sacrificed her personal happiness in order to rule the country well. Popular with the majority of her subjects, for the majority of her reign, Elizabeth made a series of speeches during her lifetime that have gone down in history.

Late in her reign, she addressed Parliament as such, 'There is no jewel, be it of never so high a price, which I set before this jewel; I mean your love.' The Elizabethan era is remembered primarily for world-changing voyages of discovery and exploration and the flourishing of the arts in England. Theatre, literature, and painting thrived and Queen Elizabeth attended Shakespeare's first performance of A Midsummer Night's Dream.

Films and TV Shows Featuring Elizabeth I

- Elizabeth: The Golden Age (2007)
- Elizabeth I (2005) TV Show
- The Tudors (2007) TV Show
- Elizabeth (1998)

- Shakespeare in Love (1998)
- Orlando (1992)
- The Virgin Queen (1955)

Further Research

- Somerset, Anne (2003) Elizabeth I
- Stanley, Diane (2001) Good Queen Bess: The Story of Elizabeth I of England
- Weir, Alison (1999) Who Was Queen Elizabeth I?
- Maclaren, A. N. (1999) Political Culture in the Reign of Elizabeth I
- Jones, Norman (1993) The Birth of the Elizabethan Age
- MacCaffrey, Wallace T. (1993) Elizabeth I.

Locations Related to Elizabeth I

- Many portraits of Elizabeth were made during her reign, some of which can be seen at the National Gallery in London, UK.
- Elizabeth was born at the Palace of Placentia in Greenwich, London. Although the palace was demolished in the seventeenth century, a plaque marks the site of the former palace.
- She was raised at Hatfield House in Hertfordshire. The house is open to visits from the public.
- Elizabeth spent much of her time at Richmond Palace in Surrey. She died there in 1603.
- The tomb of Elizabeth I can be found in Westminster Abbey.

JAMES I
(1603–1625)

First known as James VI of Scotland, James was the first monarch to rule both Scotland and England. He was born on June 19, 1566, in Edinburgh Castle, Scotland, and was the only son of Mary, Queen of Scots, and her second husband, Henry Stuart, Lord Darnley. His mother was forced to abdicate the throne when James was only one year old, and he was crowned King of Scotland at the tender age of 13 months.

Key Facts about James I

- James I was the first monarch to rule over both Scotland and England, effectively unifying the two nations (the union under the United Kingdom would come later under Queen Anne).
- He was only 13 months old when he was crowned King of Scotland, making him the youngest Scottish monarch to ever ascend to the throne.
- James was a patron of the arts and literature, and his court was a hub of culture and learning. Some of the greatest playwrights and poets of all time, including William Shakespeare, Ben Jonson, and John Donne, flourished under his patronage.
- James I was a staunch Protestant and believed in the divine right of kings, which gave him absolute power over his subjects.
- One of James's most significant accomplishments was the publication of the King James Bible in 1611, which became the standard version used by many Protestant churches and is still widely read today.

A Brief Biography of James I

James grew up in a turbulent time in Scottish history, with religious and political strife causing chaos throughout the country. However, he was known as a precocious child and received an excellent education in languages, history, and theology. In 1586, he married Anne of Denmark, and they eventually had seven children together. James was already King of Scotland when he ascended to the English throne, and his reign marked the beginning of the Stuart dynasty in England. This was a union of the crowns of England and Scotland. The nations would not be united politically until Queen Anne's reign in the next century.

When Elizabeth I died in 1603, James succeeded her as King of England, uniting the two countries under one monarch for the first time. James was a staunch Protestant and believed in the divine right of kings, which gave him absolute power over his subjects. He was also a patron of the arts and literature, and his court was a hub of culture and learning.

During his reign, James faced many challenges, including religious conflicts, political upheavals, and economic difficulties. He was forced to deal with the Gunpowder Plot in 1605, a failed attempt by a group of Catholics to blow up the Houses of Parliament and assassinate the king.

Despite these challenges, James was able to consolidate his power and establish a stable government. He was known for his wise and fair rule, and he was respected for his intelligence and wit. James was also a patron of the arts, and during his reign, some of the greatest playwrights and poets of all time, including William Shakespeare, Ben Jonson, and John Donne, flourished.

One of James's most significant accomplishments was the publication of the King James Bible in 1611. This translation of the Bible into English became the standard version used by many Protestant churches and is still widely read today.

King James Bible and James I

The King James Bible, also known as the Authorized Version, is one of the most widely read and influential translations of the Bible in English. It was first published in 1611 during the reign of King James I of England. The translation was commissioned by the king in response to concerns about the accuracy of existing translations and the need for a new authoritative version.

The project to produce the King James Bible was undertaken by 47 scholars who were divided into six committees, each responsible for a different section of the Bible. The scholars worked from the original Hebrew and Greek texts and used previous translations as a guide, but aimed to produce a more accurate and elegant version. The translation was completed in 1611 and was immediately popular, thanks in part to the high quality of the language and the beauty of the prose.

The King James Bible had a profound impact on English literature and language. Its elegant and poetic language influenced writers such as William Shakespeare, John Milton, and John Bunyan, and helped to shape the development of modern English. The King James Bible is also notable for its influence on religion and society. It played a key role in the development of Protestantism and helped to spread the Christian message throughout the English-speaking world.

Despite its enduring popularity, the King James Bible has been criticized over the years for its inaccuracies and inconsistencies. Some of the language used in the translation is now archaic and difficult to understand, and the translation has been revised and updated over the centuries to reflect changes in the English language and to improve its accuracy.

Today, the King James Bible remains an important part of English literary and religious heritage and is still widely read and studied by scholars and laypeople alike. Its influence can be seen in everything from literature and art to politics and popular culture, and it continues to shape the way we think about the world and our place in it.

American Connections of James I

James's reign also saw the establishment of the first permanent English colony in North America at Jamestown, Virginia, in 1607. James I played a significant role in the founding of Jamestown, the first permanent English settlement in North America. In 1606, he granted a charter to the Virginia Company, a group of investors who were tasked with establishing colonies in the New World. The Virginia Company established Jamestown in 1607, naming the settlement after the king. James' support for the venture was driven by his desire to expand English trade and territory, and to spread Christianity to the native peoples of the New World. Despite early struggles with disease, starvation, and conflict with the native Powhatan people, Jamestown survived and paved the way for the eventual colonization of North America by the English.

James I's Legacy Today

James's reign was not without controversy, and he faced criticism from both his own subjects and foreign powers. He was accused of being too lenient towards Catholics and too friendly with Spain, which led to tensions with France. James was also criticized for his extravagant spending, which left the country in debt.

Despite these criticisms, James's reign had a profound impact on English history and left a lasting legacy. He played a key role in establishing the modern concept of the British monarchy, which continues to this day. His patronage of the arts and literature helped to create a golden age of English culture, which has influenced the world to this day. His religious beliefs and commitment to the divine right of kings played a crucial role in shaping the political and social structures of England for centuries to come.

James I was a significant figure in English history who played a crucial role in shaping the modern concept of the British monarchy. His reign was marked by political and religious turmoil, but it was also a time of great cultural and artistic achievement. James's legacy is still felt today, and his impact on English history cannot be overstated.

Movies and TV Shows Featuring James I

- "The Witch" (2015) – a horror film that takes place during James I's reign
- "Anonymous" (2011) – a historical drama that explores the authorship of Shakespeare's plays during James I's reign
- "Gunpowder" (2017) – a BBC miniseries that tells the story of the Gunpowder Plot
- "Elizabeth: The Golden Age" (2007) – a historical drama that features a brief appearance by James I
- "The Virgin Queen" (2005) – a miniseries that features James I as a minor character

Further Research

- "James I: The Phoenix King" by Thomas Cogswell
- "James I: Scotland's King of England" by John Matusiak
- "James I and the Politics of Literature" by Anthony Parr
- "James VI and I: Ideas, Authority, and Government" edited by Ralph Houlbrooke
- "King James VI and I: Political Writings" edited by Johann Sommerville
- "James I and the English Court: A Study in Political and Cultural History" by David L. Smith
- "James I: The Masque of Monarchy" by Graham Parry
- "King James and the History of Homosexuality" by Michael B. Young
- "King James's Bible: A Selection" edited by Robert Carroll and Stephen Prickett
- "The King's Bed: Sex, Power and the Court of Charles II" by Don Jordan and Michael Walsh (includes a section on James I)

Locations Related to James I

- Edinburgh Castle, Scotland – James I was born here on

June 19, 1566.
- Holyrood Palace, Scotland – James I was crowned King of Scotland here in 1567.
- Westminster Abbey, England – James I was crowned King of England here in 1603.
- Hampton Court Palace, England – James I's primary residence and the site of many important events during his reign.
- Tower of London, England – James I imprisoned several notable figures here, including Sir Walter Raleigh.
- Jamestown, Virginia – The first permanent English colony in North America was established during James I's reign.
- Royston, England – James I frequently visited this hunting lodge during his reign.
- The Palace of Whitehall, England – James I's main residence in London, which burned down in 1698.
- The Globe Theatre, England – James I was a patron of William Shakespeare and other playwrights who performed at this famous theatre.
- Oxford University, England – James I visited Oxford several times during his reign and was a patron of the university.

CHARLES I
(1625–1649)

Charles I was not the most successful King in the history of the British monarchy but he was certainly the most stubborn. Ruler of the Kingdoms of England, Ireland, and Scotland during the mid-seventeenth century, Charles' unwavering belief in the king's divine right to rule his country unencumbered by the demands of democracy and the rights of parliament led to a devastating civil war.

Charles's attempts to convert the religious practices of the British Isles to those of Catholicism combined with his levying of taxes without parliamentary consent made him an unpopular king with the public. Charles's megalomaniacal tendencies eventually led him to attempt to rule his kingdoms as a dictator, the final straw for his parliamentarian opponent Oliver Cromwell who helped lead the country into a brutal civil war that ended with Charles' inglorious beheading.

Key Facts about Charles I

- Charles I was born on November 19th, 1600 in Dunfermline Palace, Fife, Scotland.
- He ascended to the throne on March 27th, 1625 at the age of 24.
- Charles married Henrietta Maria, daughter of King Henri IV of France shortly after his coronation when she was 15 years old.
- Charles died by execution on January 30th, 1649 at Whitehall and is buried at Windsor.

The Life of Charles I

King James VI of Scotland had two sons: the elder, popular and manly Henry, Prince of Wales, and the younger, small and sickly Charles. Unable to make the journey to England as a child, Charles was left behind in Scotland, only reunited with his family once he was able to walk the length of the Great Hall at Dunfermline without assistance. After Henry's death in 1612, Charles became heir to the English, Scottish, and Irish thrones of King James VI.

Charles was placed under the protective wing of King James' closest advisor, Lord Buckingham. Often referred to as James's 'favorite', there is much evidence to suggest that Buckingham was James' lover and was lavished with affection and patronage from the King. In 1623 Charles and Buckingham travelled to Madrid in order to negotiate for a marriage between Charles and the daughter of Philip III of Spain.

Tensions between Catholics and Protestants in Europe were high, with disagreements over the heir to the throne of Bohemia eventually igniting the Thirty Years War. The trip was unpopular with the English public and parliament and proved to be unsuccessful. Charles and Buckingham returned to the UK frustrated and humiliated and tried to convince King James to declare war on Spain.

James took the suggestion to Parliament which rejected his request for funds to raise an army. In retaliation Charles and Buckingham called for the impeachment of the high-ranking officials who opposed the war, a move James was furious about, warning the pair that they would live to regret it. By the time Charles succeeded his ailing father to the throne in 1625, he and Buckingham were already in de facto control of the kingdom. In their unpopular negotiations with Spain, thirst for war in Europe, and behavior towards officials in parliament, the pair had already made many powerful enemies.

Charles's contentious attitude towards religion in the English, Scottish, and Irish kingdoms became apparent in his marriage to French princess Henrietta Maria. The pair were married on the 13th June 1625 in Canterbury and Charles delayed the opening of his first parliament until after the ceremony to avoid any objections to the match. Henrietta Maria was a Catholic and refused to take part in Charles's coronation in 1626 at Westminster Abbey as the ceremony was a Protestant one.

On his engagement to Henrietta Maria, Charles had agreed in secret to provide the French with an English naval force to suppress the Protestant Huguenots at La Rochelle. But once they were married he gave orders for an English attack on the French coast to defend the very army he had agreed to suppress. The attack, led by the now universally hated Buckingham, was disastrous and led to Louis XIII's siege of La Rochelle.

In 1628 Buckingham was assassinated, an occurrence that is thought to have devastated the King. Following Buckingham's demise, Charles's relationship with his wife is said to have grown from strength to strength, and within a few months, Henrietta Maria was pregnant with the first of their nine children.

Charles's open support of ecclesiastic Richard Montagu, whose religious propaganda supported a Catholic-derived, anti-Calvinist doctrine, increased tensions between the monarchy and state. The Commons refused to deliver finance for Charles' proposed war with Spain and France and in retaliation Charles levied the public with arbitrary taxes. Parliament responded with the Petition of Right, an act that declared that Charles' innovations in religion, taxation without the consent of parliament, unfair imprisonment and the application of martial law to civilians were illegal. In a further act, parliament declared any citizen who took part in any of the activities named above to be an enemy of the state.

Charles immediately dissolved parliament and ruled as a dictator for almost 11 years. During this time the conditions for a full-scale revolt and civil war steadily matured. Charles attempted to force the Church of Scotland to adopt High Anglican practices which they strongly opposed. In 1639, the Scottish Parliament abolished episcopacy and established an army in the North of England. Charles was forced to call a 'long parliament' to deal with the invasion during which he impeached some of his most able advisors, accusing them of colluding with the Scots. On 4th January 1642, Charles stormed the House of Commons with an armed guard intending to arrest the 'five members' he had charged with high treason. The men had already escaped and the King was forced to withdraw having committed a grave rebuff to parliament and lost further credibility in the eyes of his supporters.

Execution of Charles I

Civil war ensued. For more background on the English Civil Wars, this article will help. The English Parliamentary army combined with the Scottish to create a formidable force with Oliver Cromwell, the famously fierce and cruel leader, at the helm. Three years of fighting that tore England apart led to Charles' surrender to a Scottish force in 1646. Charles refused to approve Presbyterianism as the official religion of Scotland and refused his captor's demands for a constitutional monarchy. The King was handed over to the English Parliamentarian commanders who spent two years negotiating the terms of a new relationship between monarchy and state. Charles would not budge on his position and would make no concessions. Cromwell's New Model Army had control of England by 1648 and soon after, in 1649, Charles was tried, convicted, and beheaded for treason. The English Commonwealth was born.

The Legacy of Charles I

Charles, I's reign challenged the powers of parliament to such a point that civil war broke out in England, the effects of which were felt by its people for many decades afterwards. Charles' capture and execution left Oliver Cromwell in a position whereby he was able to extinguish all military opposition in Britain and Ireland and establish The Protectorate with himself as Lord Protector. For the first time England became a Commonwealth.

Charles was repeatedly ineffectual in his engagement with Europe from a political and military point of view and his exploitation of the British citizens to fund his war campaigns made him very unpopular with the common man.

Charles believed that he stood for social stability and was a pious defender of his faith so for some, his death was a martyrdom. Following his execution a memoir emerged named The Royal Portrait. An effective piece of Royalist propaganda, the book helped to turn Charles I into a martyr King who died for his religious and political beliefs.

Throughout his lifetime Charles amassed one of the most

impressive art collections in the world. On his death, Charles is thought to have had a collection of over 1700 paintings by the likes of Titian, Caravaggio, and Rembrandt, an expensive hobby that added to the financial strain of the monarchy on the nation.

Films and TV Shows Featuring Charles I

- Queen of Sorrow (1923)
- The Royal Oak (1923)
- The Vicar of Bray (1937)
- The Scarlet Blade (1963)
- Cromwell (1970)
- Children of the New Forest (1977) TV Series
- The Return of the Musketeers (1989)
- Civil War: England's Fight for Freedom (1997) Drama/Documentary
- The Devil's Whore (2008) TV Drama

Further Research

- Starkey, David and Hibbert, Christopher (2007) Charles I: A Life of Religion, War and Treason
- Kishlansky, Mark (2014) Charles I: An Abbreviated Life
- Spencer, Charles (2014) Killers of the King: The Men who Dared to Execute Charles I
- Scarboro, Dan (2005) England 1625-1660
- Adamson, John (2001) The Noble Revolt: The Overthrow of Charles I

Locations Related to Charles I

- Dunfermline Castle in Fife, Scotland was Charles I's birthplace. The ruins of the castle are in the care of Historic Scotland and are open to the public.
- The Palace of Whitehall was once the largest palace in the world, rivaling the Vatican and Versailles in scale. Charles I lived at Whitehall throughout his reign. Although few

parts of the original palace remain, it is possible to visit the current Whitehall government building complex and the original banqueting hall, in front of which Charles was executed.
- Carisbrook Castle on the Isle of Wight is one of the places Charles was held prisoner at the end of the English Civil War. The castle is still standing and it is possible to visit the Constables Chamber in which he lived.
- Charles I's tomb is located at St George's Chapel at Windsor Castle.
- There is a statue of Charles I on horseback located at Charing Cross in London. Sculpted by Hubert Le Sueur, the statue was probably cast around 1633 and marks the official center of London.

OLIVER CROMWELL
Lord Protector
(1653-1658)

The man who deposed a king, and then ruled as a King in all but name. Oliver Cromwell was an English military and political leader and later Lord Protector of the Commonwealth of England, Scotland, and Ireland. He ruled as Lord Protector and was Britain's only non-monarch ruler (during the Interregnum period). He ruled as essentially a genocidal dictator and he's very controversial to this day but his legacy is alive and well in Britain's vibrant parliamentary democracy.

Key Facts about Oliver Cromwell

- Born April 25, 1599, died September 3, 1658
- Led the Parliamentary army to victory over the Royal army and presided over the execution of Charles I
- Briefly dictator of England
- Remains highly controversial in British history but important in Britain's constitutional development.

A Short Biography

The British are usually considered to be moderate in their views, very tolerant, and open-minded. But that was not always so. In the 17th century, intolerance was widespread on a scale that today we would consider to be religious fanaticism. It led to a Civil War, the execution of the King, and the establishment of a dictatorship. Oliver Cromwell was a key figure of that period, whose actions remain highly controversial while he is at the same time considered an important figure in British history.

Cromwell was born in 1599, on the cusp of the new century. He was a member of the gentry – a land-owner and therefore of some social rank, but not a member of the nobility.

His early life was relatively uneventful. He married in 1620 and fathered nine children. His wife, Elizabeth Bourchier, came from a family of somewhat higher social position and the network of associations Cromwell made through his wife's family served him well in his later political career.

During the 1620's Cromwell, seems to have had a personal crisis. He was treated for depression (called at that time valde melancolicus) and discovered God. This turned him from a moderate figure into someone who believed that God had chosen him to carry out God's will on earth – which he proceeded to do.

In 1628 he became a Member of Parliament but seems to have made only one speech before the Parliament was dissolved by the King, Charles I. The King ruled without Parliament for the next decade, but in 1640 he called a new one to pass financial bills since he had bankrupted himself waging war with Scotland. This parliament became known as the Long Parliament because it continued in various forms until after Cromwell's death in 1658.

There were several divisive issues in British society at the time. On the religious front, there was a battle between two views of church governance. On one side were the episcopal churches – Catholics and Anglicans – who believed in centralized church control through the system of bishops appointed by a leader such as the Pope or an Archbishop. On the other were the Presbyterian Churches – particularly the Church of Scotland – that had a more democratic system of elected elders running the church.

A growing third side was the Puritans, who believed in a congregationalist approach with direct control of each church by its members and no centralized power structure. Cromwell belonged to this last group although he was not as extreme in his views as some other Puritan Churches.

There were also a number of serious issues between the King and the Parliament, involving taxation, religious freedom, the introduction of Presbyterianism in Scotland, and an apparent plot by supporters of the King to raise an army in Ireland to suppress freedoms in Britain. Finally, in 1642 Parliament declared itself able to pass laws without Royal Assent and began to raise an army to defend its rights.

Cromwell had very little military experience but he quickly joined the army of Parliament, which won some early victories over the Royalist forces. Cromwell quickly showed himself to be a brave leader, riding at the head of his cavalry and using novel tactics to ensure victory. He led with the authority of his own commitment and developed more disciplined tactics for what were basically amateur soldiers. By 1644 he had risen to the rank of Lieutenant General of the cavalry.

Following a period of indecisive military campaigns, the Parliament created a brand new centralized form of the military, called the New Model Army. This was the beginning of a national army and developed into the present British Army. This new force quickly defeated the royalist troops at the decisive Battle of Naseby in 1645.

Parliament attempted to reach a political settlement with the King, but they were hampered by factions within their own side, most notably the Levellers, a radical group that had developed within the New Model Army and who demanded universal suffrage for men. The King escaped from imprisonment and pro-Royalist uprisings broke out in Wales and Scotland, where a Royalist army invaded Britain. Cromwell quickly put down the Welsh uprising and finally in sole control of the army, defeated a Scottish force twice his size just below the Scottish border.

Following a military coup by Thomas Pride, only those MPs who supported a trial of the King were allowed to sit in Parliament. Cromwell returned to London to lend his support and along with the other remaining MPs he signed the death warrant for Charles I, who was beheaded on January 30th, 1649.

A republic was declared, called the Commonwealth of England. As the royalists had re-grouped in Ireland Cromwell was ordered to invade and crush this opposition. While organizing for the invasion he destroyed the Levellers, whose demands for universal suffrage were denounced as anarchy. The vote was restricted to male landowners only and Leveller leaders were executed.

Cromwell had both religious and political reasons to attack Ireland. He was vehemently anti-Catholic and his nine-month campaign in Ireland is still remembered by the Irish for the slaughter of captured soldiers and civilians. Many historians consider Cromwell's actions in Ireland to be genocidal. Perhaps 600,000 Irish died from battle, disease, and famine.

Having dealt with Ireland, Cromwell turned his attention to Scotland, where in a relatively gentler campaign he seized control of the country for the Commonwealth. Presbyterianism was allowed, but the powers of the Scottish Church were reduced.

After a period of transition, a new constitution was adopted for the Commonwealth, which made Cromwell Lord Protector. In all but name he was a King – he was even addressed as 'Your Highness' – or as we would say today, a dictator. As dictators do, he took power with the declared aim of 'restoring order' to the country. In 1657 there was a coronation of Cromwell as Lord Protector, complete with a throne, ermine robes, and a sword of justice.

However the following year Cromwell fell ill with malaria and kidney infections and he died on September 3rd, 1658. He was buried in Westminster Abbey.

Cromwell was succeeded as Lord Protector by his son Richard but he lacked a strong power base and the Commonwealth was short-lived. The attempts to impose Puritanism on the public were hated and in 1660 Parliament invited Charles II back from exile in France to restore the Monarchy. Cromwell's corpse was dug up, hung in chains, and beheaded. The body was thrown into a churchyard crypt and his head was put on a pole outside Parliament, where it remained until 1685.

His Legacy

Cromwell is perhaps the most controversial figure in British history. To some, he is an admirable early republican, to others a genocidal fascist dictator. In Ireland in particular he is universally hated.

He was perhaps best described by one Royalist writer as a "Brave Bad Man". At a time when brutal executions and slaughter were more 'normal,' it is perhaps difficult to judge him by modern standards, but his fanatical religious intolerance seems strangely familiar in the present period.

At such an early time theories of equality and democracy were so poorly developed that it is no surprise that the Commonwealth failed. A hundred years later the same ideas succeeded with the French and American Revolution and a little after that in Britain with universal suffrage and women's suffrage in the 19th and early 20th centuries.

Sites to Visit

- Some of the Civil War Battlefields have monuments, but most are now simply agricultural land often with limited access.
- Banqueting House, in Whitehall, London is all that remains of the Palace of Westminster where Cromwell's Parliaments met. Charles I was executed on the balcony of this building.
- The Museum of London has a large collection of Cromwell artifacts, including his bible and death mask. This collection was made by Richard Trevithick Tangye, a Victorian businessman.
- There are statues of Cromwell which were erected in the 19th century outside Parliament, in London, and also in Manchester, St-Ives, and Warrington.
- There is a small stone in Westminster Abbey recording his brief burial there. In what is now the RAF chapel at St Margaret's, Westminster there is a stone in the floor marking the pit where his body and those of his family were buried.
- There is a Cromwell Museum in Cambridgeshire but it is threatened with closure in 2016 so visit soon.

Further Research

- A film called Cromwell, starring Richard Harris was made in 1970.
- He is a main character in a TV miniseries called "The

Devil's Whore" (2008)
- Some recent biographies are Oliver Cromwell: King in All But Name by Roy Sherwood (1997), Cromwell by Antonia Fraser (2011), and "Oliver Cromwell: God's Warrior and the English Revolution" by Ian Gentles (2011).

CHARLES II
(1660–1685)

Known as the 'Merry Monarch', the reign of Charles II differed dramatically from what had come before. Following the English Civil War, the execution of Charles I, and years of Cromwellian dictatorship, the populace of the Kingdoms of England, Scotland, and Ireland welcomed Charles II's return from exile and hoped for a return to normality. What they got was a lively, hedonistic king who enjoyed a close friendship with Louis XIV and enjoyed a similar taste for the finer things in life. Charles II's approach to ruling his Kingdoms was one of flexibility, indulgence, and cynicism. Ruling through the two greatest crises of the 17th century, the Great Plague and the Great Fire of London, Charles II was a relatively popular king whose attitude to England's eternal religious divide was one of 'live and let live'.

Key Facts about Charles II

- Charles II was born on May 29th, 1630 at St James' Palace, London, and was the eldest son of Charles I.
- Charles technically became King of England, Scotland, and Ireland on his father's execution on January 30th, 1649 but his rule was not acknowledged until Parliament invited him back from exile in 1660.
- He married Catherine of Braganza on 21st May 1661. Although she died childless, Charles II acknowledged 12 illegitimate children with various mistresses.
- Charles died on February 6th, 1685 at the age of 54 and is buried at Westminster Abbey.

The Life of Charles II

Charles was born under the stormy skies of the English Civil War. His father, King Charles I, fought against the parliamentary and Puritan forces in England and Scotland throughout the 1640s. Young

Charles joined his father in battle during the campaigns of 1645 when he was made commander of the English forces in the West Country at the age of just fourteen.

By 1646, it was clear that King Charles I's cavalier forces were unable to defeat the might of Oliver Cromwell's army and young Charles went into exile in France where he was to remain for nine years. Diplomatic efforts by the young Charles were fruitless and in 1649, King Charles I was beheaded in front of Whitehall Palace. Young Charles automatically became King Charles II of England, Scotland, and Ireland but his kingdom remained under the control of dictator Oliver Cromwell England and entered a period known as the English Commonwealth. Charles II was forced to remain in exile throughout his twenties, reputedly living the enjoyable life of an idle royal libertine.

At Oliver Crowell's death, England fell into a state of political chaos. It was hoped that the restoration of the monarchy would bring peace and stability. On May 29th 1660, Charles II returned to England and was restored to the throne to public acclaim. For the purposes of law, all documents were re-dated as though Charles II had succeeded his father in 1649. For those born after Oliver Cromwell's England came to an end, it was as though it had never happened.

Charles was received less warmly by the powerful 'cavalier parliament', who were cautious and skeptical of the new king's tolerance and reluctance to punish his political enemies. Members of the commonwealth regime went more or less unpunished under Charles and in response, parliament limited the king's access to funds and powers to effect law. Parliament also enacted the Clarendon Code, with Charles's reluctant support, re-establishing the dominance of the Church of England.

Charles' family and personal life had great significance for his reign. Soon after Charles' restoration, his youngest brother Henry, and his sister Mary died of smallpox. Charles' oldest brother James secretly married Anne Hyde, the daughter of Lord Chancellor Edward Hyde, who quickly became pregnant. Charles responded by making Edward Hyde the Earl of Clarendon and pulling him further into his close circle of advisors.

In 1661 Charles was married to Catherine of Braganza, daughter of King John IV of Portugal. Charles acknowledged at least twelve illegitimate children with various mistresses and ladies of court but in his marriage, he remained childless. This complicated matters as it became clear that his brother James, who was a vocal Roman Catholic, was now heir to the English throne.

During negotiations for Catherine of Braganza's hand in marriage, Charles formed an alliance with Portugal which had been fighting a war against Spain since 1640 to restore its independence. Catherine's dowry included Tangier in North Africa, Bombay (strategic for the British Empire), trading privileges in Brazil and East Indies, and a lump sum in cash.

In 1665 Charles embarked upon the Second Anglo-Dutch War in the hope of taking control of major sea routes and ending the Dutch domination of world trade. The English royal navy was inadequate and with the Dutch's surprise attack on the English fleet docked on the River Thames, the venture was a failure.

Charles promised to aid his first cousin King Louis XIV of France in warfare and convert to Catholicism in exchange for Louis' financial support in the Third Anglo-Dutch War, which turned out to be similarly costly and fruitless. This agreement was known as the 1670 secret treaty of Dover. At the same time, Charles encouraged the global domination of the British East India Company by drawing up a series of five charters that promised the company the right to mint money, gain territory, wage war, and exercise criminal jurisdiction in acquired areas of India.

Charles II's reign is remembered for two of the biggest crises in England in the 17th century, the Great Plague of London and the Great Fire of London. In September 1665, the death toll in London reached over 7,000 in one week. Sanitation and living standards in London were poor and the disease spread quickly. Charles fled London for Salisbury, taking his family and entire court with him while Parliament met in Oxford. The plague spread rapidly, taking over 100,000 lives in one year, about 15% of London's population.

Believed now to have been spread via bites from fleas living on rats, the plague was only stopped by the next disaster, the Great Fire of London. Rumored at the time to have been started by Catholic conspirators, it was later discovered that the fire had started in a bakery on Pudding Lane. Raging from September 2nd of 1666 for five days, the fire engulfed the Medieval City of London, consuming an estimated 13,200 houses and 90 churches, including St Paul's Cathedral. The death toll is thought to have been small but the fire left up to 80,000 of London's inhabitants homeless.

In the succeeding years, Charles did not convert to Catholicism and still refused to take a hard line on religion in his kingdom. Strong anti-Catholic protests gripped the country throughout his reign but Charles refused to punish non-conformists to the Established Church of England. Charles even attempted to introduce religious freedom for dissenters with his 1672 Royal Declaration of Indulgence which parliament promptly forced him to withdraw.

Anti-Catholic dissent followed him throughout the remainder of his reign with the country divided by the pro-exclusion Whig political party and the anti-exclusion Tory party. Charles dissolved parliament in 1681 and ruled alone for the next four years. In 1683, a plot to murder Charles and his brother James was discovered and Charles reacted by having leaders and prominent members of the Whig party executed.

In a final twist to his generally antagonistic rule, Charles deferred to Roman Catholicism on his deathbed, leaving the fallout of his shrewd tactical move for his brother James to deal with.

Legacy of Charles II

Charles's legacy is primarily one of benevolence. At worst, he is seen as a lovable rogue, prone to saying one thing and doing another, but always acting in the interests of peace. Charles dissolved three parliaments during his reign, all of which tried to introduce Exclusion Bills to stamp out Catholicism in England with the advice, 'we are not like to have a good end'.

Despite producing no legitimate heir, Charles did father many children whom he bestowed with gifts of dukedoms and earldoms. The public resented paying taxes to fund the King's extended illegitimate family but nevertheless, many of Charles's children went on to occupy prominent positions in English politics and society. Charles is thought to have ruled admirably during the two great crises of the 17th century, the Great Plague and the Great Fire of London, playing a role in organizing containment and rescue efforts.

A patron of the arts and sciences Charles founded the Royal Society to promote scientific research and the Royal Observatory. He also Royal Hospital Chelsea, dedicating it to the welfare of wounded soldiers.

Films and TV Shows Featuring Charles II

- Bonnie Prince Charlie (1923)
- Nell Gwyn (1934)
- Hudson's Bay (1941)
- Lorna Doone (1951)
- The First Churchills (1969) TV Show
- Restoration (1995)
- King Charles II (2003)
- The Libertine (2004)
- The Great Fire (2014) TV Show

Further Research

- Walsh, Michael & Jordan, Don (2015) The King's Bed: Sex, Power and the Court of Charles II
- Frasier, Antonia (2011) King Charles II
- Hanrahan, David C. (2006) Charles II and the Duke of Buckingham: The Merry Monarch and the Aristocratic Rogue
- Harris, Tim (2005) Restoration: Charles II and his kingdoms, 1660–1685
- Keay, Anna (2008), The Magnificent Monarch: Charles II and the Ceremonies of Power
- Wilson, Derek (2003) All The King's Women: Love, sex and politics in the Life of Charles II

Locations Related to Charles II

- There is a statue of Charles II by Grinling Gibbons in the court of Royal Hospital Chelsea. Unusually the King is wearing ancient Roman dress. There are also statues of Charles II in London's Soho Square, Edinburgh's Parliament Square and near Lichfield Cathedral.
- Charles II was born at St James's Palace in London.
- For some of his life, Charles II lived at the Palace of Whitehall of which only the Banqueting Hall survives in its original form.
- Charles II also lived at Hampton Court Palace in London.
- Charles II is buried at Westminster Abbey.

JAMES II
(1685–1688 - Deposed)

James II was the last Catholic monarch to reign over England, Scotland (as James VII), and Ireland. He ascended the throne in 1685 following the death of his brother, Charles II. As the last Catholic monarch, James II was a controversial figure whose reign was marked by religious turmoil, political conflict, and military setbacks. Despite his many challenges, James II left an indelible mark on English history and continues to be a subject of fascination for historians, scholars, and popular culture enthusiasts.

Key Facts about James II

- James II was the last Catholic monarch to reign over England, Scotland, and Ireland.
- James II faced significant opposition from his Protestant subjects due to his Catholic faith and policies.
- James II issued the Declaration of Indulgence in 1687, which granted religious toleration to Catholics and Protestants.
- James II was deposed in the Glorious Revolution of 1688 and replaced by William III and Mary II.
- James II spent the rest of his life in exile in France, where he died in 1701.

Early Life of James II

James II was born on October 14, 1633, in St. James's Palace, London. He was the second son of King Charles I and his wife, Henrietta Maria of France. James II was raised in a turbulent period of English history, marked by civil war, political upheaval, and religious conflict. In 1649, James II's father was executed by Parliamentarians, and the monarchy was abolished. James II and his brother, Charles, spent the next decade in exile in Europe, where they received military training and learned about politics and diplomacy.

The Accession and Early Challenges

James II ascended to the throne upon the death of his brother, Charles II, in 1685. His accession was met with cautious optimism, as many hoped that his experience as the Duke of York and Lord High Admiral would translate into a stable and prosperous reign. However, concerns over his Catholic faith soon emerged, fueling fears of a potential return to religious persecution and the erosion of Protestant rights.

One of James's earliest challenges was the Monmouth Rebellion, led by his illegitimate nephew, the Duke of Monmouth. Monmouth, a Protestant and popular figure among the gentry, claimed the throne on the grounds of his alleged legitimacy. While the rebellion was swiftly quashed, it exposed the deep-seated religious divisions within the kingdom and foreshadowed the challenges that lay ahead for James's reign.

Religious Tensions and the Struggle for Tolerance

James II was an unwavering Catholic, and his commitment to his faith shaped many of his actions as monarch. He sought to promote religious tolerance and extend civil rights to his fellow Catholics, a stance that put him at odds with the predominantly Protestant Parliament and the Church of England.

In 1687, James issued the Declaration of Indulgence in an effort to achieve greater religious freedom. This declaration suspended penal laws against Catholics and Nonconformists. The Anglican establishment fiercely opposed this move, viewing it as a direct threat to the established Church and a violation of parliamentary authority.

James's appointment of Catholics to prominent positions, including the universities of Oxford and Cambridge, further fueled resentment and mistrust among the Protestant majority. This perceived "Catholicization" of the government and institutions raised concerns about a potential return to the religious persecutions of the past and galvanized opposition against the king.

The Glorious Revolution and the Overthrow of James II

The mounting tensions between James II and his Protestant subjects reached a boiling point with the birth of his son, James Francis Edward, in 1688. This event raised fears of a Catholic succession and prompted a group of influential Protestants, known as the "Immortal Seven," to invite William of Orange, the Protestant husband of James's daughter Mary, to intervene.

William's invasion, later dubbed the "Glorious Revolution," was a pivotal moment in English history. As James's support crumbled and his army deserted him, he fled to France, paving the way for William and Mary to assume the throne as joint monarchs in 1689.

The aftermath of the Glorious Revolution saw the enactment of the Bill of Rights, which limited the power of the monarchy and enshrined the principles of parliamentary sovereignty and the protection of Protestant rights. This historic document laid the foundations for the constitutional monarchy that exists in Britain today.

The Legacy and Consequences

While James II's reign was relatively brief, it had far-reaching consequences that shaped the political and religious landscape of England for generations to come. His unwavering commitment to Catholicism and his efforts to promote religious tolerance ultimately led to his downfall, as the Protestant majority perceived his actions as a threat to their faith and liberties.

The Glorious Revolution, sparked by James's actions, marked a significant shift in the balance of power between the monarchy and Parliament. The Bill of Rights established the supremacy of Parliament and the principles of constitutional monarchy, ensuring that future monarchs would be bound by the will of the people and their elected representatives.

Moreover, James II's reign and the events that followed solidified the position of Protestantism as the dominant religion in England. The ascension of William and Mary, both staunch

Protestants, ensured the continuation of the Protestant faith and the preservation of the Church of England's primacy.

In the aftermath of the Glorious Revolution, James II and his supporters, known as Jacobites, continued to pose a threat to the new regime. Jacobite rebellions and attempts to restore the Stuart dynasty persisted for several decades in Scotland, underscoring the enduring religious and political divisions that had characterized James's reign.

The reign of James II remains a complex and controversial chapter in English history, one that exemplifies the tensions and conflicts that arose from the clash between religious beliefs and political ambitions. While his efforts to promote religious tolerance and civil rights for Catholics were admirable, his unwavering commitment to his faith ultimately alienated the Protestant majority and sowed the seeds of his downfall. The legacy of James II serves as a reminder of the delicate balance that must be struck between religious freedom and the preservation of individual liberties, a lesson that continues to resonate in modern times.

Movies and TV Shows Featuring James II

- The Last King: The Power and the Passion of Charles II (2003)
- The Glorious Revolution (2011)
- Charles II: The Power and the Passion (2003)

Books and Documentaries About James II

- James II: The Last Catholic King (2017) by David Womersley
- James II: The Triumph and the Tragedy (2019) by John Miller
- The Glorious Revolution (2007) by Edward Vallance
- James II and the Three Questions: Religious Toleration and the Landed Classes, 1687-1688 (2018) by Mark Knights

Locations Related to James II

- St. James's Palace, London: James II was born here in 1633.
- Whitehall Palace, London: James II's court was located here during his reign.
- Windsor Castle, Windsor: James II was imprisoned here after his deposition.
- Palace of Versailles, France: James II spent the rest of his life in exile here.

WILLIAM & MARY
William III (1689–1702) and Mary II (1689–1694)

William and Mary's marriage and joint reign over England, Scotland, and Ireland were the product of lengthy political machinations. Parliament was in agreement that King James II, Mary's father, had to go, and what better solution than to join the protestant cousins, William and Mary, in holy matrimony, have William invade England and place the crown on Mary's head? Mary insisted on a co-regency but the Bill of Rights that followed, an important document that hugely limited the sovereign's power over tax, legislation, the military, and the treasury, may have been more than she bargained for. William spent eight months out of every twelve fighting a war with France and survived two Jacobite attempts to overthrow him, but his reign was short at just 13 years. Mary died after just five years on the throne, and as she died childless, the couple had failed to begin a dynasty of their own, and the crown was passed promptly to Mary's sister, Anne upon William's death.

Key Facts about William and Mary

- William, son of William II of Orange, was born on 14th November 1650 (Georgian Calendar) at The Hague. Mary, the eldest daughter of King James II, was born on the 30th of April 1662 at St. James' Palace.
- William III and Mary II succeeded as the King of England and Ireland and Queen of England and Ireland on 13th February 1689.
- William and Mary were married on the 4th of November 1677 in London. William was 27 at the time, and Mary was 15.
- William died on 8th March 1702, having reigned in England for thirteen years. Mary died on the 28th of December 1694, having reigned just five years.

About Britian's Joint Monarchy

Both William and Mary's childhoods were sadly lacking in parental influence. William's father, William II, died a week before he was born meaning William was the Sovereign Prince of Orange from the moment of his birth. Mary also grew up motherless from the age of ten and was separated from her father James, then Duke of York, because it was thought imperative that Mary remain a Protestant while James was an open and dedicated Catholic.

In 1677, William and Mary were married despite the fact that they were first cousins. Mary was William's mother's niece and the daughter of his maternal uncle, James, Duke of York. The circumstances of William and Mary's succession to the English throne were unconventional, to say the least. King James II of England and II of Ireland, and VII of Scotland, Mary's father, was overthrown and militarily defeated in the so-called Glorious Revolution of 1688 by a union of English Parliamentarians led by William III of Orange who just happened to be Mary's husband.

James II and the other Stuart kings who came before him were accused by Parliament of repeated and gross abuses of their sovereign power. Several long centuries of conflict between the parliament and the crown came to a head in 1688 as the question of succession and, most importantly, the religion of the next king or queen came into focus. William of Orange's successful invasion of England forced King James II to flee to France and allowed Parliament to depose him on the grounds of desertion.

Despite the fact that James II had an infant son, James Francis Edward, who should have succeeded him by hereditary principle, it was Mary to whom the English throne was offered by parliament. This was not an oversight but a tactical move by parliament who wanted to restrict the succession to a Protestant line, ensuring an end to the idea that England may be restored to Roman Catholicism. To make it official, William and Mary accepted a Parliamentary Act of Settlement that meant their title to the throne was only valid by an act of Parliament.

Although William had militarily defeated James II and invaded England, Mary was senior to her husband in her claim to the English throne and could have reigned independently. However, her insistence that she wished to resign her rights altogether to William resulted in Parliament offering the crown to the couple jointly as king and queen regnant.

The English Bill of Rights (1689) was drawn up by Parliament and signed by William and Mary in 1689. The bill was conceived to ensure that the power of the monarchy would be, in the future, limited and that Parliament could function free from royal interference. Importantly the bill reaffirmed Parliament's control of taxation and legislation in England meaning the Sovereign was forbidden from levying taxes without Parliamentary consent or interfering with laws already passed by Parliament. The royal court was abolished, and the proper court was forbidden from imposing cruel punishments or excessive bail. Freedom of speech was to be upheld, and the sovereign was banned from having anything to do with elections or from maintaining their own army. Finally, Parliament put an end to the monarchy's use of England's treasury as a personal piggy bank and tightened control over the sovereign's expenditure.

This magnificent document inspired the English colonists in the Thirteen Colonies who would later become part of the United States of America, to revolt against King James II and his stance on colonial government. Revolts occurred in New York, Massachusetts, and Maryland in 1689.

One of the main factors that motivated William's marriage to Mary and the seizing of the English throne was to embroil the English in the ongoing war between the Netherlands and Louis XIV of France. The Dutch and the English joined the coalition against France during the Nine Years' War, hoping to limit France's expansion in Europe. This long and costly war came to an end in 1697 with The Peace of Rijswijk treaty. William immediately formed an alliance with England, Holland, and Austria in an attempt to prevent France and Spain from uniting. This move led to the 'War of the Spanish Succession.'

Soon after Mary and William's wedding Mary had become pregnant but miscarried and due to a later illness was unable to give birth to a child. In 1694 Mary died of smallpox, aged just 32 years and childless. With Mary, dead William's popularity with the English public dwindled further. Already criticized for his conflict with France which was a venture more beneficial to the Netherlands than England, William now became a target for more Jacobite plots. William and Mary had already fought two Jacobite rebellions in 1689. Scottish Jacobites defeated the Scottish army at Killiekrankie and James II fought with French troops in Londonderry. William's navy defeated James,' and he led an English army to victory at the Battle of the Boyne in 1690.

In 1701 James II died, and Louis XIV recognized his son, James, Duke of York, the Catholic son who had been skipped in the succession for Mary, as King of England. This move created a surge in popularity for William's war with France with many patriots and politicians rallying to protect their nation and its sovereign. Just a year later though, on the 8th March 1702, William died of bacterial pneumonia following a fall whilst riding at Hampton Court. It was Mary's younger sister Anne's turn to take to the throne.

Legacy Today

The most significant event of William and Mary's reign was the signing of the English Bill of Rights in 1689. This bill dramatically increased the English Parliament's influence and ended many centuries of hostility between parliament and the crown. It also comforted a nation of Protestants who were now satisfied that England would not be returned to Roman Catholicism and inspired English colonists in the Thirteen Colonies to make their first loud steps towards American Independence. William's victory over James II at the Battle of the Boyne ensured the Protestant faith kept its hold in Britain and his war with France, although costly and beneficial to his native Netherlands, did put a stop to Catholic Louis XIV's ambitions to expand his territory.

Film & TV Appearances

William III

- The League of Gentlemen's Apocalypse (2005)

- Blood Royal: William the Conqueror (1990) TV play
- Orlando (1992)
- Peter the Great (1986) TV series
- The First Churchills (1969)
- Against All Flags (1952)
- Captain Kidd (1945)
- The Black Tulip (1937)

Mary II

- The League of Gentlemen's Apocalypse (2005)
- England, My England (1995)
- Orlando (1992)
- The First Churchills (1969)

Further Research

- Waller, Maureen (2006). Sovereign Ladies: The Six Reigning Queens of England
- Van der Kiste, John (2003) William and Mary
- Van der Zee, Henri, and Barbara. William and Mary (1973)
- Baxter, Stephen B, William III and the Defense of European Liberty, 1650–1702 (1966)
- Chapman, Hester W., Mary II: Queen of England (1953)

Locations to Visit

- Mary II was born at St James's Palace, died at Kensington Palace, and is buried at Westminster Abbey.
- William III was born at Binnenhof, The Hague, died at Kensington Palace, and is buried at Westminster Abbey.
- William and Mary lived primarily between their palaces at Whitehall and Kensington in London.

ANNE
(1702–1714)

Queen Anne is remembered more for the events that took place during her reign, such as the Acts of Union that united Scotland and England as one nation and made Queen Anne the first sovereign of Great Britain or the development of the two-party parliamentary system, than anything that she herself did. As Queen, Anne seemed to have little insight or influence in the important political matters of the day, and in her personal life, she suffered almost constant loss, first in the deaths of her siblings and mother and later with all seventeen of her pregnancies ended in miscarriage, stillbirth or infant death. In a letter from Queen Anne's doctor to author Rev. Dr. Jonathan Swift, he wrote, "I believe sleep was never more welcome to a weary traveler than death was to her."

Key Facts about Anne

- Queen Anne was born on the 6 February 1665 at St James' Palace.
- She succeeded as the Queen of England, Scotland, and Ireland on 8 March 1702 at the age of 37 and became the first Queen of Great Britain and Ireland on the 1st May 1707, the date the Act of Union came into effect.
- Queen Anne was married to Prince George of Denmark on 28 July 1683, aged 18. Together they had five children; two died in infancy, two under the age of two from smallpox, and one aged 11.
- Queen Anne died on 1 August 1714, aged 49, and was buried in Westminster Abbey.

A Brief History of Her Life

As the fourth child and second daughter of James, Duke of York, and his wife Anne Hyde, Anne seemed at first to be an unlikely candidate for the future Queen of England. However, Anne's childhood was marked by loss, and she became one of only two of her eight siblings to survive into adulthood. As the Duke of York was the younger brother of King Charles II who had no legitimate heir, Anne became third in the line of succession to the English throne.

As well as losing all of her siblings apart from one, Anne's paternal grandmother, who she lived with while in France, died in 1669. She moved to live with her aunt who died suddenly in 1670 before returning to England to be reunited with her mother who died the following year.

In 1673, the widowed Duke of York, Anne's father made his conversion to Roman Catholicism public and married a Catholic princess who was fourteen, just six years older than Anne. The new Duchess gave birth to ten children over the next ten years, but all were stillborn or died in infancy.

King Charles II took an active interest in who his niece Anne was to marry and scoured the great dynasties of Europe looking for a prince deemed suitable by both Protestant subjects and Catholic allies such as Louis XIV of France. A marriage between Anne and Prince George of Denmark was arranged to the joy of the Duke of York who saw the union as a way of limiting the power of his son-in-law, William of Orange (later William III.)

George of Denmark

The wedding of Anne and George of Denmark took place on 28 July 1683, and they immediately took up residence in London in the Palace of Whitehall. Anne became pregnant almost immediately but, unfortunately, like many of her subsequent pregnancies, the baby was stillborn. In the next two years, Anne gave birth to two daughters Mary and Anna Sophia, but both daughters died in 1687 of smallpox. In the days preceding her daughters' deaths, Anne had miscarried and her husband George became gravely ill. Anne gave birth to another stillborn child in the year after.

The Duke of York became King James II in 1685. Anne was a devoted Anglican and had become estranged from her father as he made moves towards restoring Roman Catholicism to England.

Three years after James II succeeded his brother he was deposed, and Anne's older sister Mary became Queen Regnant alongside her husband William III. During Mary's reign, the sisters became estranged, purportedly due to Mary's disapproval of Anne's choice of acquaintances and mismanagement of her finances.

By 1700, Anne had been pregnant seventeen times in eighteen years and had miscarried or had stillborn births twelve times. Four of her five surviving children had died before they were two and Anne was in very bad health with what was understood to be gout. On 30 July 1700, Anne's only surviving child, the Duke of Gloucester died at age 11.

King William III died on the 8 March 1702 and Anne became the Queen of England. The English public was enamored with the new Queen and overjoyed by her promise to focus solely on the happiness and prosperity of England, unlike her Dutch brother-in-law and predecessor. Due to her ailments, the Queen was crowned at Westminster Abbey on 13 April 1702, carried there in a sedan chair.

During her long bouts of seclusion, Anne had become very intimate with a lady called Sarah Churchill, wife of the Earl and later Duke of Marlborough who became Anne's main political advisor. Anne made Marlborough Master General of the Ordnance, Captain-General in charge of the Army and he was created a Knight of the Garter. Anne's husband, Prince George of Denmark, died in 1708 which caused ripples of discontent to emerge in both Anne's political and private life. George's handling of the navy had been unpopular amongst Whig politicians, and they used George's death to force Anne to appoint the Earl of Orford as First Lord of the Admiralty.

George's death also proved to be a turning point in the Queen's previously incredibly close relationship with the Duchess of Marlborough. The Duchess was thought to be jealous of the Queen's friendship with Abigail, a woman of the bedchamber and the pair quarreled over a letter and in person leading to the irrevocable breakdown of a long friendship.

The Treaty of Union Between England and Scotland

During Anne's reign, tension grew between Scotland and England with the two parliaments finding it increasingly difficult to agree on economic and foreign policy. As none of Anne's seventeen pregnancies had resulted in a healthy child who would live to become her heir, the issue of succession took on great importance. While the English government wanted the Stuart Protestant Sophia of Hanover to become Queen (Act of Settlement, 1701) to prevent the restoration of a Catholic line, the Scots [unhappy with this prospect given the Stuart lineage originated in Scotland] wanted to make their own decision, suggesting that they may be considering a Jacobite revolution that would welcome exiled James Francis Edward Stuart, Anne's half-brother, to the throne. To avoid revolt and promote unity, Anne pushed for an agreement between the two sides.

Finally, the Scottish and English Parliaments agreed to the Acts of Union, a series of acts that were created and passed over the course of five years and culminated in the happy uniting of the English and Scottish nations into a single kingdom called Great Britain with one parliament.

A Privy Council managed to enforce the lawful Act of Settlement and secure a Protestant King quite literally over Queen Anne's dying body when she collapsed during an angry Privy Council meeting in 1714. Two days after her collapse, Queen Anne died at Kensington Palace on 1 August 1714 having reigned for 12 years. George, Elector of Hanover, his mother Electress Sophia of Hanover having died two months prior to Anne, was summoned to assume the British crown as King George I.

Legacy Today

Queen Anne's reign saw the union of Scotland and England into one nation, Great Britain, and the creation of a two-party political system. Despite these political and diplomatic achievements, Queen Anne is generally seen as lacking in political astuteness, a Queen who picked her advisors based on personality and was less and less influential in government as the years went by. In ill health from around her thirties and almost constantly pregnant for as long as she was able to be, Anne may have been preoccupied throughout some of her reign. As the influence of powerful politicians and ministers increased, Queen Anne's influence waned, but she did not operate a petticoat government as has been suggested; Queen Anne attended more cabinet meetings than any of her predecessors or successors, and the lack of any real calamity between monarch and parliament during her reign prove she may have been much wiser than she was given credit for.

Film & TV

- Wren: The Man Who Built Britain (2004) Documentary
- The First Churchills (1969)
- The Favourite (2018)

Further Research

- Winn, James Anderson (2014) Queen Anne: Patroness of Arts
- Somerset, Anne (2012) Queen Anne: The Politics of Passion
- Waller, Maureen (2006). Sovereign Ladies: The Six Reigning Queens of England.
- Gregg, Edward (2001) Queen Anne (Yale English Monarchs Series)
- Green, David (1970). Queen Anne
- Curtis, Gila (1972). The Life and Times of Queen Anne

Locations to Visit

- Queen Anne was born at St James's Palace in the City of Westminster, London, died at Kensington Palace in the Royal Borough of Kensington and Chelsea, London and is buried at Westminster Abbey.
- There is a statue of Queen Anne in front of St Paul's Cathedral in London.

GEORGE I
(1714 - 1727)

King George I was the first of the Hanoverian monarchs who ruled over Britain from 1714 to 1727. He was born in Hanover, Germany, on May 28, 1660, and was the eldest son of Ernest Augustus, Elector of Hanover, and Sophia of the Palatinate. It marked the beginning of the Georgian era in Britain, which would have lasting effects on Britain, its role in the world, and eventually implications for the American colonies. In this article, we will take a closer look at the life, reign, and legacy of this significant historical figure.

Key Facts about George I

- George I was not born in Great Britain, but in Hanover, Germany, and he was the first monarch of the House of Hanover to rule over Britain.
- He was not fluent in English when he arrived in Britain, and he relied heavily on his ministers to conduct state affairs.
- George I was not particularly interested in British politics and preferred to spend his time in Hanover, where he was still the Elector.
- During his reign, the Whig political party emerged as the dominant force in British politics, and the Tories lost much of their influence.
- George I's reign saw the emergence of the British Empire as a major global power, laying the groundwork for the growth of British influence in the Americas, Africa, and Asia.

Early Life and Career

As a young man, George I served in the army of the Holy Roman Empire and fought in the War of the Spanish Succession.

He was not originally in line to inherit the throne of Great Britain, but after Queen Anne died childless, the Act of Settlement 1701 established him as the next in line.

George I arrived in London on September 18, 1714, and was crowned king on October 20 of that year. However, he was not particularly interested in British politics and was more focused on his responsibilities as Elector of Hanover. As a result, he left much of the decision-making in England to his ministers.

Reign

One of the most significant events of George I's reign was the Jacobite Rising of 1715, which was an attempt to overthrow him and put James Stuart, the son of James II, back on the throne. The rebellion was ultimately unsuccessful, but it did highlight the ongoing tensions between the supporters of the Stuarts and the Hanoverians.

Another important development during the reign of George I was the emergence of the Whig political party as the dominant force in British politics. The Whigs were generally more supportive of the monarchy and more tolerant of religious dissent than their Tory counterparts, which made them the natural allies of the Hanoverians.

In terms of foreign policy, George I was primarily concerned with maintaining peace in Europe. He supported the Quadruple Alliance, which was a coalition of Britain, France, Austria, and the Netherlands that sought to maintain the balance of power on the continent.

Legacy

Although George I was not a particularly popular or influential monarch, his reign did have some significant long-term effects on British politics and society. Perhaps the most notable of these was the emergence of a two-party system, with the Whigs and Tories vying for power in Parliament.

Additionally, the Hanoverian succession helped to solidify the Protestant character of the British monarchy and the British state. This was particularly important given the ongoing tensions between Protestants and Catholics in Europe at the time.

George I's reign also saw the emergence of the British Empire as a major global power. Although he was not directly involved in many of the early colonial ventures, his support for the Whigs and their pro-imperial policies helped to lay the groundwork for the growth of British influence in the Americas, Africa, and Asia.

King George I was an important historical figure who played a significant role in the development of Britain and Europe during the early 18th century. Although he was not a particularly charismatic or influential monarch, his reign saw the emergence of a new political order and helped to lay the groundwork for the growth of the British Empire. Despite his relative lack of popularity, his legacy continues to be felt in Britain and around the world to this day. One could say his most important legacy was his son and grandson, who became George II and George III, respectively, one of the longest reigns in British history.

Movies and TV Shows Featuring George I

On screen, George I of Great Britain has been portrayed by Peter Bull in the 1948 film Saraband for Dead Lovers, Eric Pohlmann in the 1953 film Rob Roy, the Highland Rogue, Otto Waldis in the 1954 film The Iron Glove, and Steve Plytas in an episode of the Granada Television series Rogues' Gallery entitled "A Bed-Full of Miracles" (1969). George was also featured in the book Isle of Fire by Wayne Thomas Batson.

Further Research

- George I: The Lucky King by Tim Blanning
- King George I by Ragnhild Hatton
- The Hanoverians: The History of a Dynasty by Jeremy Black
- George I: Elector and King by R. H. Nichols
- The First Georgians: The Kings Who Made Britain by Lucy Worsley
- George I: The German Connection by Michael De-la-

Noy
- George I: The English Monarch by Stephen Taylor
- The Reign of George I, 1714-1727 by Basil Williams
- George I: The Forgotten Monarch by Gerard Kilroy
- Hanover and the British Empire, 1700-1837 by Brendan Simms.

Locations Related to George I

- Hanover, Germany – George I was born here in 1660 and spent much of his life as Elector of Hanover before becoming King of Great Britain.
- London, England – George I arrived in London in 1714 and was crowned king later that year. He spent much of his time in England as king.
- Oxfordshire, England – In 1716, George I visited Oxfordshire and stayed at the palace of Woodstock.
- Scotland – The Jacobite Rising of 1715 was centered in Scotland and was an attempt to overthrow George I and restore the Stuart dynasty to the throne.
- The Netherlands – George I was a supporter of the Quadruple Alliance, which was a coalition of Britain, France, Austria, and the Netherlands that sought to maintain the balance of power in Europe.

GEORGE II
(1727 - 1760)

The final British sovereign to physically lead troops into battle, King George II was the last of the soldier Kings who were eager to expand their empires through warfare with European neighbors. George II's reign was long and saw the successful suppression of the Jacobites, the laying of foundations for the Industrial Revolution, a boom in overseas trade, and the expansion of the British Empire in Quebec and Bengal. A devoted husband (if you don't count mistresses), father to eight children, and King of Great Britain and Ireland for 32 years, King George II had three passions in life; his wife, his music, and his wars.

Son of George Louis and Sophia Dorothea of Celle, George was the grandson of Sophia of Hanover, an important figure in British history who, in 1701, suddenly became second in line to the British throne. Parliament's 1701 Act of Settlement restricted the succession to Protestants making Sophia heir presumptive to the crowns of the Kingdom of England and the Kingdom of Ireland, skipping around 50 Catholics in the hereditary line.

Key Facts about George II

- Reigned as King of Great Britain and Ireland from 1727 to 1760, the last British monarch born outside of Britain (born in Hanover, Germany)
- Led Britain during the War of Austrian Succession (1740-1748) and the beginning of the Seven Years' War (1756-1763), becoming the last British monarch to lead troops into battle at Dettingen in 1743
- Had a notoriously bad relationship with his son Frederick, Prince of Wales, who died before him in 1751
- Was a patron of composer George Frideric Handel, who wrote "Music for the Royal Fireworks" and "Water Music" for him
- Established the British Museum in 1753 through an act

of Parliament, using Sir Hans Sloane's collection as its foundation

A Brief History of His Life

Born in the city of Hanover in Germany, George was separated from his mother when he was around ten years old. Accused of adultery, Sophia was confined and denied access to her children who, in all likelihood, never saw her again. In 1705, George was naturalized as an English subject as part of the Sophia Naturalisation Act and in 1706 was made a Knight of the Garter and created Marquess of Cambridge, Earl of Milford Haven, Viscount Northallerton, and Baron Tewkesbury.

Unusual for the time and circumstances, George was allowed to choose his own wife. In 1705, George met Caroline of Ansbach, the former ward of his aunt Queen Sophia Charlotte of Prussia. It was love at first sight and George and Caroline were married on the August 22nd, 1705 in the chapel at Herrenhausen. During the early years of his marriage, George was keen to assert himself on the battlefield and asked for his father's permission to join the war effort against France in Flanders. George Senior refused as George Junior was yet to provide the family with an heir. George and Caroline readily obliged and on 1 February 1707, brought Frederick Louis, later the Prince of Wales, into the world.

In 1708 George went off to war and fought valiantly under Queen Anne's trusted commander Marlborough in the Battle of Oudenarde. Three more children were his reward, all girls born between 1709 and 1713 and named Anne, Amelia, and Caroline.

In 1714, Sophia of Hanover, George's grandmother, died just weeks before Queen Anne of Great Britain and George I inherited the British throne. George became the Prince of Wales, but in the early years of his father's reign, George and his father were on bad terms. Initially, a family spat that took place at the baptism of George's second son, George William led to both George and Caroline being banished from King George I's court and separated from their children.

Politically too, George opposed his father, and for the first several years of his reign, he was a key figure in the opposition to King George I's policies with his London residence, Leicester House, being used as a frequent meeting place for the king's political opponents. In 1720, King George and his son were reconciled, albeit half-heartedly, on the advice of Sir Robert Walpole, one of King George's previous opponents. Walpole was welcomed back into the ministry and later became George I's Prime Minister.

The Whig government, of which Walpole was a part, became incredibly powerful during George I's reign. This was partly due to an economic disaster known as the South Sea Bubble and partly because George I knew that the Tory government would not support the protestant succession laid down in the Act of Settlement during Queen Anne's reign. The relationship between George I and his son continued to break down as George supported the Tories and was at the center of an intrigue against Walpole.

George I died on 11th June 1727 in Hanover and George became King George II of Great Britain and Ireland at the age of 43. Walpole expected to be immediately dismissed when George II became King, but the new Queen Caroline is thought to have convinced him otherwise on the understanding that Walpole would agree to a higher civil list (amount set aside for civil expenditure) than they were entitled to. George II was crowned at Westminster Abbey on 11th October 1727 and commissioned Handel to write four new anthems fitting to the occasion.

Over the next few years, George II's relationship with his son Frederick grew strained. Frederick behaved much as George II himself had behaved when he came to England under the title of the Prince of Wales and offered immediate and open support to his father's political opposition. Each time George left England for Hanover, he left his wife as regent and not his son, and when a quarrel about Frederick's allowance broke out in Parliament, George banned him from the court.

Queen Caroline never lived to see her husband and eldest son reconciled. On the 17th of December 1737, Caroline died at St James Palace of a series of horrible ailments that included a ruptured womb and strangulated bowel, the result of complications from the birth of her final child. George and Caroline's marriage was a very loving one, and on her deathbed, Caroline implored her husband to re-marry, which he never did. George II had a pair of matching coffins with removable sides made so that when he followed her to the grave, they could lie side by side.

Following Queen Caroline's death, George turned his attention to war. Walpole had managed to keep Great Britain at peace for a generation, but the King wanted war, and a war he got. Britain began hostilities with Spain in 1739 and was deeply involved in the War of the Austrian Succession that broke out all over Europe. In June 1743, George became the last British monarch to lead an army into battle when he led allied forces to fight the French at Dettingen.

The Battle of Culloden

By 1745, George had to neglect the war in Europe in order to speed back to England and defend his throne against the Jacobite invasion of the young pretender Bonnie Prince Charlie. Charlie was supported by George's French opponents who naturally wanted to see the warring king ousted from his throne. The Jacobites marched south to invade England but due to an ambivalent British public and lack of French support were forced to turn back. Prince William [the Duke of Cumberland], George's son, faced Charlie and his army at the Battle of Culloden (17 April 1746) where William was victorious and brutally murdered all of Charlie's supporters effectively ending Jacobitism in Scotland.

Hostilities between France and Britain continued, and in 1756, a French invasion of the British-held island of Minorca prompted the Seven Years' War. The end of King George II's reign was marked by massive imperial victories in 1759 Britain defeated France at the naval battles of Lagos, and Quiberon Bay and British forces captured Quebec and Guadeloupe. On 25th October 1760, King George II died of an aortic aneurysm. He was buried on the 11th of November in Westminster Abbey and left instructions for the removable sides of his and his wife Caroline's coffins to be removed so their remains could touch.

Legacy

King George II is generally thought to have been an uncultured King with little interest in the arts and a poor handle on the English language, and yet George established many universities during his reign and was a patron of the composer Handel. After his death, George was criticized for his temper and lack of refinement, often depicted as a weak King who was overly influenced by his wife and his ministers. Although as an individual King George II was fairly uninfluential, his reign was a generally prosperous time for Great Britain; the Jacobites were stopped once and for all, production industries in Britain flourished, and British troops successfully defeated the French and expanded the Empire.

Film & TV

- The Aristocrats (1999) TV series
- King of the Wind (1989)
- Bonnie Prince Charlie (1948)
- The Last of the Mohicans (1936)

Further Research

- Thompson, Andrew (2012) George II: King and Elector (English Monarchs)
- Black, Jeremy (2007) George II: Puppet of the Politicians?
- Van der Kiste, John (1997) George II and Queen Caroline

Locations to Visit

- George II Statue in Greenwich
- George II was born in Herrenhausen in Hanover. Herrenhausen's Gardens, the heritage of the Kings of Hanover are a popular tourist attraction.
- George II died at Kensington Palace and is buried at Westminster Abbey.

GEORGE III
(1760 - 1820)

George III's life and reign were long, 81 years and 59 years respectively, but difficult, marked by a series of military conflicts all over the world and personal mental health crises that left him unable to rule in his later years. Not only King of Great Britain and Ireland, George III was Elector, and later King, of Hanover. His first public utterance is said to have been 'Born and educated in this country, I glory in the name of Briton.' His autocratic, imperialist approach to rule, both within Great Britain and the British colonies in North America, India, and Africa had the unfavorable effect of revolutionizing his subjects. During George's reign, the war against Revolutionary and Napoleonic France was won but many of Great Britain's American colonies were lost during the American Revolutionary War.

Key facts about George III

- George III was born on June 4th, 1738 at Norfolk House, St James Square.
- He succeeded as King of Great Britain, King of Ireland, and Elector of Hanover on 25th October 1760, aged 22.
- George married Charlotte Sophia, daughter of the Duke of Mecklenburg-Strelitz on September 8th
- George died at the age of 81 on January 29th, 1820 at Windsor. He had reigned as King of England for 59 years.

The Life of King George III

George was born a small and sickly child two months premature at Norfolk House in London. Son of Frederick, Prince of Wales, and Augusta of Saxe-Gotha, George was the grandchild of King George II. When the Prince of Wales died unexpectedly in 1751, George became heir apparent to the throne of Great Britain and Ireland and acquired the title of Prince of Wales. George's education is said to have been incredibly strict and thorough. Raised to be moral, according to the Anglican principles on which he was educated, self-disciplined, and proud he had the best education of any English monarch to date and studied the sciences, mathematics, Latin, history, French, geography, law, and agriculture.

George was unmarried when he took the throne, aged 22, following George II's sudden death on 25th October 1760. A king must have a wife and less than a year later George was wed to Princess Charlotte of Mecklenburg-Strelitz in the Chapel Royal at St James' Palace. King and Queen were crowned two weeks later at Westminster Abbey. Uncommon in royal matches, George and Charlotte had a long and happy marriage that lasted until George's death and resulted in fifteen children. He and Charlotte spent the majority of their lives in southern England, staying intermittently at other royal residences Buckingham House, Kew Castle, Windsor Castle, and St James' Palace.

As King of Great Britain, George's main concern was the moral health of his subjects. On taking the throne he immediately instituted a regular prayer meeting for his council and began campaigning throughout his kingdom against vice, profaneness, and immorality. The ruling nobility in England at the time was the Whig oligarchy, a political party that opposed the absolute rule of the monarchy, was against Catholicism in Great Britain, and was involved in early revolutionary activism in North American colonies. George wanted to smash the Whig's power and attain full personal power throughout his kingdom and colonies but found his match in John Wilkes, a gifted politician and propagandist who became his sworn enemy.

Wilkes challenged the King at every turn, spreading anti-monarchy propaganda, the English lower classes to fight for personal liberty and enjoying the support of prominent Whig aristocrats. George responded by having Wilkes arrested, imprisoned, and persecuted using a warrant that was later declared illegal. Wilkes's detainment, as is so often the case, only succeeded in making him a martyr for the cause and boosted his popularity and following.

George III's Stamp Act of 1765, an act that imposed a direct tax on printed materials in the colonies, led to a huge uprising against the King in North America. Specifically, the act required that printed materials in the colonies, such as legal documents, magazines, newspapers, etc, be produced on embossed and stamped paper produced in London. It was hoped this act would generate revenue for British troops stationed in North America but Americans protested against the principle of being taxed without representation in parliament and argued that American armies were able to protect themselves against Native Americans and had no foreign enemies to speak of.

George reacted by increasing his personal power on home soil, bribing servants and ministers for their loyalty, and taking an increasingly hard line against American liberty. His aim was to achieve absolute power over his subjects and he almost succeeded for a short time. George brought in four punitive Acts of Parliament against Massachusetts and Boston which incited the armed resistance of the Boston Tea Party and led to the Revolutionary War. Still, George would make concessions. He allowed no man to become a minister until he had signed the following declaration 'that he is resolved to keep the empire entire, and that no troops shall consequently be withdrawn from America, nor independence ever allowed.'

In the year 1770 Lord North became Prime Minister and supported George's stand on American liberty. In 1773, Lord North passed an act, with George's backing, taxing tea in the colonies. Tea ships moored in Boston Harbour were stormed by revolutionary colonists and boxes of tea were thrown overboard in an event now known as the Boston Tea Party.

The American Revolution began on 19th April 1775. The Americans drew up the Declaration of Independence, making legal American civilians's right to freedom and civil liberty. In 1778 America was joined by France, then Spain and the Dutch Republic while Britain had no major allies to speak of. Refusing to back down on his staunch opposition to personal and colonial liberty, George faced military defeat and prolonged the war using blockades and starvation tactics. Reluctant to come to terms with the defeat of the British army he drafted an abdication speech but in the end he signed the Treaty of Paris, recognizing the United States of America.

Following American Independence, George III enjoyed a short period of popularity in Great Britain. His appointment of William Pitt as Prime Minister was popular and the British public admired George's religious virtue and dedication to his wife and large family. But around 1788 George's health began to seriously deteriorate. Now it is thought that the King may have been suffering from a rare blood disorder called porphyria but at the time he was simply described as 'mad'. George recovered from this bout of illness although he relapsed at various times during the rest of his reign.

In 1789, the French Revolution took place. The French monarchy was overthrown and Napoleon Bonaparte took on the title of the First Consul of the French Republic. In order to strengthen Britain in the event of a French Invasion George passed the Act of Union that united Great Britain and Ireland into the United Kingdom. Although the peace Treaty of Amiens was signed in 1802, war resumed in 1803 with an invasion on English soil a real possibility until Admiral Lord Nelson defeated Napoleon's navy at the Battle of Trafalgar, thwarting any attempt at invasion.

Following the death of his youngest and favorite daughter, Amelia, aged just 27, George became seriously ill. He never recovered from the stress on his mental health and accepted the need for the Regency Act of 1811 which allowed his son, the Prince of Wales to act as regent for the remainder of George's life. George lived in seclusion at Windsor Castle, deaf, blind, and suffering from dementia until he died on the 29th of January 1820. The throne passed to his son George IV then on to William IV before passing to Queen Victoria, the last monarch of the House of Hanover.

Legacy of George III

George III was seen as a tyrant by the colonists who suffered under his fight to maintain absolute rule over North America. It was said of King George that he 'hates most cordially every American because he thinks that they have an attachment to their Liberty.' The tyranny of George's rule was cemented in time in the United States Declaration of Independence which noted George's 'tyranny' over the colonies. Others are more sympathetic towards George's war with the American colonists suggesting George was seeking only to defend the rights of parliament.

George's long reign lasted 59 years and he lived to be 81 years old. Dubbed Farmer George by commentators of the day, George took great interest in English agriculture and the rural workforce. George was also a scholar in science and industry; he funded William Herschel's 40-foot telescope and when Herchel first discovered the planet Uranus in 1781, he named it Georgium Sidus or George's Star.

Films and TV Shows Featuring George III

- America(1924)
- The Young Mr Pitt(1942)
- John Paul Jones(1959)
- Barry Lyndon(1975)
- The Madness of King George(1994)

Further Research

- Hadlow, Janice (2014) The Strangest Family: The Private Lives of George III, Queen Charlotte and the Hanoverians
- Black, Jeremy(2006). George III
- Hibbert, Christopher(1999). George III: A Personal History
- Carretta, Vincent (1990).George III and the Satirists from Hogarth to Byron
- Ayling, Stanley (1972)George the Third
- Watson, J. Steven(1960). The Reign of George III, 1760–1815
- Butterfield, Herbert(1957) George III and the Historians
- Pares, Richard (1953).King George III and the Politicians

Locations Related to George III

- George III was born in London at Norfolk House, St

James's Square. The house was demolished but parts of the 18th-century interior were salvaged and are on display in the Victoria & Albert Museum, London.
- The King's Library was assembled by George throughout his life and is on display in the British Library.
- For the majority of his life, George lived between Windsor Castle and Buckingham House, now Buckingham Palace.
- George III died at Windsor Castle in Berkshire and was buried in St George's Chapel.

GEORGE IV
(Regent 1811-1820)
(1820 - 1830)

The fourth and last Georgian king, King George IV's reputation is one of the worst of any British monarch. A wild and reckless youth, George grew into a feckless and extravagant adult. As Prince Regent, he had little to do with state affairs unless he was asking for handouts to cover his debts, and as King, his approach to sovereignty did not change. Two marriages, one secret and one failed, combined with George's taste for excess and penchant for horse racing made him unpopular with the public. The 'first gentleman of England,' George may have had fine manners and impeccable style but his reign was ineffective in every way, and he died without a friend in the world.

Key Facts about George IV

- George IV was born at St James' Palace on the 12th of August 1762.
- George succeeded as the King of Great Britain and Ireland and King of Hanover on the 29th of January 1820 at the age of 57.
- He was married in December 1785 to a twice-divorced Roman Catholic lady named Maria Fitzherbert although he repudiated the marriage. George was also married in 1795 to his cousin Caroline Amelia Elizabeth.
- George died at Windsor of various complications to do with obesity on June 26, 1830, aged 67, having reigned ten years.

A Brief Look at His Life

As the first child of King George III, George was born directly into the title of Duke of Cornwall and Duke of Rothesay. He was also given the titles Prince of Wales and Earl of Chester a few days after his birth. Said to have been a very capable student, George's education and upbringing were of a standard you would expect for a future king, and he quickly became fluent in French, German, and Italian. By age 18, George was given a house of his own, and he took to his new freedom with glee.

Wildly extravagant, the young Prince socialized constantly, drank heavily, and kept many mistresses. When he turned 21 and took up residence in Carlton House his partying and spending increased tenfold. Despite obtaining a grant of £60,000 (equivalent to £6,45 million today) from Parliament as well as a hefty annual allowance from the King, George managed to spend himself into debt. King George III despaired of his son's behavior and his political leanings which opposed the King's own conservatism.

On the 15th of December 1785, at the age of 22, George married Maria Fitzherbert, a twice-divorced Roman Catholic, and a commoner. Of course, the King did not give his consent to this union and the 1701 Act of Settlement that barred the spouse of a Catholic from succeeding was still in place making this marriage void. As a Catholic, Maria believed the laws of the Church to be superior to the law of the State and considered herself the wife of the King for the rest of her life. In 1787, overcome by debt and all but estranged from his father, George went to his political allies in Parliament for help. They came through, and on the condition that his marriage to Fitzherbert be publicly denied, gave him enough money to clear the worst of his debts and improve his residence Carlton House.

George was married again ten years later on the 8th of April 1795 to his cousin Princess Caroline of Brunswick. The marriage took place very much against George's will; he was forced to agree to the union so that his father and Parliament would pay his astronomical debts, and the marriage was disastrous. The pair separated after the birth of their only child, Princess Charlotte, and so convinced was Caroline that George hated her she claimed on her deathbed in 1821 that he had poisoned her.

By 1811, George III's mental illness had become so severe he could no longer play his role in government, and on the 5th of February 1811, the Prince of Wales became the Prince Regent of Great Britain and Ireland. Little changed in Britain as a result of this as the regent played an even lesser role than his father in governmental affairs. On 11th May 1812, Prime Minister Spencer Perceval was assassinated, and the Napoleonic Wars raged on, but George spent these years refining himself into the 'first gentleman of England,' taking an active interest in fashion and culture.

King George III died on 29th January 1820, and the Prince Regent became King George IV. In similarity with his lifestyle up to this point, King George's coronation was an obscenely costly and extravagant affair. But despite the hit to the taxpayers' pocket, it was a popular event, and the British public was relieved to see a king in the flesh after so many years under the reign of a recluse. George banned his legal wife Caroline from his coronation and refused to recognize her as Queen, even going as far as to have her name removed from the Book of Common Prayer.

The Coronation

King George IV embarked on a royal tour in 1821 visiting Ireland, the first monarch to do so since Richard II, and Scotland, the first since the mid-17th century. A born collector, George also began to establish an impressive royal art collection and transformed Windsor Castle and Buckingham Palace. The 'Catholic question,' the issue of when and how Catholic people would be emancipated from the various discriminations they faced was a major concern of parliament during George's later reign, but he intervened mainly to complicate matters. In 1829, George was forced by his ministers to agree to the Catholic Emancipation, against his will and his interpretation of his protestant coronation oath.

George's taste for excess in all things led to a massive decline in his health in his later years. Obese, addicted to laudanum, and suffering from gout, dropsy, and possibly porphyria, he became completely incapacitated. On the morning of the 26th of June 1830, King George IV took his last breath. George was buried on the 15th of July 1830 at Windsor Castle.

George may have fathered many children given his proclivity

for mistresses, but his only legitimate child was Princess Charlotte of Wales. Sadly Charlotte died of complications following the birth of a stillborn baby in 1817. Prince Frederick, Duke of York and Albany, George's younger brother had died childless, and so the third son of George III, Prince William, Duke of Clarence took to the throne as William IV.

Legacy

George IV's legacy is not a positive one. His reputation was poor amongst the British public due to rumors about his marriage to a Catholic, constant philandering, and excessive spending that saw him rack up the equivalent of millions of pounds of national debt. His moniker 'The First Gentleman of England' is an ironic one given George's indulgent lifestyle and moral weaknesses. A patron of the arts, George nevertheless had a huge influence on the architecture, fashion, and style of the day. Perhaps George IV is best summed up by the comment that ran in The Times newspaper after his death that read, he would always prefer 'a girl and a bottle to politics and a sermon.'

Film & TV

- This Charming Man (2006)
- Poldark (1996)
- A Royal Scandal (1996) TV documentary
- Vanity Fair (1987 and 1998) TV series
- Princess Caraboo (1994)
- The Madness of King George (1994)
- The Scarlet Pimpernel (1982) TV drama
- Prince Regent (1979) TV documentary
- Lady Caroline Lamb (1972)
- The First Gentleman (1948)
- The Scarlet Pimpernel (1934)

Further Research

- Hibbert, Christopher (2015) George IV
- Baker, Kenneth (2005). George IV: A Life in Caricature
- Parissien, Steven (2001). George IV: The Grand Entertainment
- David, Saul (2000). Prince of Pleasure: The Prince of Wales and the Making of the Regency.
- Smith, E.A. (1999). George IV
- De-la-Noy, Michael (1998). George IV

Locations to Visit

- George IV was born at St James's Palace in London, died at Windsor Castle in Berkshire, and was buried at St George's Chapel in Windsor. All of these locations are open to the public.
- There are many statues of George IV, but two of the most famous are located in Trafalgar Square, London, and the Royal Pavilion in Brighton.

WILLIAM IV
(1830 - 1837)

King William IV, born William Henry on August 21, 1765, was the third son of King George III and Queen Charlotte. His life, reign, and legacy spanned a period of significant change in British history, marked by political and social transformations. It was also a very short reign, which led to one of Britain's longest (Queen Victoria's). This article explores the key aspects of King William IV's life, his reign, and the lasting impact he left on the British monarchy.

Key Facts About William IV

- William IV was born on August 21, 1765, as the third son of King George III and Queen Charlotte.
- He joined the Royal Navy at the age of thirteen and served in various capacities, gaining valuable experience that would later shape his approach to leadership.
- William ascended to the throne in 1830 at the age of 64, after his older brothers, George IV and Frederick, Duke of York, both died without living heirs (George IV reigned, but Frederick did not have the chance to).
- One of the defining moments of his reign was the Reform Crisis, during which he supported the passage of the Reform Act of 1832, which transformed Britain's electoral system.
- King William IV's personal life was marked by his long-standing relationship with the actress Dorothea Jordan, with whom he had ten illegitimate children together, and his genuine concern for the well-being of his subjects endeared him to many.

Early Life and Education

William Henry was born at Buckingham Palace in London. His early life was characterized by the tumultuous events of the late

18th century, including the American War of Independence and the French Revolution. William's father, King George III, faced challenges to his rule, and the young prince witnessed the changing political landscape of the time.

Despite being the third son, William received a relatively good education. His naval career began at the age of thirteen when he joined the Royal Navy. He served in various capacities, gaining valuable experience that would later shape his approach to leadership.

Naval Career

William IV was known as the "Sailor King," because had a long and distinguished naval career before ascending to the throne in 1830. He joined the Royal Navy at the age of thirteen and quickly rose through the ranks, serving on a number of ships and participating in several important naval engagements. One of his early assignments was on the HMS Alarm, where he served as a midshipman and gained valuable experience in navigation and gunnery.

In 1789, William was promoted to lieutenant and assigned to the HMS Pegasus, which was tasked with patrolling the English Channel. He later served on the HMS Royal George, which was one of the largest and most powerful ships in the navy at the time. During his time on the Royal George, William participated in the Battle of Cape St. Vincent, which was a decisive victory for the British navy over the Spanish fleet.

In 1790, William was promoted to commander and given his own ship, the HMS Andromeda. He was later promoted to captain and given command of the HMS Valiant, which he sailed to the West Indies to protect British interests in the region. William continued to serve in the navy for many years, eventually rising to the rank of Lord High Admiral. His naval career was marked by bravery, skill, and dedication to duty, and he was widely respected by his fellow sailors and officers.

Rise to the Throne

William's older brothers, George IV and Frederick, Duke of York, were next in line to the throne. Frederick died in 1827 childless. Then, in 1830, King George IV died, and William ascended to the throne at the age of 64. His reign marked the end of the Hanoverian line, as he had no legitimate children to succeed him. This fact added a layer of significance to his rule, as it paved the way for the next era of British monarchy (The Victorian era).

The Reform Crisis

One of the defining moments of King William IV's reign was the Reform Crisis. The demand for parliamentary reform gained momentum during this period, with calls for a more representative and democratic system. The existing electoral system was widely criticized for being outdated and unrepresentative of the changing social and economic landscape.

Despite initial resistance, King William IV played a crucial role in navigating through the crisis. He ultimately accepted the need for reform and supported the passage of the Reform Act of 1832. This landmark legislation transformed the British electoral system, expanding the voting rights of a significant portion of the male population and redistributing parliamentary seats to better reflect population changes.

Personal Life and Family

King William IV's personal life was marked by his long-standing relationship with the actress Dorothea Jordan. Although they never married, they had ten children together. The couple's unconventional union was well-known, and their descendants faced challenges in terms of social acceptance.

Despite his personal affairs, William was well-regarded for his affable nature and genuine concern for the well-being of his subjects. His genuine interest in the lives of ordinary people endeared him to many, creating a unique connection between the monarch and the public.

Later Years of Reign

As King William IV continued his reign, the country faced economic challenges and social changes. The Industrial Revolution was in full swing, bringing about shifts in employment, urbanization, and living conditions. The monarch navigated these changes with a pragmatic approach, recognizing the importance of adapting to the evolving landscape.

King William IV's short years on the throne were also marked by international developments. The geopolitical landscape of Europe was undergoing transformations, with tensions and conflicts shaping the continent. Britain, under William's rule, maintained a relatively stable foreign policy, avoiding major entanglements and prioritizing diplomatic solutions.

Cultural Contributions

Beyond his political and social impact, King William IV also made cultural contributions during his reign. The era saw advancements in literature, art, and architecture. Notable figures such as Charles Dickens and William Wordsworth were active during this time, contributing to the rich cultural tapestry of the period.

In architecture, the reign of William IV witnessed the continuation of the neoclassical style while also paving the way for the emergence of the Victorian Gothic style. These architectural developments reflected the changing tastes and sensibilities of the time, leaving a lasting imprint on the built environment of Britain.

The End of the Hanoverian Line

One of the most significant aspects of King William IV's legacy is the end of the Hanoverian line of Kings. With no legitimate heir, the throne passed to his niece, Victoria, marking the beginning of the Victorian era. This transition had profound implications for the monarchy and the nation, as Queen Victoria's long reign would go on to define an entire era of British history.

The end of the Hanoverian line also highlighted the complexities of royal succession and the importance of securing a stable line of succession. The absence of a direct heir prompted discussions on the monarchy's role and the need for a clear system of succession.

Lasting Impact on the British Monarchy

While King William IV's reign might not have been as eventful or as long as some of his predecessors, his legacy lies in the stability he provided during a period of significant change. The compromises made during the Reform Crisis and the acknowledgment of the need for societal and political evolution contributed to a more resilient monarchy.

In hindsight, King William IV's reign can be seen as a bridge between eras. He's sort of a forgotten king. When you think of 19th-century history – you tend to think of the Regency and then Queen Victoria. His commitment to adaptation and his willingness to navigate challenges set the stage for the Victorian era's grandeur and influence. The lessons learned during his rule influenced subsequent monarchs, contributing to the monarchy's ability to endure and adapt in the face of evolving societal dynamics.

Movies and TV Shows Featuring

In Patrick O'Brian's final novel of the Aubrey-Maturin series, Captain Jack Aubrey is obliged to accept a midshipman who is the bastard son of the Duke of Clarence. This young man is referred to as a "first voyager." The novel provides readers with an interesting portrayal of the Duke and acknowledges his reputation as a competent seaman and commander. However, in other novels in the series, the Duke is depicted in a far less flattering light. In fact, in the penultimate novel of the series, one of the protagonists – Stephen Maturin – characterizes him as "…a bounding, confident, foul-mouthed scrub."

Bernard Bastable's "Mozart Mysteries" – Dead, Mr. Mozart, and Too Many Notes, Mr. Mozart – involves an alternate version of Wolfgang Mozart, who survives in the 1820s and has settled in England. Here, odd circumstances draw him into Hanoverian intrigue and cover-ups. William IV is a significant character in the second book, where he effectively makes Mozart his personal spy against rival factions within the royal family.

On-screen, William is portrayed as a king by Ernst G. Schiffner in the 1936 German film Mädchenjahre einer Königin, which is based on the play by Geza Silberer about Queen Victoria's early life, by Peter Ustinov in the 2001 TV miniseries Victoria and Albert, and by Jim Broadbent in the 2009 film The Young Victoria.

He has been depicted as a prince by Scott Forbes in Mrs. Fitzherbert (1947), by Tom Gill in The First Gentleman (1948), and by Toby Jones in Amazing Grace (2006).

There are several extant statues of the king: at Greenwich Park, London; at Montpellier Gardens, Cheltenham; and on the Wilhelmsplatz, Göttingen, Germany.

Further Research

- William IV (The English Monarchs Series) by Roger Fulford
- William IV by Philip Ziegler
- The Last King: William IV and the Georgian Monarchy by Jonathan Dimbleby
- William IV: A King at Sea by W.A. Speck
- King William IV by Arthur Bryant
- The Life and Times of William IV by Christopher Hibbert
- The Life of William IV by Percy Hetherington Fitzgerald
- William IV and the Irish Question by John Belchem
- William IV: A Brief History by Wallace T. MacCaffrey
- William IV: A Political Life by Stephen Taylor

Locations Related to William IV

- Buckingham Palace, where King William IV was born and

spent part of his early life.
- The Palace of Westminster, where the Reform Act of 1832 was passed during King William IV's reign.
- Kensington Palace, where William IV's long-standing partner, Dorothea Jordan, lived for many years.
- St. George's Chapel at Windsor Castle, where King William IV's funeral was held after his death in 1837.
- The Royal Pavilion in Brighton was built during the reign of King George IV and was a popular destination for William IV during his reign.

VICTORIA
(1837 - 1901)

Queen Victoria was Queen of the United Kingdom of Great Britain and Ireland for 63 years, overseeing six decades of huge change in the industry, economy, and society of Great Britain. Born and raised to take over the British throne, Victoria was known as a strong and principled monarch and a dedicated mother and wife. In 1876, Victoria became the Empress of India; her empire expanded so dramatically during her reign that it was said that the sun never set over the British Empire.

Known affectionately as the Grandmother of Europe, Victoria's marriage to Prince Albert of Saxe-Coburg and Gotha produced nine children, all of whom married into royal and noble families across Europe. After Prince Albert's sudden death at the age of 42, Victoria entered a period of mourning from which she never fully emerged.

Key Facts about Queen Victoria

- Queen Victoria was born on May 24th, 1819 at Kensington Palace.
- She succeeded as Queen of Great Britain and Ireland on the 20th of June 1837 and became Empress of India in 1877.
- Victoria was married to Albert, Prince of Saxe-Coburg-Gotha on the 10th of February, 1840 at Chapel Royal, St James Palace. They had nine children together.
- Queen Victoria died of old age at 81 after a reign lasting 63 years. She is buried at Frogmore, Windsor.

Highlights of Queen Victoria's Life

The birth of Queen Victoria was a carefully planned affair. George IV had only one daughter, Charlotte, who died in childbirth in 1817. Suddenly there was no legitimate heir to the British throne.

King George III was near his death and although he and his wife had produced a mighty brood of 12 children, the five princesses and seven princes were all remarkably without legitimate offspring. Four of the seven princes were not even married and so, in the interests of securing a suitable heir to the throne, parliament made an official appeal to the four Dukes to marry immediately and procreate.

One of the Dukes was partnered in a morganatic marriage (a marriage in which the spouse of lower rank has no claim to the titles or assets of the higher-ranking partner) and the other three dukes had long-term partners who were understandably aghast to read a public exhortation for their lovers to marry in the morning papers. Regardless, in the coming months, Adolphus Duke of Cambridge married Princess Augusta of Hesse-Cassel, Edward Duke of Kent abandoned his long-term lover and proposed to Victoria of Saxe-Coburg, Princess of Leiningen, and William of Clarence married Adelaide of Saxe-Meiningen. Now the race was on to produce an heir. The Kents, of course, won and produced Victoria who was born on the 24th of May 1819, at Kensington Palace and went on to live for 81 years, 63 of them as Queen of Great Britain.

Victoria was born fifth in line for the British throne. The Duke of Kent died just months after Victoria's birth and George III had died days earlier, leaving the throne to George IV who was already acting as King's Regent. The Duke of York died in 1827 and George IV died in 1830, leaving Victoria next in line to the throne after William IV.

Victoria's childhood is said to have been a sad and somewhat lonely one. Raised by her mother, the Duchess of Kent, and Sir John Conroy, who is thought to have been the Duchess's lover, Victoria was educated at home in seclusion. The Duchess did not have a good relationship with King William IV, who publicly declared that he hoped to live until Victoria's 18th birthday to ensure the Duchess would not rise to the position of Regent.

William got his wish and died at the age of 71 on the 20th of June, 1837. Victoria was crowned Queen of Great Britain at her coronation on the 28th of June, 1838, and immediately took up residence in Buckingham Palace. The title of Monarch of Hanover could not be passed down the female line and so went to her uncle, the Duke of Cumberland, who became King Ernest Augustus I of Hanover. A young queen who had experienced a very secluded childhood, Victoria immediately sought the advice and influence of the then-prime minister Lord Melbourne.

Victoria and Albert

Victoria married Prince Albert of Saxe-Gotha and Coburg on February 10, 1840. In a bold move for the time, Victoria proposed to Prince Albert of Saxe-Gotha and Coburg and they were married at the Chapel Royal of St James' Palace. Victoria and Albert are known to have been besotted with each other and their long and happy marriage produced nine children, each of whom were married into every royal house in Europe.

At the time of Queen Victoria's reign, Great Britain was already a constitutional monarchy in which the Queen had little to no real political power. She did, however, have the power of influence and she exerted this influence regularly, particularly when it came to the appointment of Britain's prime minister. Victoria's popularity with the British public waxed and waned depending on public scandals and political circumstances. Various attempts were made on Victoria's life throughout her early years as Queen and the courageous way in which she dealt with such threats led to a peak in her popularity. However, her popularity plummeted during the Irish Potato Famine of 1845, during which time she was thought to have offered little in the way of assistance to the millions of Irish men, women, and children who suffered. This antagonism towards the monarchy led directly to the growth of Irish Nationalism.

In 1861, Victoria's beloved husband Albert died and she entered a period of mourning from which she never fully recovered. Victoria wore black for the remainder of her life, avoided London, and made few if any, public appearances. Queen Victoria became known as the 'Widow of Windsor' and her self-imposed seclusion from the public sphere helped to encourage Britain's lean towards republicanism in the mid-nineteenth century. By 1870, with the establishment of the Third French Republic, republican sentiment in Britain had reached its peak. A rally in Trafalgar Square demanded the Queen's removal and radical MPs criticized her publicly.

During Victoria's long reign, steps were taken towards democracy as political power moved away from the sovereign and a series of parliamentary acts gave more power to the electorate. Most notably, the introduction of the secret ballot in 1872 and the Representation of the Peoples Act of 1884, which gave certain members of society the right to vote, sought to create a fairer system of political representation. Queen Victoria, however, did not support the suffragette movement which demanded the right to vote be extended to women.

Queen Victoria became Empress of India in 1877 when the British East India Company was dissolved and Britain's lands and resources in India were incorporated into the British Empire. Victoria supported Prime Minister Benjamin Disraeli's foreign policy of expansion and colonialism which led to conflicts such as the Anglo-Zulu War and Anglo-Afghan War. Victoria's view of expanding her empire was that it was a necessary and benign act by the British, essentially protecting native people from themselves. The British Empire became vast and in 1887, they celebrated Victoria's Golden Jubilee.

Ten years later, Victoria celebrated her Diamond Jubilee which was made a festival of the British Empire with the Queen's procession through London featuring troops from all over the empire. Queen Victoria was as popular as she had ever been but this popularity was short-lived and the last few years of Victoria's reign were overshadowed by the unpopular Boer War.

Victoria was buried at Windsor in the Frogmore Royal Mausoleum, which she had built especially for herself and Prince Albert's final resting place. Victoria's words, "Farewell best beloved, here at last I shall rest with thee, with thee in Christ I shall rise again."

Legacy of Queen Victoria

Victoria and Albert had a total of 42 grandchildren, but Victoria's careful management of her children's marriages into the most powerful houses in Europe was undone within the next generation, as this regality was washed away into republicanism and communism. Nevertheless, Victoria became an icon of the reach and might of the British Empire, as well as a symbol of strong moral values in family and public life.

Victoria was a natural diarist and wrote up to 2500 words a day during her adult life. Many of her journals and letters are still in existence in various forms, edited mostly by her daughter, Princess Beatrice, and Lord Escher. Through these diaries, we are able to see her real influence behind the scenes of British politics.

The Victorian Era was one of substantial and rapid change. The world Victoria left behind after 81 years, 63 years and seven months of which she spent as Queen of Great Britain, was very different then the one she was born into. The Victorian Era was one of rapid and monumental change in all spheres of public and private life and memorials to Victoria's reign exist all over the world.

Films and TV Shows Featuring Queen Victoria

- Mr Turner (2014)
- Hysteria (2011)
- Young Victoria (2009)
- Around the World in 80 Days (2004)
- Mrs Brown (1997)
- Disraeli (1978) TV Show
- Edward the Seventh (1975) TV Show
- Victoria the Great (1937)

Further Research

- Wilson (2014) Victoria: A Life
- Matthew Dennison (2012) Queen Victoria: A Life of Contradictions
- Giles Lytton Strachey (2012) Queen Victoria
- Christopher Hibbert (2010) Victoria: A Personal History

Locations Related to Queen Victoria

- Some of the most notable places named after Queen Victoria include the states of Queensland and Victoria in Australia, Victoria Falls, the capitals of British Columbia, Newfoundland, and Saskatchewan in Canada, and the capital of the Seychelles.
- In the UK and Scotland, there are a huge number of streets, bridges, hospitals, and other buildings named after the Queen.
- Victoria was born in Kensington Palace.
- As soon as she was crowned Queen, she took up residence in Buckingham Palace.
- Balmoral Castle was Victoria and her family's country home for the majority of her life and is open to visits from the public when the royal family is not in residence.
- The Albert Memorial in London's Kensington Gardens is a beautiful and moving tribute to Victoria's beloved husband.

EDWARD VII
(1901 - 1910)

Known as both the 'Peacemaker' and the 'Playboy Prince', Edward VII is an enigma. A thoroughly modern monarch Edward VII was the Uncle of Europe, the first truly constitutional British sovereign and also the last sovereign to exercise any real political power. Living for 59 years as the Prince of Wales, longer than any other monarch (though now Prince Charles has been waiting longer), Edward's reign was short but influential. Dandy of the British upper classes Golden Age, Edward was loved by the British populace for his diplomatic skills, easy-going charm, and, perhaps, his headline-grabbing transgressions.

Key Facts about Edward VII

- Edward VII was born on the 9th of November 1841 at Buckingham Palace.
- He succeeded as King of Great Britain and Ireland and Emperor of India on the 22nd of January 1901, aged 59.
- Edward married Alexandra, daughter of King Christian IX of Denmark on the 10th of March 1863.
- Edward died on the 6th May 1910 at Buckingham Palace of pneumonia and a heart attack having reigned just 9 years.

A Brief Biography

The eldest son of Queen Victoria and her husband Prince Albert of Saxe-Coburg and Gotha, Edward was born the Duke of Cornwall and Duke of Rothesay. Christened Albert Edward but known to the family as Bertie, Edward was also the Prince of Saxe-Coburg and Gotha, Duke of Saxony, and the Prince of Wales, a title he would come to hold longer than any of his predecessors. As direct heir to the throne, Edward was given an education fit for a King but did not take to his studies as well as some of his siblings and was thought to have rebelled against the strict severity of his parent's and tutors' methods.

In atonement for the wild and wicked ways of the previous long-time Prince of Wales, King George IV, Edward was expected to grow into a model constitutional monarch. But as soon as he was free of formal education Edward set about finding ways to enjoy himself and quickly found himself with a reputation as a playboy prince. This reputation was not helped when in 1861 under the guise of getting 'army experience' in Ireland Edward had a liaison with actress Nellie Clifden. Prince Albert found out, was furious, and traveled to Cambridge to reprimand Edward. Albert died just two weeks after his altercation with his son and Queen Victoria is thought to have blamed Edward for her beloved Albert's death.

During the rest of his mother's long reign, Edward was side-lined and excluded from political power but, as his mother isolated herself in mourning after Prince Albert's death, Edward took on most of Queen Victoria's public duties and represented Britain throughout the world. Although Edward resented his mother's withholding of political influence in foreign policy he used his position to his advantage, creating personal relationships with important players around the world and cultivating his many family connections in Europe. During an extensive tour of India in 1875, Edward pushed for the issuing of new guidance on the treatment of native Indians by British officials, and, partly as a result of the tour's success, Victoria was given the title Empress of India by Parliament.

By his early twenties, Edward's marriage had already been arranged and following an extensive tour of the Middle East in 1862 he married Alexandra on the 10th March 1863 at St George's Chapel, Windsor Castle. Because of tension between Denmark and Germany, Edward and Alexandra's marriage was unpopular with some but the marriage appeared to be a happy one, and the young couple regularly entertained on a lavish scale. Edward became the pinnacle of London society spending his time gambling, shooting, sailing, and enjoying good food and good wine.

Edward had six children with Princess Alexandra of Denmark, two of which sadly died, but in his devotion to a life of personal indulgence, he may have fathered many more children with a number of mistresses. Some of Edward's mistresses were long-term, such as the actress Lily Langtry, but he also enjoyed short affairs and visiting prostitutes. Edward is said to have been a regular in a series of legal Parisian brothels, most famously Le Chabanais. During the middle years of his life Edward found himself in financial difficulties but thanks to some good investments and success as a race-horse owner he was finally made solvent.

An extrovert and a charmer, Edward made the monarchy more visible to the public than ever before by making constant 'public appearances', opening the Thames Embankment, the Mersey Tunnel, and the Tower Bridge personally. A patron of the arts and sciences, Edward hoped to ease class tension in Britain with the opening of the Royal College of Music. But where Edward went scandal was never too far behind and thanks to a baccarat scandal in which the prince was accused of playing an illegal card game and endless revelations regarding intimacies with women other than his wife the relationship between Edward and his mother remained strained.

In January 1901, Victoria died and Edward stepped tardily up the throne as Edward VII. Edward's coronation was held on 9th August 1902 and from the outset, Edward's reign was focused on changing foreign policy. Known as the 'Uncle of Europe', Edward was able to use his family connections to most European royalty to engineer alliances and agreements that were favorable to British interests. In 1903 Edward managed to gain the goodwill of the French, no small feat, and lay the foundation of what would become the Anglo-French Entente Cordiale (1904) that ruled out any aggression between the countries over colonies in North Africa. Not only that, Edward convinced the French to begin active rearmament against the military aggrandizement of Germany under Kaiser Wilhelm II who, although he was his nephew, Edward thoroughly despised.

Edward was not as deeply involved with politics on home soil as he could have been but he did play an active role in initiating military and naval reforms. The failings of the Boer War had made it clear to everyone that the British Army and Royal Navy needed a complete overhaul. On social issues, Edward's views were notably liberal although inconsistent. Edward repeatedly condemned prejudice and discrimination on the basis of race but did not support votes for women. He intended to vote for Gladstone's Representation of the People Bill in 1884 but was persuaded to maintain an objective stance.

During the final year of his reign, Edward was involved in a constitutional crisis. The House of Lords majority, the Conservatives, refused to pass the Liberal government's 'People's Budget' and the King was forced to intervene. The January 1910 election resulted in a hung parliament eventually the crisis led to the removal of the Lord's right to veto legislation.

Around 1908 Edward began to suffer from ill-health thought to be related to his heavy smoking habit. Already suffering from severe bronchitis, Edward VII had a series of heart attacks on the 6th of May 1910. He was put to bed, became unconscious, and died peacefully in his sleep. His funeral held on the 20th May 1910 attracted 400,000 mourners including a delegate of the most high-ranking royals and politicians in Europe.

Legacy Today

King Edward VII's legacy is overwhelmingly positive. Although forced to wait in the wings as far as foreign policy went during Queen Victoria's long reign, as heir apparent Edward was the first King to foster a truly public persona. The face of the British monarchy at home and abroad long before he took to the throne, Edward VII was a seasoned diplomat and a smooth talker. To the chagrin of royal biographers, Edward VII ordered for his letters to be destroyed after his death leaving much of the more colourful detail of his private life up for speculation. A devoted father, Edward prepared his son George for an uncertain future perhaps foreseeing that within four years of his death World War One would devastate Europe.

Film & TV

- The Lost Prince (2003) TV series
- Mrs. Brown (1997)

- 1871 (1990)
- Edward the King (1975) TV Series
- The Pallisers (1974) TV series
- Young Winston (1972)
- Mayerling (1968)
- Sixty Glorious Years (1938)

Further Research

- Ridley, Jane (2013) Bertie: A Life of Edward VII
- Hattersley, Roy (2004), The Edwardians
- Thomas, Hugh and Hibbert, Christopher (2007) Edward VII: The Last Victorian King
- Bentley-Cranch, Dana (1992), Edward VII: Image of an Era 1841–1910
- Hough, Richard (1992), Edward & Alexandra: Their Private and Public Lives
- Lee, Sidney (1927), King Edward VII: A Biography

Locations to Visit

- Edward VII was born and died at Buckingham Palace, London
- Edward and his family lived between Marlborough House in London and Sandringham House in Norfolk. Both houses are open to the public.
- He is buried at St George's Chapel in Windsor Castle.

GEORGE V
(1922-1936)

George V was the second son of King Edward VII and Queen Alexandra, and he was born on June 3, 1865. He became King of the United Kingdom and the British Dominions and Emperor of India after the death of his father in 1910. George V's reign lasted from 1910 to 1936, and he is remembered as a monarch who played an important role in the First World War, and who made significant contributions to the development of the British monarchy.

Key Facts about George V

- George V changed the royal family's surname from Saxe-Coburg-Gotha to Windsor in 1917 due to anti-German sentiment during World War I.
- He was the first British monarch to make a Christmas Day broadcast to the nation, starting the tradition that continues to this day.
- George V was an avid stamp collector and had one of the most extensive collections in the world at the time.
- He was a heavy smoker, and his addiction to cigarettes is believed to have contributed to his death from bronchitis in 1936.
- George V was the first monarch to fly in an airplane, taking a flight in 1918 to visit troops on the Western Front during World War I.
- First British King to be Photographed with a US President

Early Life and Education

George was born in Marlborough House, London, and he was christened George Frederick Ernest Albert. He was the second son of King Edward VII and Queen Alexandra, and he had five siblings. His older brother, Albert Victor, was the heir to the throne but died of influenza at the age of 28 in 1892. George V was educated privately at home by tutors, and he was later sent to the Royal Naval College, Osborne, and then to the Royal Naval College, Dartmouth. He also attended the University of Cambridge, where he studied history, economics, and politics. He served in the Royal Navy until his brother's death as he was never meant to be King.

Marriage and Family Life

In 1893, George married Princess Mary of Teck, who was his cousin (she had originally been engaged to his brother). They had six children together, including the future Edward VIII and George VI. George and Queen Mary had a happy marriage, and they were known for their love of family life. They were also passionate about charity work, and they supported many causes throughout their lives.

Prince of Wales

As the Duke of York, George fulfilled a diverse range of public duties. Following Queen Victoria's death in 1901, George's father became King Edward VII, and George became the Prince of Wales and second in line for the throne (and also the Duke of Cornwall).

In 1901, the Prince and Princess of Wales embarked on an extensive tour of the British Empire, covering destinations like Gibraltar, Malta, Port Said, Aden, Ceylon, Singapore, Australia, New Zealand, Mauritius, South Africa, Canada, and the Colony of Newfoundland. The tour, orchestrated by Colonial Secretary Joseph Chamberlain and supported by Prime Minister Lord Salisbury, aimed to reward the Dominions for their participation in the South African War. Despite elaborate receptions, not all residents responded favorably, especially in South Africa, where the display was met with resentment among white Cape Afrikaners.

His father, King Edward VII, intended to prepare George for his future role as king, granting him extensive access to state documents. As Prince of Wales, George advocated for naval training reforms, emphasizing equal education for cadets regardless of class. The reforms were implemented by Sir John Fisher, the then Second (later First) Sea Lord.

From November 1905 to March 1906, George and Mary toured British India, where he denounced racial discrimination and campaigned for increased Indian involvement in government. Subsequent international travels included attending the wedding of King Alfonso XIII in Spain and the coronation of King Haakon VII in Norway, demonstrating George's engagement with global affairs.

Reign

George became King of the United Kingdom and the British Dominions, and Emperor of India, after the death of his father, King Edward VII, in 1910. He was initially considered a conservative and reserved monarch, but he quickly gained popularity by showing concern for the welfare of his subjects, especially during the First World War. George V worked closely with his Prime Ministers, and he was known for his strong sense of duty and his commitment to public service.

During the First World War, George V played an important role in boosting morale and supporting the troops. He visited the front lines, and he made speeches to encourage the soldiers. He also established the Order of the British Empire to recognize service to the country, and he gave out medals to soldiers who showed bravery on the battlefield.

After the war, George V worked to rebuild the country and strengthen the British Empire. He visited many parts of the empire, including India, Australia, and Canada. He also played an important role in the establishment of the Irish Free State, which was created in 1922.

During the reign of George V, Britain underwent significant changes and transformations. The First World War had a profound impact on the country, and it brought about many changes in British society and politics. The war had a devastating effect on the economy, and many industries were forced to close down or reduce their workforce. The government responded to the crisis by introducing new policies and programs, including the first-ever income tax to be levied on ordinary citizens.

The war also had a significant impact on the role of women in British society. With so many men serving in the military, women were called upon to take on new roles and responsibilities. They worked in factories, offices, and hospitals, and they played a vital role in keeping the country running. The war helped to break down some of the traditional barriers that had prevented women from entering the workforce, and it paved the way for greater gender equality in the years to come. Women fought for and won the right to vote after the war.

Another significant change that took place during the reign of George V was the rise of the Labour Party. The party was founded in 1900, but it wasn't until after the First World War that it began to gain significant support. The war had exposed many of the social and economic problems facing the country, and the Labour Party offered a vision of a fairer, more equal society. The party's policies included the introduction of a minimum wage, the provision of free healthcare, and the creation of a welfare state to support those in need.

The reign of George V also saw the beginning of the decline of the British Empire. Although the empire was still vast and powerful, it was beginning to show signs of weakness and instability. The First World War had drained Britain's resources, and many of its colonies and territories were demanding greater autonomy and independence. India, in particular, was becoming increasingly restless, and there were growing calls for self-rule and independence.

Despite these challenges, George V worked tirelessly to maintain the unity and stability of the British Empire. He traveled extensively throughout the empire, and he was known for his ability to connect with people from all walks of life. He recognized the need for change and reform, and he worked to modernize the monarchy and make it more accessible to ordinary people. His legacy as a king who cared deeply about his people and his country continues to inspire and guide us today.

Legacy

George V is remembered as a monarch who played an important role in the First World War, and who made significant contributions to the development of the British monarchy. He was a popular and respected king, who was known for his sense of duty, his kindness, and his commitment to public service. He was also a family man, who was devoted to his wife and children, and who loved spending time with them.

George V's legacy lived on through his children and grandchildren. His son, Edward VIII, abdicated the throne in 1936, and George V's second son, George VI, became King. George VI's daughter, Queen Elizabeth II, was the longest-reigning monarch in British history until her death in 2022.

Movies and TV Shows Featuring George V

- George V has been portrayed on screen by:
- Derek Erskine in the 1925 silent film The Scarlet Woman: An Ecclesiastical Melodrama
- Carleton Hobbs in the 1965 film A King's Story
- Michael Osborne in the 1975 ATV drama series Edward the Seventh
- Marius Goring in the 1978 Thames Television series Edward & Mrs. Simpson
- Keith Varnier in the 1978 LWT drama series Lillie
- Rene Aranda in the 1980 film The Fiendish Plot of Dr. Fu Manchu
- Terence Brook in the 1981 drama series The Life and Times of David Lloyd George
- Guy Deghy in the 1981 Southern Television drama series Winston Churchill: The Wilderness Years
- Andrew Gilmour in the 1985 Australian miniseries A Thousand Skies
- David Ravenswood in the 1990 Australian TV miniseries The Great Air Race
- John Warner in the 1991 RTÉ TV drama The Treaty

- David Troughton in the 1999 BBC TV drama All the King's Men
- Rupert Frazer in the 2002 TV miniseries Shackleton
- Alan Bates in the 2002 Carlton Television drama Bertie and Elizabeth
- Tom Hollander in the 2003 BBC miniseries The Lost Prince and in the 2021 film The King's Man
- Clifford Rose in the 2005 TV drama Wallis & Edward
- Julian Wadham in the 2007 TV drama My Boy Jack
- Michael Gambon in the 2010 film The King's Speech
- James Fox in the 2011 film W.E.
- Guy Williams in the 2013 Christmas episode of Downton Abbey
- Simon Jones in the 2019 film Downton Abbey
- Richard Dillane in the 2022 fifth season of The Crown

Further Research

- "George V" by Kenneth Rose
- "George V: The Unexpected King" by David Cannadine
- "George V and the Edwardian Age" by John Turner
- "George V: The First Modern Monarch" by Harold Nicolson
- "George V" by Christopher Hibbert
- "The Last Courts of Europe: A Royal Family Album 1860-1914" by Robert K. Massie
- "The King's Speech: How One Man Saved the British Monarchy" by Mark Logue and Peter Conradi
- "The Windsors: A Dynasty Revealed" by Mark Logue and Catherine Mayer
- "The King's War: 1917-1919" by Mark Logue and Peter Conradi
- "The Royal Family at War" by Jessica Fellowes

Locations Related to George V

- Marlborough House, London – where George V was

born
- Royal Naval College – where George V received his education
- University of Cambridge – where George V studied history, economics, and politics
- Buckingham Palace – the official residence of George V during his reign
- Sandringham House – the country estate of George V and Queen Mary
- Balmoral Castle – the Scottish residence of the royal family, which George V frequently visited

EDWARD VIII
(1936 - Abdicated)

Edward VIII was the eldest son of King George V and Queen Mary, and he succeeded his father as the King of the United Kingdom and the Dominions of the British Empire in January 1936. However, his reign lasted only 326 days, making him one of the shortest-reigning monarchs in British history. He is perhaps best known for his abdication in December 1936, which was caused by his desire to marry the American socialite Wallis Simpson. This decision had far-reaching consequences for the British monarchy and the political establishment, and it remains a topic of fascination for historians and the public alike.

Key Facts about Edward VIII

- Edward VIII was born on June 23, 1894, and he was christened Edward Albert Christian George Andrew Patrick David.
- He was educated at the Royal Naval College in Osborne and the Royal Naval College in Dartmouth, and he joined the Royal Navy in 1913.
- During World War I, he served in the Mediterranean and the North Sea, and he was promoted to lieutenant in 1916 and to commander in 1922.
- After his accession to the throne, he became known for his interest in social issues and his support for the unemployed and the poor.
- Edward VIII was succeeded by his younger brother, George VI, who went on to become one of the most beloved monarchs in British history.

Early Life

Edward VIII was born on June 23, 1894, at White Lodge in Richmond Park, London. He was the eldest son of King George

V and Queen Mary, and he was initially third in line to the throne, behind his grandfather, King Edward VII, and his father, the Duke of York. Edward was educated at home by private tutors until the age of 13 when he went to the Royal Naval College in Osborne. He later attended the Royal Naval College in Dartmouth, where he was known for his athleticism and his love of sports.

After leaving Dartmouth, Edward joined the Royal Navy as a midshipman, and he served on various ships in the Mediterranean and the North Sea. He was promoted to lieutenant in 1916, and he saw action in the Battle of Jutland, the largest naval battle of World War I. After the war, Edward traveled extensively and became known for his love of parties, fashion, and socializing.

Reign and Abdication

Edward VIII became king on January 20, 1936, upon the death of his father, George V. He was initially popular with the British public, who saw him as a modern and charismatic monarch. However, his relationship with Wallis Simpson, an American socialite who was still married to her second husband, soon caused controversy and scandal.

The British establishment, including Prime Minister Stanley Baldwin and the Archbishop of Canterbury, opposed the idea of Edward marrying Simpson, who was seen as a divisive and unsuitable figure for a queen. Edward was determined to marry her, however, and he abdicated on December 11, 1936, in order to do so. His younger brother, George VI, succeeded him as king.

Legacy

The abdication crisis of 1936 had a profound impact on the British monarchy and the political establishment. It raised questions about the role of the monarch, the power of the government, and the influence of the media. It also highlighted the tensions between tradition and modernity, and it showed the importance of public opinion in shaping the destiny of the monarchy.

After his abdication, Edward was given the title of Duke of

Windsor, and he lived in France with Simpson, whom he married in June 1937. He remained a controversial figure and persona non grata with the Royal Family. He died in Paris on May 28, 1972, and he was buried in the Royal Burial Ground at Frogmore, Windsor.

Movies and TV Shows Featuring

Edward VIII has been portrayed in numerous films and TV shows over the years, including The King's Speech (2010), which focuses on the reign of his brother, George VI, and the abdication crisis. He has also been depicted in The Crown (2016-), a popular Netflix series about the reign of Queen Elizabeth II.

Further Research

For those interested in learning more about Edward VIII, there are many books and documentaries available. Some of the most popular include The Duke of Windsor's War (2017) by historian Michael Bloch, and The Queen Mother: The Official Biography (2009) by William Shawcross. Most recently Once a King: The Lost Memoir of Edward VIII by Jane Tippett.

Locations Related to Edward VIII

There are several locations that are associated with Edward VIII, including Buckingham Palace, where he lived as a member of the royal family; Fort Belvedere, a country house in Surrey where he signed his abdication papers; and Frogmore House, where he is buried. Other notable locations include the Château de Candé in France, where he married Wallis Simpson, and the Bahamas, where he served as governor during World War II.

GEORGE VI
(1936 - 1952)

George VI's reign is remembered as a time of hardship, suffering, and uncertainty. After serving in the Royal Navy and Royal Air Force during World War One, George unexpectedly found himself as the King of The United Kingdom during World War Two. Following his older brother Edward VIII's shocking abdication of the throne, George embarked on a fifteen-year-long reign that saw the eventual break-up of the British Empire, the beginning of the Commonwealth, the Second World War, and the Independence of India and Pakistan. For his public displays of support for the besieged people of London during the Blitz, his respectable family life, and his belief in equal rights for all men and women, George VI is one of Britain's best-loved monarchs.

Key Facts about George VI

- King George VI was born on 14th December 1895 at York Cottage, Sandringham.
- He succeeded as George VI King of The United Kingdom and the British Dominions overseas on December 11th
- George VI married Lady Elizabeth Bowes-Lyon on April 26th, 1923 in Westminster Abbey when he was age 28 and she was 22.
- King George VI died of cancer aged 56 on February 6th, 1952 following a reign of 15 years.

The Life of George VI

George VI, known informally as Albert, was born the second son of King George V, formerly Prince George Duke of York, and Queen Mary. George was the great-grandson of Queen Victoria and was born on the 14th of December, the anniversary of the death of Victoria's beloved husband, Albert. In memory of his great-grandfather George, was named Albert Frederick Arthur George and known formally as "His Highness Prince Albert of York" from birth. Behind his grandfather, father, and older brother, Albert was fourth in line to Victoria's throne.

As with most aristocratic families of the early 20th century, Albert was mostly separated from his mother and father during his childhood. Young Albert suffered from ill health and was beset by various developmental problems. The young prince had stomach issues that lasted well into adulthood, problems with his legs that forced him to wear corrective splints, and a stammer that made speaking in public difficult. It was this verbal tic that inspired the 2010 film The King's Speech in which the King, played by Colin Firth, overcomes his stammer with the help of a therapist in order to address the nation at the outbreak of World War Two.

Albert trained to become a naval officer on board HMS Cumberland and HMS Collingwood. In 1916, Albert saw active duty during the World War One Battle of Jutland. In 1918, he transferred from the Royal Navy to the Royal Air Force where he became a fully qualified pilot and commanding officer of a squadron on the cadet wing. Albert studied at Trinity College, Cambridge following the First World War and took a more active role in the duties of the royal family. As President of the Industrial Welfare Society, Albert became interested in British Industry, particularly the working conditions of people from low-income backgrounds, and was nicknamed the 'Industrial Prince'.

In 1923 Albert finally married the woman he had been pursuing for the last three years, Lady Elizabeth Bowes-Lyon. Albert chose Lady Elizabeth to be his wife without the permission of his family or the church and as Lady Elizabeth was not of royal blood this was considered a modernizing move. The couple's marriage was a great success and with Elizabeth's support, Albert sought the help of professional speech therapist Lionel Logue and gradually overcame the stammer that had plagued his adult life. Albert and Elizabeth had two children, Elizabeth, who succeeded Albert as Queen Elizabeth II, and Margaret. Both girls were raised by their parents within the close family household of 145 Piccadilly.

When King George V died on 20th January 1936, Prince Edward succeeded him to the throne as King Edward VIII. For many Edward was an undesirable King. King George V himself had expressed his wish that Albert become King before he died but Edward ascended as the law dictated. Less than a year later, Edward abdicated his right to the throne in order to marry his lover Wallis Simpson, an American socialite and divorcée. Some believe Edward was forced to abdicate his position while others believe that he was happy to do it. Either way, the crown now belonged on Albert's head and he reluctantly took control of the kingdom.

The transfer of power was not straightforward as Edward thought he should retain the title of 'His Royal Highness' as well as the titles, positions, and properties he had formerly enjoyed. King George VI disagreed and although he bestowed Edward with the new title 'His Royal Highness the Duke of Windsor', he also ensured that the new title made any wife or children of Edward's ineligible for royal titles. King George was forced to buy Balmoral Castle and Sandringham House from Edward as these were private properties that once belonged to Queen Victoria and did not pass automatically with the crown.

During his first years as King George, as Albert was now known, he made state visits to France, Canada, and the United States of America, becoming the first British monarch to ever set foot in the USA. These public displays of friendship were timely as within the year, Great Britain was at war with Germany. King George VI worked closely with Prime Minister Winston Churchill in the war effort and remained resident at Buckingham Palace in London throughout the war, despite the palace being bombed nine times.

Keeping a high profile and instilling in the public a strong sense of British identity, the King and Queen visited heavily bombed areas of East London and munitions factories throughout the United Kingdom during the war. King George also made visits to military forces abroad in France, North Africa, and Malta. In June 1944, King George visited British troops on the beaches at Normandy, ten days after D-Day.

On VE day, the King and Queen's official residence of Buckingham Palace was at the center of the country's celebrations with crowds reportedly chanting 'We want the King' outside the building. The King emerged and invited Prime Minister Winston Churchill to appear on the balcony alongside him to the crowd's rapturous applause; an act that secured King George VI's popularity with the people.

Clement Atlee took over as Prime Minister of the United Kingdom following the Second World War and, overseen by King George, was responsible for ushering in the rapid transformation of the British Empire from one kingdom into a series of associated but independent states known as the Commonwealth. The segregation of India and Pakistan took place in 1947 and King George was no longer known as the Emperor of India but was instead the Head of the Commonwealth. Three independent states left the commonwealth in the next few years including Burma, now Myanmar, Palestine, and the Republic of Ireland.

The intense stress and hardship of George VI's reign severely damaged his health. The war had ruined Britain's economy, a situation made bleaker by the dismantling of the British Empire and the beginning of the Cold War. The tensions of the post-war period exasperated King George's health problems, which by this time included lung cancer and arteriosclerosis. The King failed to recover from an operation to remove his left lung which contained a malignant tumor and he died in his sleep on 6th February 1952, aged 56. King George's daughter Elizabeth and her husband, the Duke of Edinburgh, were part-way through a tour of Africa when she heard of his death and she returned to the UK as Queen Elizabeth II.

Legacy of George VI

Despite the hardships experienced by the British people during King George VI's reign, the public opinion of the monarch was a favorable one. The people had endured the desperation and loss of World War Two and saw the influence of imperial power wane and yet public faith in the monarchy was high. King George spoke at the first UN assembly of 1946 in London, proclaiming 'our faith in the equal rights of men and women and of nations great and small'.

The King instituted the George Cross and George Medal

during his reign in acknowledgment of the bravery of individual citizens and nations during warfare. George was awarded the Ordre de la Liberation by the French government following his death, Winston Churchill was the only other individual to receive the award following 1946.

Films and TV Shows Featuring George VI

- A Royal Night Out (2015)
- Hyde Park on Hudson (2012)
- E. (2011)
- The King's Speech (2010)
- Bertie and Elizabeth (2002) TV Series
- The Royal Family at War (1995) TV Series

Further Research

- Philip Zeigler (2014) George VI: The Dutiful King
- Judd Dennis (2012) George VI
- Sarah Bradford (1989) King George VI
- C.G. Matthew (2004) George VI (1895 – 1952)
- Duke of Windsor (1952) A King's Story
- Sir John Wheeler-Bennet (1958) King George VI: His Life and Reign

Locations Related to King George VI

- During his reign, George lived primarily at Buckingham Palace, parts of which are open to visits from the public.
- King George was born and died at Sandringham House in Norfolk. Sandringham still belongs to the royal family but is open to visits from the public.
- A statue of George VI is located at Carlton Gardens in London.
- Many places have been named after George VI since his death. These include the King George Hospital in London, King George VI Reservoir in Surrey, and the King

George VI Chase, a horse race in the United Kingdom.
- King George VI is buried in St George's Chapel in Windsor Castle, the chapel is open to visitors.

ELIZABETH II
(1952 - 2022)

Elizabeth Alexandra Mary Windsor was arguably the world's most recognizable monarch, serving as Queen of the United Kingdom and Head of the Commonwealth for over 70 years. Her reign spanned post-war austerity, the transformation of empire into Commonwealth, and the dawn of the digital age, making her both a link to Britain's past and a symbol of its modern identity.

Key Facts about Elizabeth II

- Born: April 21, 1926, at 17 Bruton Street, London
- Became Queen: February 6, 1952, aged 25
- Coronation: June 2, 1953, at Westminster Abbey
- Married: Philip Mountbatten (later Duke of Edinburgh) on November 20, 1947
- Children: Charles, Anne, Andrew, and Edward
- Died: September 8, 2022, at Balmoral Castle, Scotland
- Notable for: Longest-reigning British monarch, modernizing the monarchy, stabilizing the Commonwealth

Early Life

Born third in line to the throne, Princess Elizabeth was not expected to become Queen. The abdication of her uncle Edward VIII in 1936 placed her father on the throne as George VI and made her heir presumptive. Her childhood was marked by the growing shadow of World War II, during which she and her sister Margaret were moved to Windsor Castle for safety. At 14, she made her first radio broadcast to evacuated children, and at 18, she joined the Auxiliary Territorial Service, training as a driver and mechanic.

Accession and Early Reign

Elizabeth was in Kenya when she learned of her father's death on February 6, 1952. Her coronation the following year was the first to be televised, marking a new era of royal accessibility. Her early reign saw her navigate the challenges of being a young female monarch in a male-dominated world, while also raising a young family.

Modernizing the Monarchy

Throughout her reign, Elizabeth worked to modernize the monarchy while preserving its traditions. She initiated the "walkabout," meeting people face-to-face on royal visits. In 1969, she allowed cameras into the palace for the documentary "Royal Family," though she later regretted this level of access. She opened parts of Buckingham Palace to the public to help fund Windsor Castle's restoration after the 1992 fire.

Challenges and Triumphs

The Queen faced numerous challenges during her reign. 1992, her "annus horribilis," saw three of her children's marriages collapse and Windsor Castle severely damaged by fire. The death of Diana, Princess of Wales in 1997 created a crisis when the Queen's traditional reserve seemed out of step with public emotion. Yet she adapted, making an unprecedented broadcast to the nation that helped heal the rift between palace and public.

Constitutional Role

Elizabeth II took her role as constitutional monarch seriously, holding weekly audiences with fifteen Prime Ministers from Winston Churchill to Liz Truss. She never gave interviews or expressed political opinions publicly, maintaining the neutrality essential to a constitutional monarch. Her Christmas broadcasts became a tradition, offering rare glimpses of her personal views on faith and society.

Commonwealth Leadership

As Head of the Commonwealth, Elizabeth II helped transform the organization from a remnant of empire into a voluntary association of independent nations. She visited every Commonwealth country multiple times and was particularly proud of the Commonwealth's growth and evolution during her reign.

Personal Life

The Queen's marriage to Philip, Duke of Edinburgh lasted 73 years until his death in 2021. Their partnership was central to her reign's success, with Philip's support allowing her to fulfill her duties while raising their four children. She was known for her love of horses and dogs, particularly corgis, and maintained a private persona despite living such a public life.

Legacy

Elizabeth II's reign saw Britain transform from a post-war imperial power to a modern European state. She provided stability through decades of social change, adapting the monarchy while maintaining its essential character. Her dedication to duty and service set a standard for modern monarchy, while her personal qualities of steadfastness and dignity earned respect worldwide.

The Queen died at Balmoral on September 8, 2022, ending the second Elizabethan age. Her death prompted global mourning and reflection on how she had shaped both monarchy and nation through seven decades of service.

Viewing History

Films and TV shows featuring Elizabeth II include "The Queen" (2006), "A Royal Night Out" (2015), and "The Crown" (2016-2023). The various actresses who have portrayed her include

Claire Foy, Olivia Colman, Imelda Staunton, and Helen Mirren, who won an Oscar for her portrayal.

Places to Visit

- Buckingham Palace: The Queen's official London residence
- Windsor Castle: Her preferred weekend home
- Sandringham House: Where the royal family traditionally spends Christmas
- Balmoral Castle: Her beloved Scottish residence and place of death
- Westminster Abbey: Site of her coronation and marriage
- St. George's Chapel, Windsor: Her final resting place alongside Prince Philip

CHARLES III
(2022-present)

The longest-waiting heir in British history, Charles III spent over 70 years as Prince of Wales before ascending to the throne in 2022. His life has encompassed dramatic social change, personal controversies, and pioneering environmental advocacy, making him one of the most scrutinized and complex royal figures of modern times.

Key Facts about Charles III

- Born: November 14, 1948, at Buckingham Palace
- Created Prince of Wales: July 1, 1958 (Invested 1969)
- First Marriage: Lady Diana Spencer, July 29, 1981 (Divorced 1996)
- Second Marriage: Camilla Parker Bowles, April 9, 2005
- Children: William (1982) and Harry (1984)
- Became King: September 8, 2022
- Coronation: May 6, 2023

Early Life and Education

Born to Princess Elizabeth and Prince Philip during the reign of his grandfather George VI, Charles became heir apparent at age three when his mother became Queen. Breaking with royal tradition, he attended school rather than being educated by tutors, first at Gordonstoun in Scotland (though he reportedly disliked its spartan regime) and later at Trinity College, Cambridge, becoming the first heir apparent to earn a university degree.

Prince of Wales

Created Prince of Wales in 1958, Charles was formally invested with the title at Caernarfon Castle in 1969. As Prince of Wales, he developed a wide range of interests and initiatives, particularly in environmental causes, architecture, and youth opportunity. His Prince's Trust, founded in 1976, has helped hundreds of thousands of young people into education and employment.

First Marriage and Family

Charles's marriage to Lady Diana Spencer in 1981 was dubbed a "fairy tale wedding," watched by millions worldwide. The couple had two sons, William and Harry, but the marriage became troubled. Their separation was announced in 1992, followed by divorce in 1996. Diana's death in 1997 created a crisis for the royal family and left Charles as a single father to two grieving teenagers.

Second Marriage and Later Years

In 2005, Charles married Camilla Parker Bowles, who became Duchess of Cornwall. This marriage proved more successful, with Camilla gradually winning public acceptance. As Prince of Wales, Charles increasingly took on more of the Queen's duties in her later years, particularly representing her at Commonwealth events.

Environmental Advocacy

Charles has been a consistent environmental advocate since the 1970s, long before it became mainstream. He converted Highgrove House to organic farming, launched sustainable initiatives, and has spoken frequently about climate change. His early warnings about plastic pollution and climate change, once dismissed as eccentric, are now seen as prescient.

The Working Prince

As Prince of Wales, Charles developed a unique working style, writing to ministers about concerns (the "black spider memos"), establishing charities, and speaking out on issues from architecture to alternative medicine. His approach sometimes proved controversial, raising questions about the proper role of the heir to the throne.

Architectural and Urban Planning Interests

His interventions in architectural debates and the creation of Poundbury, an experimental new town in Dorset built according to his architectural principles, demonstrated his willingness to put ideas into practice. While controversial among modernist architects, his advocacy for traditional design and sustainable urban planning has influenced discussions about how communities should be built.

Becoming King

Charles became King immediately upon his mother's death on September 8, 2022. His first acts as monarch showed both continuity with his mother's style and his own distinctive approach. His coronation in 2023 was notably shorter and more inclusive than his mother's in 1953, reflecting his desire for a modernized monarchy.

Properties and Residences

- Clarence House: His London residence as Prince of Wales
- Highgrove House: His beloved country home in Gloucestershire
- Birkhall: His private residence on the Balmoral estate
- Buckingham Palace: Now his official London residence as King

Legacy as Prince of Wales

Charles's long tenure as heir gave him time to develop initiatives and interests that have had lasting impact. His environmental advocacy, though once mocked, proved ahead of its time. The Prince's Trust has helped over a million young people. His willingness to engage with controversial issues, while sometimes criticized, showed a determination to make the role of Prince of Wales meaningful.

Looking Forward

As King, Charles III faces the challenge of maintaining the monarchy's relevance while respecting its traditions. His decades of preparation and clear vision for the role suggest he will continue to adapt the institution while maintaining its essential character.

The reign of Charles III represents both continuity and change - continuity with his mother's dedication to service, but change in his more outspoken approach to issues he considers important. How he balances these aspects may define not just his reign but the future of the monarchy itself.

Places Associated with Charles III

- Buckingham Palace: His birthplace and current official residence
- Highgrove House: His personal creation, known for its organic gardens
- Clarence House: His London home as Prince of Wales
- Caernarfon Castle: Site of his investiture as Prince of Wales
- Poundbury: The town he created as an experiment in urban planning

Screen Portrayals

Notable dramatizations of Charles's life have focused primarily on his years as Prince of Wales, particularly his relationship with Diana. Key portrayals include:

Films

- "The Queen" (2006) - Alex Jennings portrayed Charles

during the aftermath of Diana's death
- "Diana" (2013) - Douglas Hodge as Charles opposite Naomi Watts as Diana
- "Spencer" (2021) - Jack Farthing played Charles in this psychological drama about Diana
- "William & Catherine: A Royal Romance" (2011) - Victor Garber as Charles
- "Whatever Love Means" (2005) - Laurence Fox in a TV movie about Charles and Camilla's early relationship

Television Series

- "The Crown" (1990s-2020s) - Multiple actors have played Charles:
- Josh O'Connor (Seasons 3-4) - Won an Emmy for his portrayal of young Charles
- Dominic West (Seasons 5-6) - Portraying middle-aged Charles
- "Charles & Diana: A Royal Love Story" (1982) - David Robb as Charles
- "The Royal House of Windsor" (2017) - Documentary series featuring extensive coverage of Charles
- "King Charles III" (2017) - Tim Pigott-Smith in an adaptation of Mike Bartlett's speculative play about Charles becoming king
- "Charles: The Private Man, The Public Role" (1994) - Documentary with unprecedented access to Charles himself

Documentary Appearances

Charles has appeared as himself in numerous documentaries, notably:

- "A Prince Among Men" (2008)
- "Prince Charles at 70" (2018)
- "The Prince's Trust: 30 Years" (2006)

- "The Prince and the Composer" (2011) - About his appreciation of Hubert Parry's music
- "Harmony: A New Way of Looking at Our World" (2012) - Based on his book about sustainable living

These portrayals reflect changing public perceptions of Charles over time, from romantic leading man in the 1980s, through the troubled years of his first marriage, to more sympathetic recent depictions of his environmental advocacy and preparation for kingship.

Charles III's story is still being written, but his long apprenticeship as Prince of Wales has already left a significant legacy in areas from environmental awareness to youth opportunity. His reign offers the possibility of a monarchy that combines tradition with engagement in modern concerns.

APPENDIX I
CURRENT LINE OF SUCCESSION

King Charles III currently reigns as Britain's monarch, having ascended to the throne in September 2022. Below him, a clear line of succession ensures the continuity of the British monarchy. Here are the first 26 people in line to the throne:

1. William, Prince of Wales (b. 1982)

The eldest son of King Charles III and the late Princess Diana, William serves as heir apparent. A former air ambulance pilot, he now works full-time as a senior royal, focusing on environmental causes, mental health awareness, and homelessness. Married to Catherine (Kate) Middleton, he balances royal duties with raising their three children.

2. Prince George of Wales (b. 2013)

William and Catherine's eldest child, George represents the future of the monarchy. Currently attending Lambrook School, he's being gradually introduced to royal duties while maintaining as normal a childhood as possible within his unique position.

3. Princess Charlotte of Wales (b. 2015)

The second child of William and Catherine benefits from the Succession to the Crown Act 2013, which ended male preference primogeniture. A student at Lambrook School alongside her brothers, Charlotte has shown early poise at public events.

4. Prince Louis of Wales (b. 2018)

The youngest child of William and Catherine has captured public attention with his spirited appearances at royal events. Like his siblings, he attends Lambrook School.

5. Prince Harry, Duke of Sussex (b. 1984)

The younger son of King Charles III and Princess Diana now resides in California with his family. Despite stepping back from senior royal duties in 2020, he retains his place in the succession.

6. Prince Archie of Sussex (b. 2019)

Harry's eldest child with Meghan Markle lives in California. His birth marked a significant moment as one of the first mixed-race members of the British royal family.

7. Princess Lilibet of Sussex (b. 2021)

Named after her great-grandmother Queen Elizabeth II's family nickname, Lilibet lives in California with her parents and brother.

8. Prince Andrew, Duke of York (b. 1960)

The second son of Queen Elizabeth II stepped back from public duties in 2019 due to controversies surrounding his associations. Despite this, he remains in the line of succession.

9. Princess Beatrice (b. 1988)

The elder daughter of Prince Andrew and Sarah Ferguson works in business while maintaining some charitable patronages. She married Edoardo Mapelli Mozzi in 2020.

10. Sienna Mapelli Mozzi (b. 2021)

Daughter of Princess Beatrice and Edoardo Mapelli Mozzi, Sienna represents the next generation of the extended royal family.

11. Athena Elizabeth Rose Mapelli Mozzi (b. 2025)

The second child of Princess Beatrice and Edoardo Mapelli Mozzi.

12. Princess Eugenie (b. 1990)

The younger daughter of Prince Andrew and Sarah Ferguson works in the art world while supporting various charities. She married Jack Brooksbank in 2018.

14. August Brooksbank (b. 2021)

Son of Princess Eugenie and Jack Brooksbank, August was named partly in honor of Queen Victoria's consort Prince Albert, who had Augustus as a middle name.

14. Ernest Brooksbank (b. 2023)

The second son of Princess Eugenie and Jack Brooksbank, Ernest was named after his paternal great-great-great-grandfather.

15. Prince Edward, Duke of Edinburgh (b. 1964)

The youngest son of Queen Elizabeth II works full-time as a senior royal, having taken on many of his late father's responsibilities, particularly with the Duke of Edinburgh's Award scheme.

16. James, Earl of Wessex (b. 2007)

The son of Prince Edward and Sophie, James maintains a relatively private life while attending school.

17. Lady Louise Mountbatten-Windsor (b. 2003)

Edward and Sophie's elder child, Louise is a university student who occasionally participates in royal events.

18. Princess Anne, The Princess Royal (b. 1950)

The only daughter of Queen Elizabeth II is known for her extensive charitable work and was previously an Olympic equestrian. She's consistently ranked as one of the hardest-working royals.

19. Peter Phillips (b. 1977)

Anne's son works in sports and event management. Despite being the Queen's eldest grandchild, he holds no royal title due to his mother's wish for her children to live more normal lives.

20. Savannah Phillips (b. 2010)

Peter's elder daughter with his former wife Autumn Kelly lives a relatively private life while occasionally appearing at major royal events.

21. Isla Phillips (b. 2012)

Peter's younger daughter also maintains a private life while participating in family gatherings.

22. Zara Tindall (b. 1981)

Princess Anne's daughter followed in her mother's footsteps as an accomplished equestrian, winning an Olympic silver medal. She's married to former rugby player Mike Tindall.

23. Mia Tindall (b. 2014)

Zara and Mike's eldest daughter often appears at equestrian

events supporting her mother.

24. Lena Tindall (b. 2018)

The second daughter of Zara and Mike Tindall continues the family's tradition of living a relatively normal life while maintaining royal connections.

25. Lucas Tindall (b. 2021)

The youngest child and only son of Zara and Mike Tindall was born at home in a surprise delivery.

26. David Armstrong-Jones, 2nd Earl of Snowdon (b. 1961)

The son of the late Princess Margaret and Antony Armstrong-Jones, he works as a furniture maker and businessman while occasionally attending royal events.

This line of succession represents the evolving face of the British monarchy, combining traditional roles with modern lives and careers. While some members maintain active royal duties, others pursue private careers while retaining their places in this historic lineage.

APPENDIX 2
BURIAL PLACES OF THE MONARCHS

England's rich history is filled with stories of monarchs and their legacies. The burial places of England's kings and queens are a testament to the country's royal heritage and offer a glimpse into the lives of those who ruled over the nation. From Westminster Abbey to St George's Chapel at Windsor Castle and even as far away as Germany and France, the final resting places of these rulers reveal a fascinating narrative of power, religion, and tradition. This article presents a comprehensive list of the burial locations of England's kings and queens, from the early Plantagenets to the present-day Windsors. Join us on a journey through time to discover where the likes of Henry VIII, Elizabeth I, and Queen Victoria were laid to rest and explore the symbolism and significance of their final resting places.

- King William the Conqueror: Saint-Étienne Abbey (Abbaye-aux-Hommes), Caen, France
- King William II: Winchester Cathedral, Hampshire, England
- King Henry I: Reading Abbey, Berkshire, England (ruins)
- King Stephen: Faversham Abbey, Kent, England (destroyed)
- Empress Matilda: Rouen Cathedral, Normandy, France
- King Henry II: Fontevraud Abbey, Anjou, France
- King Richard I: Fontevraud Abbey, Anjou, France (heart at Rouen Cathedral)
- King John: Worcester Cathedral, Worcestershire, England
- King Henry III - Westminster Abbey
- King Edward I - Westminster Abbey
- King Edward II - Gloucester Cathedral
- King Edward III - Westminster Abbey
- King Richard II - Westminster Abbey
- King Henry IV - Canterbury Cathedral

- King Henry V - Westminster Abbey
- King Henry VI - Windsor Castle
- King Edward IV - St George's Chapel, Windsor Castle
- King Edward V - Unknown (disappeared in 1483)
- King Richard III - Leicester Cathedral
- King Henry VII - Westminster Abbey
- King Henry VIII - St George's Chapel, Windsor Castle
- King Edward VI - Westminster Abbey
- Queen Mary I - Westminster Abbey
- Queen Elizabeth I - Westminster Abbey
- King James I - Westminster Abbey
- King Charles I - St George's Chapel, Windsor Castle
- King Charles II - Westminster Abbey
- King James II - St. Germain-en-Laye, France
- King William III - Westminster Abbey
- Queen Mary II - Westminster Abbey
- Queen Anne - St George's Chapel, Windsor Castle
- King George I - Hanover, Germany
- King George II - Westminster Abbey
- King George III - Windsor Castle
- King George IV - St George's Chapel, Windsor Castle
- King William IV - St George's Chapel, Windsor Castle
- Queen Victoria - Frogmore Mausoleum, Windsor Castle
- King Edward VII - St George's Chapel, Windsor Castle
- King George V - St George's Chapel, Windsor Castle
- King Edward VIII - Frogmore Estate, Windsor
- King George VI - St George's Chapel, Windsor Castle
- Queen Elizabeth II - St George's Chapel, Windsor Castle

APPENDIX 3
TURNING POINTS: TEN EVENTS THAT SHAPED THE CROWN

The thousand-year history of the British monarchy has been marked by moments of dramatic change that transformed not just who wore the crown, but what that crown meant. Here are the ten most pivotal moments that shaped the institution we know today.

Norman Conquest

The Norman Conquest of 1066 was perhaps the most transformative moment in English history. When William the Conqueror defeated Harold Godwinson at Hastings, he didn't just change who sat on the throne – he revolutionized English society. The Norman invasion brought feudalism, transformed the English language, and established a new dynasty that connects directly to today's monarchy. Every British monarch since has traced their legitimacy back to William's conquest.

Wars of the Roses

The Wars of the Roses (1455-1487) tore apart medieval England as the houses of Lancaster and York fought for the crown. The conflict destroyed the Plantagenet dynasty that had ruled since 1154 and gave rise to the Tudors when Henry VII united the warring houses through his marriage to Elizabeth of York. The wars demonstrated how destructive dynastic uncertainty could be and led to stronger emphasis on clear succession rules.

The English Reformation

Henry VIII's Break with Rome in 1534 redefined the very nature of English monarchy. By declaring himself Supreme Head of the Church of England, Henry transformed the crown from a purely political institution into a religious one as well. This dual role as both political and religious leader remains part of the monarchy today, with the Sovereign still serving as Supreme Governor of the Church of England.

The Civil Wars

The Civil Wars and Interregnum (1642-1660) represented the greatest challenge to monarchical rule in British history. The conflict between Crown and Parliament led to the execution of Charles I, Britain's only experiment with republicanism under Cromwell, and ultimately the restoration of Charles II. The period permanently weakened the doctrine of divine right and established Parliament's role in governing alongside the monarch.

The Glorious Revolution

The Glorious Revolution of 1688 created constitutional monarchy as we know it. When Parliament invited William and Mary to replace James II, it established its right to determine succession and limit royal power. The Bill of Rights of 1689 codified these principles, creating a system where monarchs reign with Parliament's consent rather than by divine right alone.

The Act of Union

The Act of Union in 1707 transformed the nature of British monarchy by uniting the English and Scottish crowns permanently. Though the crowns had been held by the same person since 1603, this act created a new Kingdom of Great Britain, fundamentally changing what it meant to be British monarch. No longer ruler of separate kingdoms, the Sovereign became head of a united nation.

The Victorian Era

The Victorian Era marked perhaps the most important peaceful transformation of the monarchy. Queen Victoria and Prince Albert redefined the institution's role, moving it away from direct political power toward ceremonial leadership and moral example. They created the model of monarchy as a symbol of national unity and family values that continues today.

Empire to Commonwealth

The evolution from Empire to Commonwealth fundamentally changed the monarch's global role. As the British Empire transformed into the Commonwealth of Nations, the Crown adapted from an imperial institution to a symbolic head of a voluntary association of independent nations. This transformation, largely complete by 1949, created the modern Commonwealth role that remains one of the monarchy's most important functions.

The Abdication Crisis

The Abdication Crisis of 1936, when Edward VIII chose to give up the throne to marry Wallis Simpson, established modern expectations about royal duty. The crisis demonstrated that personal desires must be subordinate to the role's responsibilities, a principle that has guided royal behavior ever since. It also unexpectedly gave Britain one of its most dedicated monarchs in George VI.

The UK as We Know It

Finally, the creation of the modern United Kingdom in 1922 following Irish independence established the current territorial scope of the monarchy. The partition of Ireland and creation of the United Kingdom of Great Britain and Northern Ireland defined the modern state over which the monarch reigns, though their role as Head of the Commonwealth maintains their global influence.

These events collectively transformed the British monarchy from a medieval institution of personal rule into a modern constitutional monarchy. Each crisis or change forced the institution to adapt, demonstrating the remarkable resilience that has allowed it to survive while other European monarchies fell. Understanding these pivotal moments helps us comprehend both how the British monarchy reached its current form and why it continues to evolve.

APPENDIX 4
A GUIDE TO BRITAIN'S ROYAL PALACES

From Medieval Fortresses to Modern Homes: Here's your complete guide to Britain's royal residences, both past and present.

Currently Used Royal Residences

Buckingham Palace

The most famous royal building in Britain, Buckingham Palace has been the official London residence of British monarchs since Queen Victoria's reign. Originally built as Buckingham House in 1703, it was acquired by George III in 1761 as a private residence. The palace we know today was largely designed by John Nash and completed in 1837. The State Rooms are open to visitors during summer months, and the iconic Changing of the Guard ceremony takes place in the forecourt. The palace has 775 rooms and the largest private garden in London.

How to visit: State Rooms are open typically July-October. Book through Royal Collection Trust.

Windsor Castle

The oldest and largest inhabited castle in the world, Windsor has been a royal residence for over 900 years. William the Conqueror chose the site, and every monarch since has added to or modified the castle. It's still used regularly by the Royal Family, particularly for weekends, and became King Charles's primary residence. The castle survived a devastating fire in 1992 and was magnificently restored.

How to visit: Open year-round except for specific dates. The State Apartments, Queen Mary's Dolls' House, and St. George's Chapel are highlights.

Palace of Holyroodhouse

The official residence of the monarch in Scotland, Holyroodhouse sits at the end of Edinburgh's Royal Mile. The palace began as a monastery in 1128 but is most famous for its associations with Mary, Queen of Scots. The State Apartments reflect the palace's baroque makeover by Charles II and are used by Charles III during 'Holyrood Week'.

How to visit: Open year-round except during royal visits.

Historic Royal Residences

Hampton Court Palace

Perhaps the most magnificent Tudor palace remaining, Hampton Court is forever associated with Henry VIII. Originally built for Cardinal Wolsey (who gave it to Henry to try to retain favor), it features Tudor kitchens, a famous maze, and beautiful gardens. The palace was later partly rebuilt in baroque style by William III and Mary II.

How to visit: Open daily, managed by Historic Royal Palaces.

Tower of London

More fortress than palace, the Tower has served as castle, prison, mint, and menagerie. Built by William the Conqueror to dominate London, it housed medieval kings in the White Tower. Today it's home to the Crown Jewels and the famous ravens.

How to visit: Open daily, managed by Historic Royal Palaces. Book ahead to avoid queues.

Kensington Palace

Currently home to the Prince and Princess of Wales among others, Kensington Palace became a royal residence when William III and Mary II bought it in 1689. Queen Victoria was born here. The State Rooms are open to the public while other areas remain private royal apartments.

How to visit: State Rooms open daily, managed by Historic Royal Palaces.

St James's Palace

The most senior royal palace, built by Henry VIII. While no longer the Sovereign's primary residence, it remains the official seat of the monarchy where foreign ambassadors are accredited. Parts are used as royal apartments but it's not open to the public.

Former Royal Residences

Palace of Whitehall

Once the largest palace in Europe with over 1,500 rooms, Whitehall was the main residence of English monarchs from 1530 to 1698. Destroyed by fire, only the Banqueting House remains, featuring a magnificent ceiling painted by Rubens.

How to visit: Banqueting House open to visitors most days.

Palace of Westminster

Before becoming the Houses of Parliament, this was the primary royal residence in London from the 11th to 16th centuries. Westminster Hall remains from the medieval palace.

How to visit: Tours available when Parliament isn't sitting.

Private Royal Residences

Highgrove House

Located near Tetbury in Gloucestershire, Highgrove House has been the private residence of King Charles III since 1980, when he purchased it while still Prince of Wales. The house itself is a nine-bedroom, Georgian neoclassical building dating from the 1780s, but it's the gardens that have made Highgrove famous. Over more than 40 years, Charles transformed the grounds into a stunning example of organic and sustainable gardening, creating what many consider his most personal legacy.

How to visit: While the house itself remains private, the gardens are open to the public through pre-booked tours from April to October. Tours must be booked in advance through the Highgrove Gardens website. All visitors must bring photo ID, and no photography is permitted. The estate's shop and restaurant, the Orchard Room, are open to visitors. All profits from garden tours and the shop go to The Prince's Foundation.

Highgrove represents something unique among royal residences - it's perhaps the most personal expression of a monarch's interests and beliefs, transformed from a typical country house into a showcase for sustainable living and organic gardening principles. It's also unusual in that it was purchased by Charles himself, rather than being an inherited royal property or owned by the Crown Estate.

Sandringham House

The private Norfolk estate of the Royal Family since 1862, this is where they traditionally spend Christmas. The house and gardens are open to visitors when not in use by the family.

Balmoral Castle

The Scottish private residence of the Royal Family since Prince Albert purchased it for Queen Victoria. The grounds and gardens are open to the public from April to July, but the castle's main rooms are private.

Bonus:

The Royal Yacht Britannia

Often referred to as "The Queen's Floating Palace," HMY Britannia served the Royal Family for over 44 years, traveling over a million nautical miles and completing 968 official voyages. Launched in 1953 and decommissioned in 1997, Britannia was a unique combination of royal residence, diplomatic venue, and working ship.

The yacht measured 412 feet in length and was crewed by 240 Royal Yachtsmen. The interior was designed with both comfort and function in mind, featuring:

The decision to decommission Britannia was made by the government in 1994, and her last official voyage was to retrieve the last Governor of Hong Kong, Chris Patten, following the handover to China in 1997. The Queen notably shed a tear at the decommissioning ceremony, one of the rare public displays of emotion in her reign.

How to visit:

Britannia is now permanently moored in Edinburgh's port of Leith and is one of Scotland's most popular tourist attractions. Visitors can tour five decks with an audio guide (available in multiple languages). The tour includes the State Apartments, crew's quarters, engine room, and Royal Deck Tea Room where visitors can enjoy tea and cakes.

APPENDIX 5
ROYAL FILMS: A GUIDE TO THE BEST MOVIES ABOUT THE BRITISH MONARCHY

The King's Speech (2010)

Colin Firth's Oscar-winning portrayal of George VI shows the future king struggling with his stammer while facing the crisis of his brother's abdication and the looming threat of World War II. Notable for its historical accuracy and intimate portrayal of the relationship between the King and his speech therapist Lionel Logue (Geoffrey Rush). This film masterfully captures both the personal struggles and public duties of monarchy.

The Queen (2006)

Helen Mirren delivers a masterful performance as Elizabeth II during the week following Princess Diana's death. The film explores the tension between traditional royal protocol and public expectations of emotional display, offering a nuanced look at how the monarchy adapted to changing times. Particularly notable for showing the relationship between the Queen and Prime Minister Tony Blair.

Elizabeth (1998)

Cate Blanchett's breakout role as the young Elizabeth I, following her journey from vulnerable princess to powerful queen. The film focuses on the early years of her reign, including the challenges of being a female monarch in a male-dominated world and the political intrigue surrounding her court. While it takes some historical liberties, it captures the essence of Elizabeth's transformation into the "Virgin Queen."

Elizabeth: The Golden Age (2007)

The sequel follows Elizabeth I during the Spanish Armada crisis and her complicated relationship with Sir Walter Raleigh. While more dramatically stylized than its predecessor, it showcases Elizabeth at the height of her power and the personal sacrifices required by her position.

The Young Victoria (2009)

Emily Blunt stars as Victoria in her early years as queen, focusing on her romance with Prince Albert and her early struggles to assert herself as monarch. The film is particularly strong in showing how a teenage queen learned to navigate political power and find her own voice.

The Madness of King George (1994)

Nigel Hawthorne gives a remarkable performance as George III, exploring the king's mental illness and its impact on both his family and the nation. The film provides insight into 18th-century attitudes toward mental health while examining the vulnerability of royal power.

Mrs. Brown (1997)

Judi Dench plays Queen Victoria during her period of intense grief following Prince Albert's death, focusing on her controversial relationship with Scottish servant John Brown. The film explores themes of duty, grief, and the human side of monarchy.

Spencer (2021)

Kristen Stewart's portrayal of Princess Diana focuses on three days during Christmas at Sandringham, as she decides to end her marriage to Prince Charles. While taking creative liberties with historical facts, the film is an artistic exploration of Diana's emotional state and the pressures of royal life.

The Other Boleyn Girl (2008)

While more focused on the Tudor court than royalty itself, this film starring Natalie Portman and Scarlett Johansson explores the political machinations that brought Anne Boleyn to the throne and her eventual downfall. Though historically questionable at times, it captures the dangerous nature of Tudor politics.

Honorable Mentions:

- The King (2019) - A revisionist take on Henry V starring Timothée Chalamet
- Victoria & Abdul (2017) - Judi Dench returns as Victoria in her later years
- Mary Queen of Scots (2018) - Saoirse Ronan and Margot Robbie as Mary and Elizabeth I
- A Royal Night Out (2015) - A lighthearted look at Princess Elizabeth and Princess Margaret on VE Day

APPENDIX 6
ROYAL TELEVISION: THE BEST SHOWS ABOUT THE BRITISH MONARCHY

While films offer snapshots of royal life, television series have the luxury of exploring the monarchy in greater depth. Here are the most significant TV shows about Britain's royal family:

The Crown (2016-2023)

Netflix's flagship royal drama stands as the most ambitious portrayal of the British monarchy ever attempted. Starting with Elizabeth II's marriage and early reign, the series spans decades with different actors portraying the royals at various ages. Claire Foy, Olivia Colman, and Imelda Staunton each brought their own interpretation to Elizabeth II, while the show tackled everything from the Suez Crisis to Diana's death. While historically controversial at times, its production values and attention to detail are unprecedented.

Victoria (2016-2019)

Jenna Coleman stars as the young Queen Victoria, following her from her accession at age 18 through her marriage to Prince Albert and into her role as mother and monarch. The series excels at showing Victoria's personal growth and the challenges of balancing duty with family life. Particularly strong on the political aspects of Victorian era monarchy.

The Tudors (2007-2010)

Jonathan Rhys Meyers leads this stylized take on Henry VIII's reign. While taking considerable liberties with historical accuracy (and everyone's appearance), it captures the drama and intensity of Tudor court life. The series particularly excels at showing the political and religious upheavals of Henry's reign.

Wolf Hall (2015)

Based on Hilary Mantel's acclaimed novels, this BBC adaptation stars Mark Rylance as Thomas Cromwell and Damian Lewis as Henry VIII. Notable for its historical accuracy and psychological depth, it offers a more nuanced view of Tudor politics than The Tudors.

Edward & Mrs. Simpson (1978)

This classic series remains one of the best examinations of the abdication crisis, with Edward Fox as Edward VIII. It takes a more sympathetic view of the relationship than modern portrayals while exploring the constitutional crisis it created.

The White Queen (2013)

Based on Philippa Gregory's novels, this series covers the Wars of the Roses from the perspective of the women involved. It's followed by The White Princess and The Spanish Princess, forming a trilogy that explores the transition from Plantagenet to Tudor rule.

The Virgin Queen (2005)

Anne-Marie Duff stars as Elizabeth I in this BBC series that follows her entire reign. Notable for its attention to historical detail and its exploration of Elizabeth's relationships with her advisors and courtiers.

Six Wives with Lucy Worsley (2016)

While technically a documentary series, Worsley's unique approach of combining traditional documentary elements with dramatic reconstructions (in which she appears as a silent servant) offers fresh insight into Henry VIII's marriages.

Elizabeth R (1971)

Glenda Jackson's portrayal of Elizabeth I in this BBC series set the standard for all future depictions. Known for its historical accuracy and powerful performances, it remains influential fifty years later.

Charles III (2017)

This BBC adaptation of Mike Bartlett's controversial play imagines Charles's accession to the throne and the constitutional crisis that follows. While speculative, it raises interesting questions about monarchy in modern Britain.

Remember that no television show can perfectly capture historical truth - they're interpretations influenced by both the period they're depicting and the period in which they're made. The best approach is to watch critically and use these shows as starting points for learning about the actual history they portray.

APPENDIX 7
ROYAL PROTOCOL: A GUIDE TO TITLES, STYLES, AND ETIQUETTE

The world of royal protocol can seem daunting at first glance, filled with complex titles and seemingly arcane rules of behavior. However, understanding the basics of how to address and interact with members of the Royal Family isn't as complicated as it might appear.

At the apex of the royal hierarchy stands the monarch. Currently, King Charles III is addressed as "His Majesty" (HM), and should first be addressed in person as "Your Majesty," followed by "Sir" in subsequent references. This same principle applies to the Queen Consort, Camilla, who is addressed as "Your Majesty" and then "Ma'am" (pronounced to rhyme with "jam," not "palm").

The children of the sovereign hold the style "His/Her Royal Highness" (HRH) and are princes or princesses in their own right. When meeting them, the first address should be "Your Royal Highness," followed by "Sir" or "Ma'am." The Prince and Princess of Wales, as heir apparent and his wife, follow this same protocol, though they hold a unique position in the hierarchy.

Grandchildren of the monarch present an interesting case. Those born to male heirs (like Prince William's children) receive the HRH style and prince/princess titles, while those born to female heirs traditionally take their father's title unless specifically granted royal status by the monarch.

When it comes to meeting members of the Royal Family, certain basic protocols are observed, though they're generally more relaxed than in previous generations. Physical contact should be limited to a handshake if offered by the royal. The traditional neck bow for men or small curtsy for women is customary but not mandatory for British citizens, and many choose simply to shake hands.

Conversation with royals follows its own etiquette. The golden rule is to allow them to initiate conversation and respond naturally but respectfully. Gone are the days when people were expected to walk backwards from the royal presence or follow elaborate rules about which piece of cutlery to use first (though formal dinners still follow standard formal dining etiquette).

Dress codes remain important when meeting royalty. For formal occasions, conservative business attire is appropriate unless otherwise specified. State banquets call for white tie and decorations, while garden parties typically require morning dress or lounge suits for men and day dresses with hats for women.

Written communication with the Royal Family maintains more traditional formality. Letters to the monarch should begin with "May it please Your Majesty" and end with "I have the honour to be, Sir/Madam, Your Majesty's most humble and obedient servant." Similar formal constructions are used when writing to other royal family members, though with appropriate adjustment to their titles.

The modern Royal Family has worked to make themselves more accessible while maintaining the dignity of their positions. Many traditional protocols have been relaxed, particularly at public events, and social media has brought new informality to royal communications. However, core principles of respect and recognition of the monarchy's constitutional role remain important.

Perhaps the most crucial thing to remember is that these protocols exist as guidelines rather than strict rules. Royal staff are always on hand to guide visitors through appropriate behavior, and the Royal Family understands that most people aren't familiar with every nuance of traditional etiquette. What matters most is showing sincere respect for the institution, rather than perfect adherence to every detail of protocol.

The key is to remain respectful while following the lead of royal staff and other guests. When in doubt, observe what others are doing and err on the side of formality. Remember that modern royals are generally more concerned with putting people at ease than enforcing rigid protocol. After all, these traditions exist to show respect for the institution of monarchy, not to create barriers between the Royal Family and the people they serve.

APPENDIX 8
THE UNCROWNED

Ever since the crowning of King William I in Westminster Abbey in 1066, the coronation of the British monarch has been a major affair for the United Kingdom. However, this grand ceremony has not been enjoyed by every individual to call themselves king or queen, and several never made it to this point. The reigns of these monarchs were short lived for various reasons from overthrow to abdication. Today, we're going to more deeply examine the circumstances behind four monarchs who never got the chance for their crowning glory. As you read, consider how history may have been different had their coronations occurred.

The first monarch to never receive the crown in Westminster Abbey was Empress Matilda. The daughter of King Henry I, Matilda was married off to Holy Roman Emperor Henry V, and it seemed like she was never going to have to worry about the English crown. However, when her younger brother William died, it left England with a succession crisis that was followed by the Anarchy, a civil war to determine who would be the next monarch. Henry I nominated Matilda as his heir, but that was not accepted by the Anglo-Norman court. After he died, the Norman nobles balked at the thought of Matilda as queen and instead installed her cousin, Stephen of Blois. She eventually came back in force and managed to capture Stephen. However, when she attempted to have her coronation in Westminster Abbey, Londoners rioted and threatened the safety of the proceedings. Due to the growing threat outside the church, the coronation was canceled and Matilda fled back to Normandy. However, while she was unsuccessful, her oldest son, King Henry II, succeeded in claiming the throne in 1154 after Stephen died.

Next up is King Edward V. Edward succeeded his father, Edward IV, at the age of twelve and only ruled for 86 days without being crowned. His is one of the more tragic stories in British history. King Edward IV nominated his brother, Richard, Duke of Gloucester, as Protector during his son's minority. Not long after his brother Edward died, Richard escorted the young Edward and his brother Richard, Duke of York, to the Tower of London, reportedly for their protection. Parliament then declared Richard to be the legitimate king, and the two boys were seen less and less until they disappeared altogether. What happened to the two "Princes in the Tower" has long been the subject of speculation among historians, and the most prominent theory is that King Richard III had them killed in order to secure his claim to the throne. The theory is supported by little historical evidence and mostly championed by William Shakespeare's play, Richard III. Eventually, the bones of two young children were discovered in the Tower of London and, thought to be the lost princes, were buried in Westminster Abbey.

Lady Jane Grey is another sad story in the tales of those who would be crowned. When fifteen-year-old King Edward VI was dying, he nominated his first cousin, once removed, Jane, to succeed him in his will. This cut off the claim of his sister Mary, who wasn't too happy with the result. Edward has sought to preserve a Protestant legacy by altering the succession to favor the Protestant Jane over the Catholic Mary. Mary then marched on London with an army, and the Privy Council switched their allegiance to her, imprisoning Jane in the Tower of London where she had been staying before her coronation. Originally set to be executed for treason, Mary initially spared Jane but then changed her mind and had Jane executed anyway. Mary's reason was that, following Wyatt's Rebellion against Mary's rule, she needed to remove the hope of the rebels that there could be any alternative to her. As such, Jane became another of the deaths that earned Queen Mary I the nickname "Bloody Mary".

The most recent uncrowned monarch is none other than King Edward VIII, the uncle of the late Queen Elizabeth II. Edward VIII was meant to succeed his father, George V, on the latter's death. He ascended to the throne on January 20, 1936, but his relationship with Wallis Simpson presented the British government with a problem. By law, the monarch is head of the Church of England, and the Church's as well as the Government's rules prevented the marriage of the monarch to a person who was divorced and whose ex-spouse was still living. Wallis Simpson had not one, but two divorces under her belt, and both men were alive. Edward was fully intent to go forward with both his coronation and his intended marriage to Wallis despite the protestations of Parliament. Edward's government threatened to resign in protest, which gave Edward little choice but to abdicate and name his brother, King George VI, as his successor. Edward went through with marrying Wallis, and the two spent much of World War II in the Caribbean before spending the rest of their lives in France.

APPENDIX 9
THE INTERREGNUM

After the execution of Charles I and the restoration of Charles II, England was for the first time without a monarch. The period between the two reigns, the interregnum, was an uneasy time during which the country was led by the deeply religious Oliver Cromwell. The Commonwealth was ahead of the times, but ultimately England rejected republicanism, and the restored monarchy survives to this day.

Key Facts

Key Dates

- 1649 Execution of King Charles I
- 1649 Council of State and Rump Parliament govern the Commonwealth of England
- 1653 Rump Parliament replaced with the Nominated Assembly
- 1653 Oliver Cromwell made Lord Protector
- 1655 Parliament dissolved; military rule begins
- 1658 Cromwell dies; his son Richard becomes Lord Protector
- 1659 The Protectorate ends; Parliament recalled
- 1660 Restoration of the monarchy

Key People

- King Charles I King of England, Scotland, and Ireland 1625 – 1649
- Oliver Cromwell Lord Protector 1653 – 1658
- Richard Cromwell Lord Protector 1658 – 1659
- King Charles II King of England, Scotland, and Ireland 1660 – 1685

The World Turned Upside Down

Until Charles I overplayed his divine right to rule, few in England had questioned the monarchy. Several kings had been usurped and killed, but it always followed that a new king took the place of the previous one. In the recent past, the conspirators of the Gunpowder Plot had sought to remove James I, but there was no question of the country going without a monarch as they planned to replace him with his young daughter. When Charles I fell foul of his government and the New Model Army, he was tried and executed and his son fled into exile. The Grandees of the New Model Army did not seek a successor for the king but instead decided to change the rules and find a new method of government.

The Grandees were the senior officers of the New Model Army, largely drawn from the landed gentry. Chief amongst them was Oliver Cromwell, Sir Thomas Fairfax, and Cromwell's son-in-law, Henry Ireton. The Grandees set about forcibly removing their opposition in the House of Commons using troops under the command of Colonel Thomas Pride. "Pride's Purge" left a smaller "Rump Parliament". With control of the Rump Parliament, the Grandees were able to set up the trial of the King and after his execution, create a "Commonwealth and Free State".

The Rump abolished not just the monarchy but the Privy Council and the House of Lords. In place of the Privy Council, the Rump established the English Council of State which was comprised of selected Members of Parliament. This body held the executive power and the Rump had legislative power. However, there was another power in the country that the Rump could not ultimately control: the Army.

The Army was kept busy in the period following the king's execution. There was a potential for invasion from Scotland, trouble in Ireland, and the threat of a Royalist uprising. Cromwell was occupied fighting the dangers that jeopardized the country, but by 1653 he had neutralized any threats. The Rump had done well in stabilizing the nation, but Cromwell was growing frustrated that the conservative members of the Rump had failed to call an election for a new parliament, preferring to cling on to the power that they had grabbed after the king's death. Cromwell decided to take the law into his own hands.

Cromwell was a member of the landowning gentry, whose military prowess had propelled him to the fore during the Civil Wars. His military reputation was a springboard to political power which was always exercised in accordance with his religious beliefs. He had undergone a religious conversion prior to the war, becoming a fervent yet liberal Puritan. It was his strong belief that God had chosen the New Model Army to do His will and had guided them to victory. Once victory was achieved, he felt that he should capitalize by reforming "ungodly" elements in not only England's government and legal systems but in society in general. Although he was keen to stamp out immorality he also supported what he termed "liberty of conscience" and so was tolerant of a diversity of Protestant groups as long as they did not force their views on others. His tolerance extended so far as to allow the Jews back into England but he was hostile towards Roman Catholics, persecuting them mercilessly in Scotland and Ireland.

On 20 April 1653, Cromwell moved to take power. He dissolved the Rump Parliament with the support of the Army. He was, for a time, a military dictator, ruling through an assembly chosen by Army officers. This assembly was commonly known as the Barebone's Parliament, after one of the members, Praise-God Barebones. The landed gentry ridiculed the assembly, considering it to be made up of the lowborn and puritanical, like the lay preacher Barebones. Formed in July 1653, the Barebones Parliament lasted until December of the same year. It was beset by in-fighting amongst various factions and rapidly became ineffective. Once again, Cromwell stepped in and drew the experiment to a close.

The Grandees next drew up the "Instrument of Government". This was England's first written constitution and it granted executive power to a Lord Protector. The Lord Protector was to be elected but would hold the position for life. In addition, a parliament was to be called every three years. The Instrument of Government was adopted on 15 December 1653 with Cromwell being sworn in as Lord Protector on the next day.

The first Protectorate Parliament met in September 1654

but Cromwell dissolved it as swiftly as he could under the terms of the Instrument of Government as his proposed reforms did not find sufficient support with the MPs. Cromwell decided to rule through a military government. The country was divided into 11 districts, each governed by a Major-General who reported to Cromwell alone.

The rule of the Major-Generals lasted from August 1655 to January 1657. During this time, England was kept under tight control to prevent uprisings. Popular social gatherings, including cock-fighting, bear baiting and races were banned so as to prevent people from meeting to plot against the regime. Similarly, inns were watched and sometimes shut down. Those with royalist sympathies were singled out for fines and the old clergy, both Anglican and Catholic, were banned from working as tutors or chaplains. There was some positive reform, such as allowing servants and apprentices a day off each month, but generally, the country disliked the Army extending its influence into civilian life. Cromwell too was uneasy with military rule, but felt it necessary to maintain the peace of the country during troubled times. In September 1656, Cromwell called a second Protectorate Parliament and then withdrew his Major-Generals at the beginning of the following year.

The Parliament soon presented Cromwell with a new problem; they offered him the crown. He did not immediately dismiss the idea, taking six weeks to think it over. Cromwell knew that the country needed a strong ruler, whatever the title. However, he still needed the support of the Army and they were opposed to the monarchy so he turned down the offer. Instead, he was reaffirmed as Lord Protector in a ceremony that was redolent of a royal coronation. The Lord Protector's role and powers were extended and set out in the Humble Petition and Advice, which replaced the Instrument of Government as the constitution.

Cromwell tried to sweep away many of the cherished traditions and pastimes of the English, considering them unholy and immoral. As well as closing the bear and cock pits, theatres were closed and maypoles were cut down. Holy days were no longer allowed to be celebrated as festivals but had to be quietly observed at church and with fasting. Soldiers patrolled the streets on Christmas Day and confiscated any celebratory meals. No work, even housework or walking anywhere other than to church, was banned on Sundays. Puritans would often inform their less pious neighbors who would then be fined. As time rolled on, many found the changes unpalatable.

Cromwell died in 1658. His role as Lord Protector was not hereditary but he was allowed to name his successor and he passed his title to his son Richard. Unlike his father, Richard was not a soldier and consequently did not find favor with the Army. Discontent grew as republicans within Parliament started to attack the Protectorate as being too like a monarchy. Richard Cromwell lacked his father's decisiveness and managed neither to reassure the Army nor quash dissent in Parliament. By the spring of 1659, Richard was obliged to relinquish power and an attempt was made to re-establish the Commonwealth. Watching England descend into chaos from Scotland, Cromwell's old friend and comrade General Monck, governor of Scotland, had decided against supporting the ineffectual Richard. Instead, he threw his support behind the exiled King Charles II. Monck marched to London and organized the Convention Parliament which first met on 25 April 1660. An invitation was extended to Charles to return and he arrived in London on his birthday, 29 May.

Parliament declared that Charles had legally been the monarch since his father's execution, so technically there had been no interregnum. Charles continued to erase the memory of the Commonwealth by exhuming Cromwell from Westminster Abbey and having his head struck from the body, whereupon it was put on a spike and displayed for decades as a warning to traitors. The new king also confiscated coins bearing the former Lord Protector's image. All over the country, there were people who were similarly keen to forget the past decade as for many it had turned into a gloomy time.

Legacy

Although the Commonwealth did not last, it did demonstrate that a country could operate without a monarch. The idea would reach maturity in the American colonies and later France. The

British, however, prefer not to repeat the experience of a republic with the majority of the public still favoring the monarchy.

The freedom of conscience allowed by the Commonwealth saw new religious sects spring up. Many, like the Diggers and the Ranters, died out but some, such as the Anabaptists and the Quakers, exist today.

Sites to Visit

- There is a statue of Cromwell outside the Houses of Parliament. It was erected in 1889 and such was his remaining unpopularity in Ireland that the Irish MPs blocked it being publicly funded.
- One of Oliver Cromwell's homes still survives and has been recreated to show how his family would have lived. Oliver Cromwell's House, Ely is open every day except Christmas Day and Boxing Day.
- After his head was taken from its spike, Cromwell's head passed through various owners until being buried in 1960 at Sidney Sussex College, Cambridge. A plaque marks the site.
- Cromwell's wax death mask can be seen at the British Museum in London.

Film and TV

- The 1970 film Cromwell starring Richard Harris as the Lord Protector is available on DVD.
- To Kill a King (2003) concerns the relationship of Cromwell and Fairfax at the time of the king's trial and execution. Tim Roth and Dougray Scott star. Available on DVD
- History Makers – Oliver Cromwell (2007) is available on DVD.

Further Research

- Cromwell, Our Chief Of Men (2008) by Lady Antonia Fraser explores the man behind the myth.
- God's Englishman: Oliver Cromwell and the English Revolution (1990) by Christopher Hill covers Cromwell's life from gentleman farmer to Lord Protector. The same author penned The World Turned Upside Down: Radical Ideas During the English Revolution (1991) in which he explores the different radical groups that were formed during the Interregnum.

APPENDIX 10
THE ACTS OF UNION

The creation of Great Britain in 1707 marked one of the most significant moments in British history, transforming two sometimes hostile neighbors into a single united kingdom. Yet the path to union was far from smooth, and its legacy continues to shape British politics today.

The story begins a century earlier, in 1603, when Elizabeth I died without heirs. The English crown passed to her closest relative, James VI of Scotland, who became James I of England. This created what historians call the "Union of the Crowns" - both kingdoms shared a monarch but remained separate nations with distinct parliaments, laws, and institutions.

This arrangement proved increasingly problematic. Trade disputes were common, as both countries maintained separate and often conflicting economic policies. Religious tensions simmered, with both nations fearful of the other's influence on their established churches. Perhaps most worryingly, there was no guarantee that future monarchs would inherit both crowns, raising the possibility that the kingdoms might separate again.

The push for fuller union gained momentum in the late 17th century. Scotland's economic situation had become desperate following the failed Darien Scheme, an attempt to establish a Scottish colony in Panama that bankrupted many of the nation's leading investors. Meanwhile, England wanted to secure the Protestant succession and prevent Scotland from potentially choosing a different monarch after Queen Anne's death.

Negotiations began in 1706, with commissioners from both nations meeting to hammer out terms. The resulting Acts of Union, passed by both parliaments in 1707, created a new state: the Kingdom of Great Britain. Scotland and England would share a parliament in Westminster, operate under a single economic system, and maintain free trade between them. However, Scotland retained its own legal and educational systems, as well as its Presbyterian Church.

The Acts faced fierce opposition, particularly in Scotland. Many Scots saw them as a surrender of national sovereignty, while others feared the loss of cultural identity. Riots broke out in several Scottish cities. The Acts passed the Scottish Parliament by a relatively narrow margin, amid allegations of English bribery and pressure.

The immediate effects were mixed. Scotland gained access to England's colonial markets and experienced significant economic growth in the following decades. However, many Scots remained resentful of what they saw as English dominance, contributing to the Jacobite risings of 1715 and 1745.

The union proved remarkably durable, surviving numerous challenges over the centuries. Together, England and Scotland became the core of a global empire, with Scottish entrepreneurs, soldiers, and administrators playing key roles in its expansion. The Industrial Revolution transformed both nations, with Scottish cities like Glasgow becoming major industrial centers.

Yet the union never fully erased national identities. Scotland maintained its distinctive culture, legal system, and sense of nationhood. These differences have periodically resurfaced in calls for greater Scottish autonomy or independence, leading to the creation of the Scottish Parliament in 1999 and the 2014 independence referendum.

Today's United Kingdom is very different from the one created in 1707, but many of the fundamental arrangements established by the Acts of Union remain in place. The relationship between Scotland and England continues to evolve, demonstrating both the durability and the ongoing challenges of this historic union.

The Acts of Union represent more than just a political merger - they mark the beginning of modern Britain, creating the framework within which British identity could develop alongside existing national loyalties. Their legacy reminds us that unity need not mean uniformity, and that successful political unions must respect and accommodate their constituent parts' distinct traditions and identities.

APPENDIX 11
ROYAL ERAS: A JOURNEY THROUGH BRITISH HISTORY

From Norman knights to modern monarchs, British history can be understood through distinct royal eras, each with its own character and defining events.

The Norman Era (1066-1154)

Beginning with William the Conqueror's invasion, this period saw the establishment of feudalism in England. The Normans built castles across the landscape, introduced new systems of government, and created the Domesday Book. The era ended in civil war - "The Anarchy" - between Stephen and Matilda.

The Plantagenet Era (1154-1485)

One of the longest dynastic eras in British history, the Plantagenet period saw the creation of common law, the signing of Magna Carta (1215), the development of Parliament, and the Hundred Years' War with France. The era ended in the Wars of the Roses, a dynastic conflict that tore England apart.

The Tudor Era (1485-1603)

Perhaps the most famous period of English history, the Tudor era brought profound changes. Henry VIII broke with Rome and established the Church of England, while Elizabeth I presided over a golden age of exploration, literature, and the defeat of the Spanish Armada. The period saw the English Renaissance flourish and established England as a Protestant nation.

The reign of Elizabeth I deserves recognition as its own distinct period, often called England's Golden Age. While technically part of the Tudor era, the Elizabethan period was marked by such significant developments that it stands alone in historical importance. This was a time of:

- Extraordinary cultural flowering, particularly in theater and literature (Shakespeare, Marlowe)
- Maritime expansion and exploration (Drake, Raleigh)
- The defeat of the Spanish Armada (1588)
- Religious settlement after decades of turmoil
- The birth of English Renaissance culture
- Growth in education and literacy
- Development of English national identity
- Economic prosperity and social mobility
- Advances in science and philosophy

The length and stability of Elizabeth's reign allowed for the development of a distinct court culture. The "Cult of Gloriana" saw Elizabeth portrayed as a virginal goddess-like figure, while she skillfully managed her court through a combination of reward and control. Her refusal to marry became a political tool, while her support of the arts led to an explosion of creativity.

The Elizabethan era saw England emerge as a major European power, with the foundations laid for what would become the British Empire. The period is particularly remembered for its rich cultural achievements, especially in theater and poetry, which continue to influence English literature and drama today.

The Stuart Era (1603-1714)

Beginning with the Union of the Crowns under James I, this turbulent period included the Civil Wars, the execution of Charles I, Cromwell's republic, the Restoration of Charles II, and the Glorious Revolution. It ended with the Acts of Union 1707, creating Great Britain, and the establishment of constitutional monarchy.

The Georgian Era (1714-1837)

Named for the four Georges and William IV, this period saw Britain become a global superpower. The Industrial Revolution transformed society, while the loss of the American colonies was balanced by expansion in India and elsewhere. The era was marked by elegance in architecture and fashion, but also by social upheaval and reform.

When George III's mental illness made him unfit to rule, his son served as Prince Regent until becoming George IV. The Regency era is remembered as a time of distinct cultural refinement, architectural innovation (especially in Brighton and London), and social excess. This was the age of Jane Austen, Beau Brummell, and the dandy, characterized by:

- Distinctive architecture (the development of Regent Street and Regent's Park)
- Fashion innovations (Brummell's influence on men's fashion)
- The popularity of the social season and grand balls
- Advancement in literature and the arts
- A remarkable contrast between high society's excesses and broader social problems

Victory over Napoleon at Waterloo (1815)

The Prince Regent himself epitomized the era's extravagance, with his lavish spending on clothing, buildings (especially the Royal Pavilion at Brighton), and entertaining.

The Later Georgian Period (1820-1837)

George IV's actual reign and that of his brother William IV saw the continuation of many Regency trends, but with growing pressure for social and political reform, culminating in the Great Reform Act of 1832. This period bridged the gap between the excesses of the Regency and the more sober Victorian era to come.

The Victorian Era (1837-1901)

Queen Victoria's long reign saw Britain reach the height of its global power. This was an age of rapid technological progress, social reform, and imperial expansion. Victorian values of duty, family, and morality shaped society, while the Industrial Revolution reached its peak. The monarchy became a model of respectability and family life.

The Edwardian Era (1901-1910)

Though brief, Edward VII's reign is remembered as a golden afternoon of the British Empire. Characterized by elegant society life and technological innovations like early automobiles and aviation, it was also a time of growing social tension and international rivalry that would lead to World War I.

The Georgian Revival (1910-1936)

George V's reign saw Britain through World War I and its aftermath. The monarchy proved its worth during the war, changing its name from the German "House of Saxe-Coburg-Gotha" to the more British "Windsor." The period ended in constitutional crisis with Edward VIII's abdication.

The Modern Era (1936-present)

Beginning with George VI, this period saw the monarchy adapt to a rapidly changing world. Elizabeth II's long reign (1952-2022) witnessed the transformation of empire into Commonwealth, the growth of mass media, and the monarchy's evolution into a ceremonial but vital part of British life. Now, Charles III's reign marks a new chapter in this ongoing story.

The progression of these eras shows how the British monarchy has survived by adapting to change while maintaining traditions. From feudal rulers to constitutional monarchs, from absolute power to ceremonial authority, the institution has evolved while remaining central to British identity.

Today's monarchy combines elements from many of these eras: the ceremony of the Tudors, the constitutional role established under the later Stuarts, the family values of the Victorians, and the media awareness of the modern era. Understanding these historical periods helps explain both how the monarchy reached its current form and why certain traditions persist.

APPENDIX 12
THE HOUSE OF WINDSOR: A VERY BRITISH REBRANDING

In 1917, amid the devastating conflict of World War I, Britain's royal family faced a peculiar crisis: their own German name. The House of Saxe-Coburg and Gotha, as the royal family was then known, had inherited this distinctly Germanic title through Prince Albert, Queen Victoria's husband. But with anti-German sentiment at its height and British soldiers fighting against the Kaiser (who happened to be King George V's cousin), the royal family's German connections had become a serious liability.

The catalyst for change came from an unexpected source - German air raids. When German Gotha G.IV bombers began attacking London in daylight raids during 1917, the coincidence of the royal family sharing a name with these enemy aircraft proved too much. King George V faced mounting pressure to distance the monarchy from its German roots.

The solution came on July 17, 1917, when George V issued a royal proclamation changing the name of the royal house to "Windsor," taken from the ancient castle that had been a royal residence since William the Conqueror. This wasn't just a simple name change - the King also renounced all German titles and asked his extended family to do the same. His British relatives who bore German titles were given new English peerages.

The choice of Windsor was masterful in its symbolism. Windsor Castle had stood for nearly a thousand years as a symbol of English monarchy. The name evoked strength, history, and quintessential Britishness. It was a powerful statement that the royal family's loyalty lay firmly with Britain, not their German cousins.

This rebranding went beyond just the family name. German relations were publicly downplayed, and the family embraced a more distinctly British identity. The King's children were encouraged to marry into British noble families rather than European royal houses, breaking with centuries of tradition. The King even changed the name of his male-line relatives residing in Britain to Mountbatten-Windsor, though the royal house remained simply "Windsor."

The transformation proved remarkably successful. The British public embraced their newly renamed royal family, and the House of Windsor emerged from World War I with its popularity intact. When George V died in 1936, he left behind a thoroughly British monarchy, its German origins largely forgotten by the public.

The name has served the royal family well through subsequent crises. When Elizabeth II married Philip Mountbatten (who had himself anglicized his name from Battenberg), there was brief discussion about changing the royal house to Mountbatten. However, Winston Churchill's government strongly advised against it, and Elizabeth declared that the House of Windsor would continue, though her descendants who needed surnames would use Mountbatten-Windsor.

Today's House of Windsor bears little resemblance to the German-influenced court of a century ago. The rebranding of 1917 helped transform a European royal house into a distinctly British institution, demonstrating the monarchy's remarkable ability to adapt and survive. The name change stands as one of the most successful royal rebrands in history, turning a potential crisis into an opportunity to strengthen the monarchy's British identity.

The timing and execution of the change highlight a key aspect of the British monarchy's survival: its ability to read the public mood and adapt accordingly. In choosing Windsor, George V didn't just pick a new name - he helped redefine the monarchy for the modern age, creating a more national institution that could survive in an era of rising nationalism and declining royal power.

APPENDIX 13
WHERE EVERY MONARCH WAS BORN

Here's a list of birthplaces for every British monarch since William the Conqueror:

- William I (the Conqueror) - Falaise Castle, Normandy, France
- William II (Rufus) - Normandy, France (exact location uncertain)
- Henry I - Selby, Yorkshire, England
- Stephen - Blois, France
- Henry II - Le Mans, France
- Richard I (the Lionheart) - Beaumont Palace, Oxford, England
- John - Beaumont Palace, Oxford, England
- Henry III - Winchester Castle, Hampshire, England
- Edward I - Westminster Palace, London, England
- Edward II - Caernarfon Castle, Wales
- Edward III - Windsor Castle, Berkshire, England
- Richard II - Bordeaux, France
- Henry IV - Bolingbroke Castle, Lincolnshire, England
- Henry V - Monmouth Castle, Wales
- Henry VI - Windsor Castle, Berkshire, England
- Edward IV - Rouen, France
- Edward V - Westminster Abbey Sanctuary, London, England
- Richard III - Fotheringhay Castle, Northamptonshire, England
- Henry VII - Pembroke Castle, Wales
- Henry VIII - Greenwich Palace, London, England
- Edward VI - Hampton Court Palace, London, England
- Mary I - Greenwich Palace, London, England

- Elizabeth I - Greenwich Palace, London, England
- James I (VI of Scotland) - Edinburgh Castle, Scotland
- Charles I - Dunfermline Palace, Scotland
- Charles II - St. James's Palace, London, England
- James II - St. James's Palace, London, England
- William III - The Hague, Netherlands
- Mary II - St. James's Palace, London, England
- Anne - St. James's Palace, London, England
- George I - Hanover, Germany
- George II - Hanover, Germany
- George III - Norfolk House, London, England
- George IV - St. James's Palace, London, England
- William IV - Buckingham House (now Palace), London, England
- Victoria - Kensington Palace, London, England
- Edward VII - Buckingham Palace, London, England
- George V - Marlborough House, London, England
- Edward VIII - White Lodge, Richmond, England
- George VI - Sandringham House, Norfolk, England
- Elizabeth II - 17 Bruton Street, London, England
- Charles III - Buckingham Palace, London, England

Interesting patterns emerge from this list:

- Greenwich Palace was a particularly popular royal birthplace in the Tudor period
- St. James's Palace saw many royal births in the Stuart and early Hanoverian period
- Several monarchs were born outside England, particularly in France during the medieval period and Germany during the Hanoverian succession
- Buckingham Palace and its environs became the standard royal birthplace from the 19th century onward

APPENDIX 14
ABDICATION CRISIS

In 1936, the charismatic new King, Edward VIII, announced to his advisors his intention of marrying his mistress, Wallis Simpson. Not since Henry VIII resolved to marry Anne Boleyn had a royal marriage threatened to wreak such havoc on the country. Henry was able to force his will on the kingdom. 400 years later, Edward found that his personal desires were no match for the State's, and he was obliged to abdicate, opening the way for a new royal family who would endear themselves to the nation.

Key Dates

- January 1931 First meeting of Prince of Wales and Mrs. Wallis Simpson
- 20 January 1936 Death of George V. Edward VIII succeeds him
- July 1936 Simpson leaves the family home
- August 1936 Foreign newspapers print photographs of the King and Wallis
- 27 October 1936 Simpsons granted a decree nisi
- November 1936 The King informs Prime Minister he wants a morganatic marriage
- November 1936 King's proposal was rejected by the governments of Britain and the Dominions
- 2 December 1936 King informed of the decision
- 3 December 1936 British Press breaks the story and Mrs. Simpson leaves for France
- 9 December 1936 Edward tells the government he intends to abdicate
- 10 December 1936 Instrument of Abdication signed and House of Commons informed
- 11 December 1936 Edward broadcasts his decision to the nation
- 12 December 1936 Edward's brother Albert proclaimed

- as King George VI
- 12 December 1936 Edward, now Duke of Windsor, travels to Austria
- 3 June 1937 Edward and Wallis Simpson marry in France

Key Figures

- Edward, Prince of Wales, briefly King of the United Kingdom and Dominions, Emperor of India, later Duke of Windsor.
- Bessie Wallis Warfield, later Wallis Spencer, then Wallis Simpson, and finally, Wallis, Duchess of Windsor.
- King George V
- Queen Mary
- Stanley Baldwin, Prime Minister
- Prince Albert, Duke of York, later King George VI
- Elizabeth, Duchess of York, later Queen Elizabeth

A Burden Too Heavy Without the Help and Support of the Woman He Loved

Edward, known as David to his family and friends, was born on 23 June 1894. His great-grandmother, Queen Victoria, was still on the throne and his grandfather, Edward, Prince of Wales, was waiting impatiently in the wings. Young Edward's parents were the Duke and Duchess of York, who would later become King George V and Queen Mary.

As a child, Edward enjoyed an affectionate, albeit distant, relationship with his parents and grandparents. He was taught by tutors until his early teens when he was sent first to Osborne Naval College and then Dartmouth Naval College to prepare him for a career in the Royal Navy. This plan was cut short in 1910 when his grandfather died. 16-year-old Edward was created Prince of Wales and sent to Magdalen College, Oxford to better prepare him for his role as future king. His academic career was not a great success; whilst he enjoyed the University's polo club, he did not manage to obtain a degree.

At the outbreak of the Great War, the Prince of Wales was determined to serve his country. He had joined the Grenadier Guards and appealed to be allowed to join the front line. His request was turned down since the government could not countenance the risk of the heir to the throne being captured by the enemy. Edward was allowed to serve behind the lines and occasionally managed to reach the front. Later, he flew military aircraft. Unlike the government, he was sanguine about the dangers and was said to have quipped "What difference does it make if I am killed? The King has three other sons!" This carefree attitude won him a good deal of popularity among the troops, who were proud of the Prince who won the Military Cross.

Following the war, Edward traveled around Britain and the Empire as his father's representative. Good-looking, sporty, and unattached, he became a favorite with photographers and gossip columnists, achieving celebrity status. Unlike his stern parents, he was affable and suited to the modernity of the "roaring twenties". The people may have loved his personality, but his character was giving his parents and their advisors cause for concern.

Edward, rather like his grandfather and namesake Edward VII, had grown into a womanizer. His affairs with married women appalled his strait-laced father who began to favor his second son, the quiet and respectably married Albert. King George went so far as to declare that he hoped Edward never had children so that Albert and his wife could eventually succeed to the throne. The King also predicted that Edward would ruin himself within a year of his father's death. In 1931, Edward met the woman who would turn George V's hopes and fears into reality.

Wallis Simpson was a vivacious and charming American socialite, who possessed a quick wit, effortless elegance, and, according to some, endless ambition. Early in 1931, Wallis and Edward met for the first time at a dinner party hosted by Edward's mistress, Lady Furness. Over the next few years, Edward and Mrs. Simpson chanced upon each other at society events. Edward developed a fascination with the charming American and it is likely that the pair became lovers when Lady Furness was abroad in 1934. Part of Wallis's attraction for the Prince was her lack of deference to his position and he was soon besotted.

Mrs. Simpson had captured the heart of the world's most eligible bachelor but it was never likely that she would capture his crown. Wallis was entirely unsuitable as a queen consort. Even putting aside the malicious gossip about her earlier scandalous escapades in the Far East, there was the fact that she was a divorcee. As a rule, a divorcee like Wallis would not be allowed at court, much less allowed to marry the monarch. The growing relationship between the Prince of Wales and Wallis was viewed with alarm by the King, many of the Prince's old friends, and the government. Special Branch trailed the couple, reporting back on alleged liaisons between Wallis and other men, in the hope that a wedge could be driven between the pair. Their attempts were unsuccessful. The Prince's infatuation continued unabated and began to impact his official duties. Worse was to come.

King George V died on 20 January 1936 and Edward became King Edward VIII. He and Wallis watched from a window at St James' Palace as the proclamation was read. It was a clear indication that he wanted Wallis by his side. Although the country at large remained unaware of the King's affair, to his family, the court, and the government, the unthinkable became obvious: Edward intended to marry Mrs. Simpson. Such a marriage was fraught with difficulty, largely because the monarch was the Supreme Head of the Church of England and the Church did not allow the remarriage of divorced people whose spouses were living. Edward and Wallis plowed on with their plans. Wallis sued for divorce on the grounds of her husband's adultery and was granted a decree nisi in October 1936. In Edward's mind, one hurdle to his marriage had been crossed. He turned his attention to the next and came up with a plan he felt would answer his critics.

In November 1936, Edward met his Prime Minister, Stanley Baldwin, and suggested that he might contract a morganatic marriage with Wallis. This type of marriage would allow Edward to retain the crown, but Wallis would not become queen, instead having a courtesy title. Any children of the marriage would be excluded from the line of succession. There was no precedent for such an arrangement in Britain though morganatic marriages were not unheard of in other

European kingdoms. Baldwin told the King that he doubted that the people would accept a marriage to Mrs. Simpson, but undertook to put the King's proposal to the government of Britain and her Dominions.

Baldwin put three alternatives to the various governments: that the King should be allowed to marry Mrs. Simpson and she becomes queen; that the King marry Mrs. Simpson in a morganatic marriage or; that the King abdicated the throne. With the exception of New Zealand's Prime Minister, who felt that the morganatic marriage proposal might work, the first two proposals were rejected. Mrs. Simpson was seen as an entirely unsuitable spouse for the King. In Britain, the leaders of the opposition parties also agreed that there could be no marriage between Mrs. Simpson and a reigning King. Winston Churchill was hopeful that if the matter could be delayed, the King would simply fall out of love with Wallis. Baldwin was not in favor of delay, wanting a swift resolution to the crisis.

As news spread about the King and Mrs. Simpson, Edward was not entirely without sympathizers. An unlikely alliance of politicians supported him, ranging from Oswald Mosely and his Union of Fascists to the Communist Party. Winston Churchill was rumored to be leading the King's supporters, but this was pure speculation. In the Press, and, therefore, the country, opinion was split. Broadly, the Establishment and the middle class were against Edward's marriage to Mrs. Simpson, whilst progressives and the working class were more tolerant of the idea. Perhaps buoyed by his supporters, Edward made a last-ditch attempt to keep his crown and the woman he loved.

At the beginning of December, he drafted a speech in which he put his idea of a morganatic marriage to the public, making it clear that he would prefer to stay on the throne. The government blocked him from broadcasting the speech, citing constitutional difficulties. Edward bowed to the inevitable; it was Wallis or the crown and there was no possibility of reconciling the two. He agreed to abdicate.

On 10 December 1936, Edward signed the abdication documentation with his three younger brothers as witnesses. His brother Albert became monarch, taking the regnal name George. The following day, announced as Prince Edward, he addressed the nation, telling the people that he could not carry out the heavy burden of responsibility without the support of the woman he loved.

Edward and Wallis Simpson married the following year in France. As the Duke and Duchess of Windsor, they enjoyed a lavish lifestyle, although they did court controversy for their apparent sympathy for the Nazi regime. Edward died in 1972 and was buried in the Royal Mausoleum at Frogmore. The Duchess died in 1986 and was buried with her husband.

Legacy

The abdication of Edward VIII cleared the way for George VI, the result that George V had always wanted. Although George VI was a shy man, he and his wife, Queen Elizabeth, provided the country with calm stability during World War II and the Blitz in particular. George VI also presided over the dismantling of the British Empire and, like his daughter, Elizabeth II, proved to be a popular monarch providing a steady influence in difficult times.

Sites to visit

- Fort Belvedere in Windsor Great Park was Edward's country home, given to him by his father. Edward and Wallis spent time here together and part of the television series Edward and Mrs. Simpson was filmed in the house. It was at Belvedere that Edward signed his abdication documents. The house is currently leased to private tenants, but it is occasionally open to raise money for charities.
- The Duke and Duchess of Windsor are buried at Frogmore Mausoleum which is located in the Home Park of Windsor Castle. Frogmore House, gardens, and the Mausoleum are open to the public on a very limited basis. The annual timetable for opening can be found on the Royal Collection Trust's website.

- The State Rooms at Buckingham Palace are open for tours, making the public more welcome than Mrs. Simpson once was!

Film and TV

- In 1981, Edward Fox and Cynthia Harris starred as Edward and Mrs. Simpson in Thames Television's drama series. Available on DVD.
- Wallis And Edward (2006) stars Joely Richardson and Stephen Campbell Moore. Available on DVD or to rent from LoveFilm.

Further research

- Philip Zeigler had unique access to the Royal Archives for his 2012 biography King Edward VIII. The book follows Edward from his childhood, through the playboy prince years, up to his death in exile in Paris.
- Behind Closed Doors (2011) by Hugo Vickers explores the Duchess of Windsor's later years, which were marred by the exploitation she suffered at the hands of those charged with her care.
- 17 Carnations: The Windsors, The Nazis and the Cover-Up (2015) by Andrew Morton explores Edward and Wallis' relationship with the Nazi regime.

APPENDIX 15
THE REGENCY ERA

When George III became unfit to rule in the latter part of his reign, his son Prince George took up the mantle of Prince Regent. The Prince was profligate, selfish, and vain, yet he possessed good taste and was a patron to innovators in the arts. During the Regency Era, which spilled out into his reign and that of his brother, a distinctive style was born that bridged the gap between the Georgian Era and the Victorians. The Regency Era remains the epitome of elegance and romance, and Britain owes a debt to the Prince Regent for his many building schemes that produced some of her most elegant buildings, squares, and terraces.

Key Facts about the Regency Era

Key Dates

- 1760 George III ascends the throne
- 1811 Regency begins
- 1820 George III dies; Prince Regent becomes King George IV

Key People

- George III
- Prince George Prince Regent, later King George IV
- Caroline of Brunswick Wife of the Prince Regent
- Princess Charlotte Daughter of the Prince Regent
- Beau Brummell Fashionable man about town
- John Nash – Architect
- Jane Austen – Novelist

A Time of Low Morals and High Fashion

George III was a devout and retiring man who had captured the hearts of his people. Unfortunately, at the height of his popularity, George was struck with an illness that robbed him of his mind. He may have been suffering from porphyria (a genetic disease), arsenic poisoning mental illness, or a combination of these maladies. The effect was to leave him insensible for long periods of time, prone to rages and foaming at the mouth. The king had fallen ill several times, and the question of a regency had arisen, but each time he recovered he dismissed the suggestion. In 1810, the king's youngest and favorite daughter, Princess Amelia, died. The loss of his daughter tipped George into a final bout of illness from which he would not recover.

It had generally been agreed during the king's earlier illnesses that his son, George, Prince of Wales, would act as regent. Prince George was a complete contrast to his father and the two did not get on. Extravagant, untrustworthy, and promiscuous, the Prince of Wales was unpopular with the people, as well as his parents. The Duke of Wellington described him as 'the most extraordinary compound of talent, wit, buffoonery, obstinacy, and good feeling — in short a medley of the most opposite qualities, with a great preponderance of good — that I ever saw in any character in my life.'

In addition to building up mountains of debt, despite an enormous allowance, the prince had entered into an illegal and invalid marriage with an actress, Mrs. Fitzherbert. The lady was a Catholic, so if George was to marry her, he needed to obtain his father's permission and even if this was forthcoming, he would be barred from the line of succession. George did not approach his father, but went through a secret ceremony and kept the matter quiet. Despite his love for Mrs. Fitzherbert, he had a string of mistresses and was maneuvered into an arranged marriage with his cousin, Caroline of Brunswick, in return for his father clearing his debts.

George and Caroline detested each other at first sight. Caroline was not impressed by the rotund Prince and he in turn was so repulsed by Caroline that he called for brandy when he first saw her. During the marriage ceremony, he was noticed to be looking at his mistress Lady Jersey rather than at Caroline, and the king had to coax him into completing the ceremony. Later, left alone with his bride, he drank so much that he passed out and spent the night on the floor of her chamber in a stupor. Despite their antipathy, the couple managed to conceive a daughter, born almost exactly nine months after their wedding night. The couple was legally separated after their daughter's birth. Princess Charlotte, the heir to the throne, reached adulthood and married but was to die in childbirth, along with her son, in 1817, predeceasing both her father and grandfather.

Notwithstanding the shortcomings of Prince George, he became regent for his father under the Care of the King during his Illness Act 1811. The Prince Regent, as he would be known, was to discharge his father's duties in his place until he recovered. George swore that he would be 'faithful and bear true allegiance' to the king, to maintain 'the safety, honor and dignity' of the king and 'the welfare of his people', and to keep to the Protestant religion. With typical extravagance, he attended the oath-taking ceremony in the flamboyant dress uniform of his own personal regiment, the 10th Hussars, whilst the band of the Coldstream Guards played "God Save the King".

Parliament did put some constraints on the Prince's powers, but he was to take less interest in the government of the country than his father did. George was content for his ministers to run the country. This disappointed the Whigs, who had regarded George as an ally and expected him to favor them once he was in power. In fact, he was surprisingly impartial and did not extend his patronage to any political faction.

During the Regency, Britain was battling Napoleon on the continent and adjusting to the changes wrought by the Industrial Revolution at home. There was agitation in the country for political reform, particularly for changes to parliamentary representation, which the government dealt with through repression. In 1819 at Peterloo near Manchester, the army turned a peaceful protest into a massacre. Following the "Peterloo Massacre" the government passed the Six Acts to stifle any further dissent which inspired one group of men to form the Cato Street Conspiracy with the ambitious and ultimately futile aim of murdering the entire Cabinet, overthrowing the government, and occupying the Bank of England.

The Prince Regent was living in volatile times, but he increasingly isolated himself at Windsor Castle. What he lacked in enthusiasm for politics, he made up for in his patronage of the Arts. Britain underwent a period of renaissance during the Regency and into George's reign, producing a distinctive style of architecture and fashion.

Fashion underwent a transformation during the Regency. Stiff, elaborate gowns and ornate wigs gave way to cleaner, more classical lines. Although grossly overweight by the time he became Regent, Prince George had been keenly interested in fashion as a younger man. He was fascinated by a junior officer in the 10th Hussars, George "Beau" Brummell. It was Brummell who was to set the standard for men's dress during the Regency. Brummell favoured elegant, understated outfits though simplicity came at a cost; Brummell was alleged to take up to five hours to dress and was to amass huge debts. His style of dress, which came to be known as dandyism, is synonymous with the Regency. Dandies like Brummell and the Prince wore long polished boots (the sheen allegedly achieved by buffing the boots with champagne), trousers rather than breeches and hose, dark coats, immaculate linen shirts, and elaborately tied cravats. Ladies stopped powdering their faces and left off their elaborate wigs. Instead, they favored their faces natural and pale and wore sheer, pale muslin gowns of the high-waisted Empire style, shawls, and low-heeled slippers.

As well as adorning his person, the Prince Regent set about beautifying his surroundings. He commissioned many projects using the talents of architect John Nash. The Prince's appetite for the building was such that Nash worked almost exclusively for him from 1810 until George's death. One of Nash's first schemes was the redevelopment of the area then known as Marylebone Park in London. Nash laid out a new development around Regent's Street and Regent's Park, with elegant townhouses, villas, terraces, and gardens. Regent's Canal was another of his creations. In addition to his town planning in London, Nash undertook the rebuilding of the Prince's seaside residence, Marine Pavilion. The new Royal Pavilion was an exotic and ambitious confection of Indian and Chinese styles, ideally suited to the Prince's excessive nature. Nash was also commissioned to upgrade Buckingham House to Buckingham Palace. The cost of the work was tremendous, adding to Prince's unpopularity in the country.

While the Prince and those in high society led a hugely ostentatious lifestyle, just below him the gentry were well looked after too. A window into their lives was opened by Jane Austen, who published all her novels during the Regency. She conjured up a world of country houses, balls, and the all-consuming importance of marrying well and maintaining the reputation of one's family. What she did not document were the lives of those at the bottom of the Regency world, for whom life was one of grinding poverty and hardship. There were no elegant housing developments for the lower part of society in London; they lived in violent "rookeries", such as at St Giles, where even the law feared to tread.

The Regency officially drew to a close in 1820 when George III died, turning the Prince Regent into the new king. The resurgence of art and culture sparked by the Regency Era might be said to continue through George IV's reign and into the reign of his brother William IV and up to the accession of their niece Victoria.

Legacy

Although the Prince Regent was a Georgian, the Regency Era formed a distinctive period. It had its own style, which is still recognizable today in the stylish terraces and squares of London and Bath and the words of Jane Austen. Even our modern dress owes a debt to the Regency; Beau Brummell pioneered the idea of the modern suit and necktie. The Regency has also provided us with the epitome of romance, with many romantic novels being set against a backdrop of Regency England.

Sites to Visit

- The Royal Pavilion, Brighton, the Prince Regent's seaside retreat, is open to the public and offers a glimpse into the grandeur and color of the Prince's world. Also in

Brighton is Steine House, which was built for the Prince's "wife", Maria Fitzherbert. Located on Old Steine, the house is much altered and is now a YMCA hostel. Mrs. Fitzherbert is buried at St John the Baptist Church in the town.
- Almack's Assembly Rooms was a social club for high society, or the "ton", and is featured in many Regency romances. Now redeveloped, the site at 28 King Street is an office building that bears a plaque in memory of the building.
- The Royal Mews at Buckingham Palace was designed by John Nash and is regularly open to the public.
- Romantic novelist Louise Allen has compiled an illustrated book that guides the reader through 10 Regency walks of London covering sites from notorious jails to elegant parks. Walks through Regency London is available through Amazon.
- Bath is a quintessentially Georgian city. The Royal Crescent, Queen Square, the Circus, and the Pump Room are highlights of the city's many architectural delights. The Jane Austen Centre in Gay Street (a street in which Jane Austen actually lived) has an exhibition and Regency tea rooms. Costumed events and balls are held throughout the year, most notably the Regency Costumed Promenade in September and the Annual Summer Ball.

Film and TV

- The Madness of King George (1994) stars Nigel Hawthorne as the King and Rupert Everett as Prince George in a highly acclaimed film that documents the King's descent into illness. Available on DVD.
- Beau Brummell: This Charming Man (2006) is a BBC TV film featuring James Purefoy as Beau Brummell and Hugh Bonneville as the Prince Regent. Available as a DVD.
- Series 3 of David Starkey's Monarchy (2006) covers

the Georgians. Available on DVD and through Channel Four's On Demand service (registration required).

Further Research

- There is a wealth of information about Regency England and Regency costume events in Bath to be found at http://www.janeausten.co.uk/
- George IV (2015) by Christopher Hibbert is a definitive account of George's life both before, during, and after the Regency.
- Jane Austen's novels provide a first-hand account of life for the gentry in Regency England. Sense and Sensibility (1811), Pride and Prejudice (1813), Mansfield Park (1814), Emma (1815), and the posthumous Northanger Abbey and Persuasion (1818) are enduring classics.
- For a contrasting view, novelist Jo Baker has written the entertaining Longbourn (2013) which explores the lives of the servants of Pride and Prejudice's Bennett family.
- The exploits of soldier Richard Sharpe brought up in a London rookery, are largely set in the Regency period. Bernard Cornwell has a long series of Sharpe novels, which begin chronologically with Sharpe's Tiger (1997).

APPENDIX 16
WHAT IS THE CROWN?

The Crown in the UK is both a concept and an object. The object sits on the head of the reigning Monarch. The Crown of State is kept in the Tower of London when not in use (the Queen only wears it on special occasions).

The Crown as a concept is more complicated.

The Crown, in the simplest terms, is the State of the United Kingdom and everything in it.

In legal terms, a type of corporation, the Crown is the legal embodiment of executive, legislative, and judicial governance in the monarchy of the United Kingdom. The concept of the Crown developed first in England as a separation of the literal Crown and property of the kingdom from the person and personal property of the Monarch. It spread through English and later British colonization and is now rooted in the legal lexicon of the United Kingdom, its Crown dependencies, and the other 15 independent realms.

The term is also found in various expressions such as "Crown land," which some countries refer to as "public land" or "state land,"; as well as in some offices, such as minister of the Crown, Crown attorney, and Crown prosecutor.

The Crown is immortal. It never dies. It is eternal. Even if the current Monarch dies, the Crown immediately passes to the next heir, in an uninterrupted line. The Crown can never cease. The reigning Monarch is the living embodiment of the concept of the Crown and the personification of the State.

The concept of the Crown took form under early feudal systems in the British Isles. Though not used this way in all countries that had this system, in England, all rights and privileges were ultimately bestowed by the ruler. Land, for instance, was granted by the Crown to lords in exchange for feudal services, and they, in turn, granted the land to lesser lords.

The body of the reigning sovereign holds two distinct personas in constant coexistence: that of a natural-born human being and that of the British State as accorded to him or her through law;

the Crown and the Monarch are conceptually divisible but legally indivisible, the office cannot exist without the officeholder.

The reigning king or Queen is the employer of all government officials and staff (including the viceroys, judges, members of the armed forces, police officers, and parliamentarians), the guardian of foster children (Crown wards), as well as the owner of all state lands (Crown land), buildings and equipment (Crown-held property), state-owned companies (Crown corporations), and the copyright for government publications (Crown copyright). This is all in his or her position as sovereign, not as an individual; all such property is held by the Crown in perpetuity and cannot be sold by the sovereign without the proper advice and consent of his or her relevant ministers.

The Crown also represents the legal embodiment of executive, legislative, and judicial governance. While the Crown's legal personality is usually regarded as a corporation sole, it can, at least for some purposes, be described as a corporation aggregate headed by the Monarch.

For example, the Queen does not need to carry a passport or get a driving license because they are all issued in her name. She is above the State, above the citizenry. It's a bit bizarre. To make it even more confusing, HM The Queen has her own property portfolio and collections that she owns personally and is not part of the Crown Estate.

The Crown Estate is a collection of lands and holdings in the territories of England, Wales, and Northern Ireland within the United Kingdom belonging to the British Monarch as a corporation sole, making it "the sovereign's public estate," which is neither government property nor part of the Monarch's private estate. It cannot be sold or divided by the Monarch. Now, the Crown Estate used to be under the control of the Monarch, but this was given up several hundred years ago when a monarch was deep in debt. In exchange for a yearly subsidy to run the Royal household and affairs, control of the estate was given to the British government. However, the Monarch still has possessions in their personal capacity that are not part of the Crown Estate.

As I said, it's very confusing but endlessly fascinating.

APPENDIX 17
THE CROWN JEWELS

One of the most important symbols of the Crown's authority and wealth, the Crown Jewels of the United Kingdom have a long, interesting, and sometimes controversial past. These objects have been part of royal ceremonies for centuries, most often in the coronation of kings and queens. What's more, the Crown Jewels aren't just a few accouterments, but represent over 100 objects, including crowns, tiaras, necklaces, rings, sceptres, orbs, and more. There are also different items for the Sovereign, the Prince/Queen Consort, and the Prince/Princess of Wales. It's a lot for us to cover in a simple article such as this, so we'll try to focus on the most important elements.

To that end, it's worth noting that the Crown Jewels used for the coronation are the most important and well-known. The Coronation Regalia, as they're known, include items such as St. Edward's Crown, the Imperial State Crown, the Sovereign's Sceptre with Cross, the Sovereign's Orb, and the Coronation Spoon. St. Edward's Crown has been part of the Crown Jewels since 1661 and is used for the actual crowning of the new Sovereign. Despite the name, it was actually made for King Charles II after the previous golden crown was melted down by the Parliamentarians after the English Civil War. Since St. Edward's Crown is only used for the actual crowning, the Imperial State Crown is the one the monarch wears when he/she leaves Westminster Abbey. The Imperial State Crown contains some of the most famous jewels in the collection, such as the Black Prince's Ruby, the Stuart Sapphire, and the Cullinan II Diamond. The Cullinan Diamond has a particularly controversial history as it was mined in South Africa and is seen by some as a symbol of British Imperialism.

The next three important items help to convey the authority of the new Sovereign. The Sovereign's Sceptre is a staff that conveys royal authority and, since the Medieval Period, has been topped with a cross as a symbol that the Sovereign is God's chosen instrument. The Sovereign's Sceptre contains another of the Cullinan Diamonds, the Cullinan I, which is the largest of the stones cut from the original. The Sovereign's Orb is another Christian symbol of royal authority and is meant to remind the Sovereign that their power comes from God. The orb has been a part of the Crown Jewels since Queen Mary II needed her own regalia for her joint investiture with co-monarch King William III. Lastly, the Coronation Spoon is one of the oldest items in the Crown Jewels and dates back to the 12th Century. It was saved from destruction by the Parliamentarians by an official who'd been in charge of King Charles I's wardrobe and sale of his effects. The spoon is used to anoint the monarch with holy oil, further cementing his/her divine authority.

In addition to these items, the Prince/Queen Consort also has their own crown, including the State Crown of Mary of Moderna, St. Mary's Crown (made for Mary of Teck in 1910), and Queen Elizabeth's Crown that was made for Elizabeth, the Queen Mother. Prince Philip wore his own coronet for the coronation of Queen Elizabeth II in 1953. The Prince of Wales also has his own coronet, with the first one made for King George II's eldest son, Prince Frederick of Wales, in 1727. These items are normally only used at Royal Coronations. The most recent version is the Coronet of Charles, Prince of Wales, which was made for Prince Charles in 1972 after the abdicated King Edward VIII took the previous coronet with him.

The Crown Jewels are kept under armed guard within the Tower of London, and some of them can be seen by visitors who go on the tour. Many of the jewels that are not part of the Coronation Regalia are still used for other state functions, such as the State Opening of Parliament, and will be replaced with an "In Use" sign when the Sovereign is utilizing them. So if you see the sign-out, you may miss out on seeing some of the most beautiful jewels in the world, but can be excited to know that something special is going on right at that moment.

www.ingramcontent.com/pod-product-compliance
Lightning Source LLC
Chambersburg PA
CBHW022048160426
43198CB00008B/163